SHIP TO SHORE

ART AND THE LURE OF THE SEA

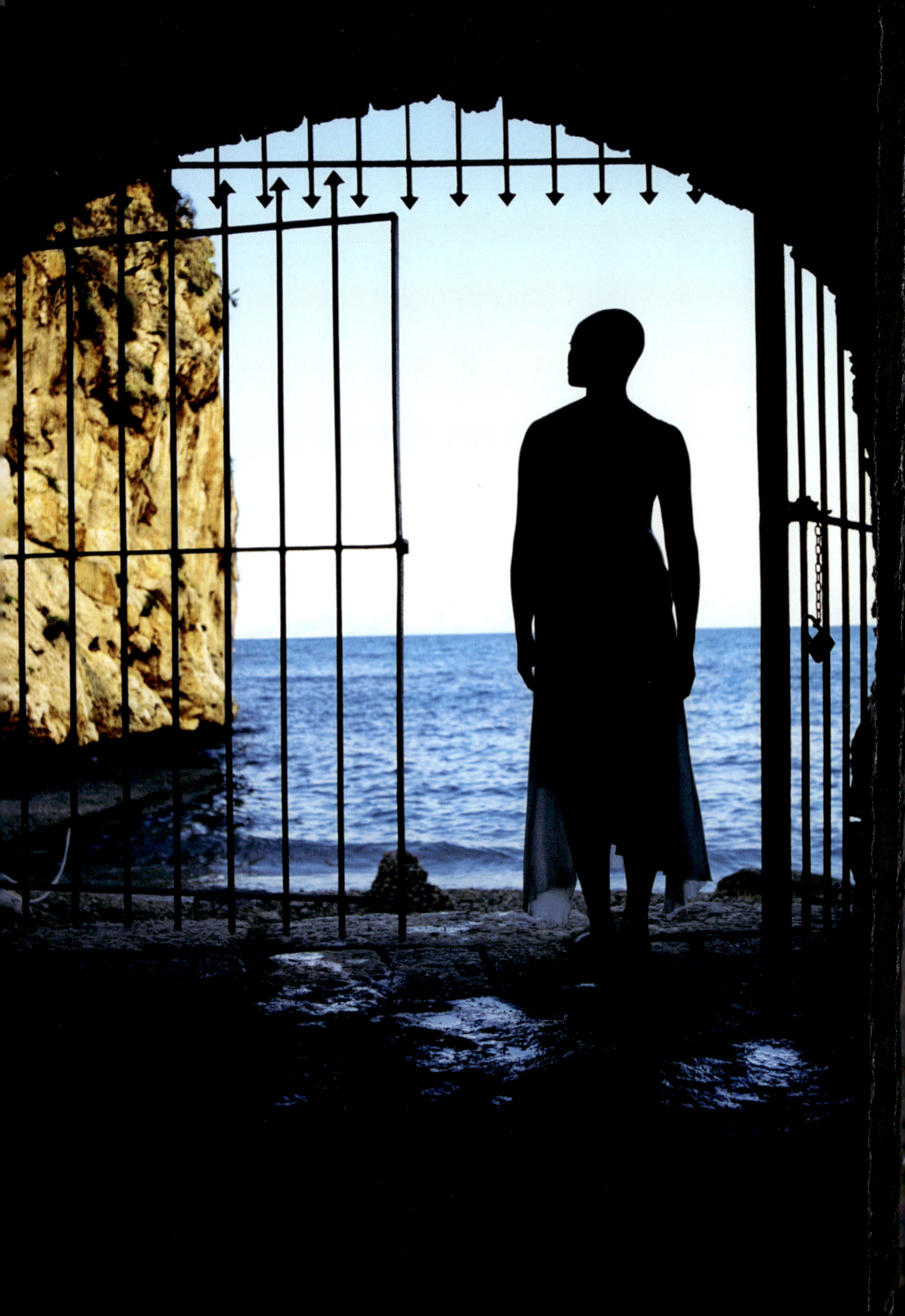

SHIP
TO
SHORE

ART AND THE LURE OF THE SEA

JEAN WAINWRIGHT

PUBLISHED BY

JOHN HANSARD GALLERY
SEACITY MUSEUM, SOUTHAMPTON

Ship to Shore: Art and the Lure of the Sea
is published in 2018 by

John Hansard Gallery at Studio 144
142–144 Above Bar Street, Southampton, SO14 7DU

and

SeaCity Museum
Civic Centre
Havelock Road, Southampton, SO14 7FY

Editor: Jean Wainwright
Project manager: Ros Carter
Designer: Adrian Hunt
Proofreader: Noreen Maconochie
Print: Belmont Press, UK
Distributed by Cornerhouse Publications, Manchester UK.
ISBN: 978 085432 9762

PREVIOUS PAGE:
Isaac Julien, *Western Union Series no.1 (Cast No Shadow)*, 2007 (detail)
Courtesy the artist and Victoria Miro, London

John Hansard Gallery is part of the University of Southampton and supported using public funding by Arts Council England

SeaCity Museum is part of Southampton City Council

This publication has been generously supported by the University for the Creative Arts

John Hansard Gallery

SEACITY MUSEUM

University for the Creative Arts

UNIVERSITY OF Southampton

SOUTHAMPTON CITY COUNCIL

Supported using public funding by ARTS COUNCIL ENGLAND

CONTENTS

FOREWORD

Ros Carter and Dan Matthews

SOUTHAMPTON HAS A LONG history as a seaport and hub for transatlantic travel, and more recently as a centre for the burgeoning cruise industry. Nicknamed 'Gateway to the World', the port has been the point of departure or return for thousands of ships on countless voyages.

The success of the port has always been inextricably linked to the fortunes of Southampton and this seafaring heritage has played a significant part in shaping the identity and culture of the city. The city's museum collections are a strong reflection of this heritage and SeaCity Museum, which opened in April 2012 – 100 years to the day after the *Titanic* steamed out of Southampton on her fateful voyage – proved a fitting location to co-host the *Ship to Shore: Art and the Lure of the Sea* exhibition in 2014, in partnership with the John Hansard Gallery at the University of Southampton. The inclusion of a mix of intriguing archival objects and oral history recordings relating to this particular maritime city brought resonance and new meanings to the artists' works, and in turn, the art brought new perspectives on the interpretation of the heritage artefacts.

The sea represents so many different things to different people: for some it represents their livelihood; for some it's a recreational playground and the route to exciting adventures; and for some it represents a long and dangerous route to what they hope will be a better life, undertaking hazardous journeys that can so often end in tragedy. Of course ocean travel for reasons of trade, migration, colonization, exploration, or (in modern times) tourism, has happened for millennia, but the sheer scale of people using the seas for evermore desperate reasons is a growing contemporary phenomenon that can't help but linger uneasily in the mind.

Ship to Shore brought to life subjects and feelings that inhabit our collective experiences and imagination in relation to the sea. This publication bears the fruit of an ongoing collaborative exploration of the ideas that were generated throughout the development and realisation of the exhibition, driven by the vision and infectious enthusiasm of its curator Jean Wainwright.

The contemporary artworks discussed in this publication reflect the complex relationship that humankind has with the sea: using it for its own purposes and gain, but at the same time constantly aware of its power and potential danger. Ultimately we know that the sea is always in charge.

ROS CARTER
Head of Exhibitions
John Hansard Gallery

DAN MATTHEWS
Lead Exhibitions Officer
Southampton City Council

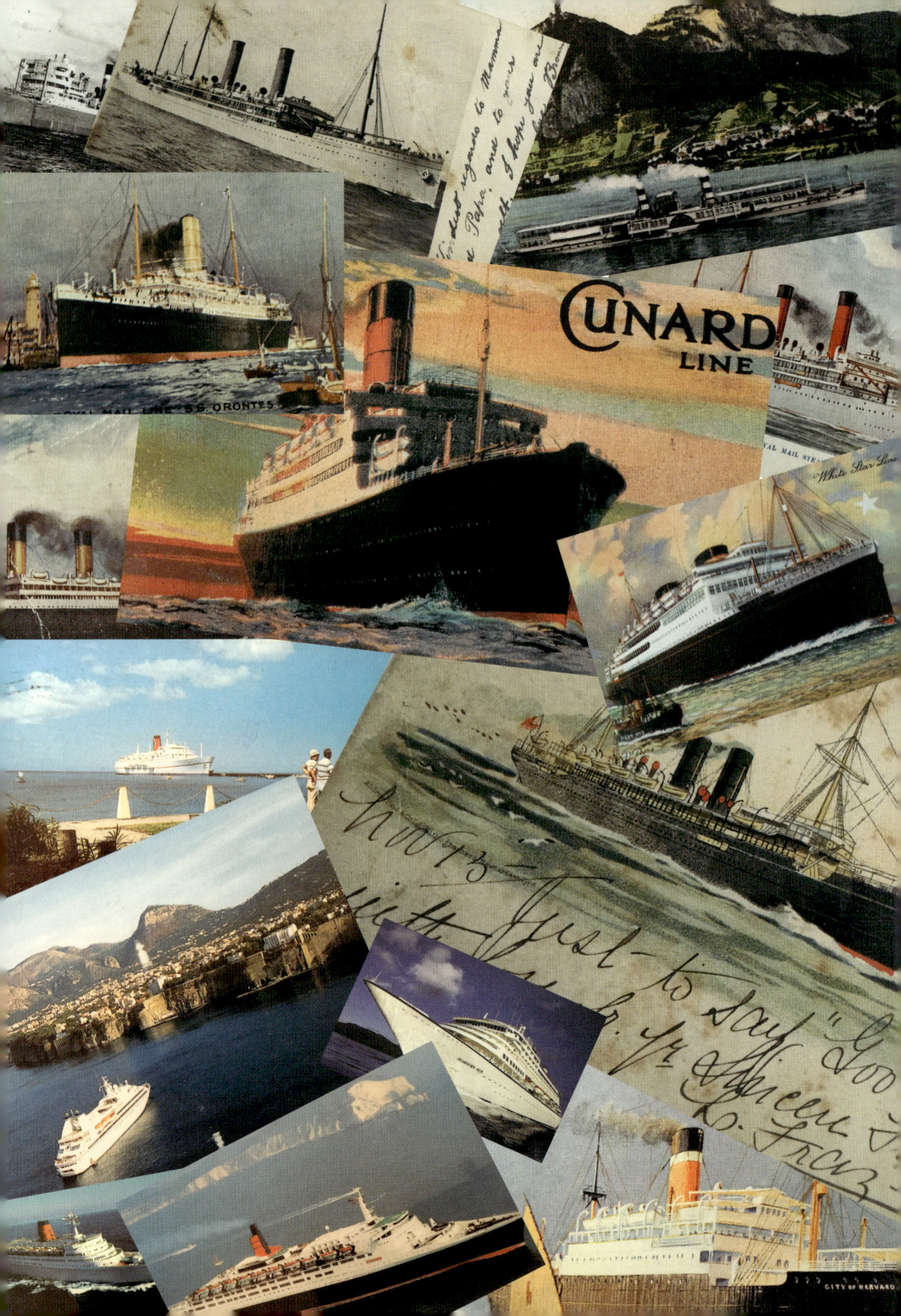
CUNARD
LINE
White Star Line

SHIP TO SHORE: ART AND THE LURE OF THE SEA

Jean Wainwright

The sea abides, never losing its most essential characteristic – the ability to lure us out of ourselves, daring us to dream of new possibilities and giving us the courage to follow those dreams beyond the furthest horizon.
Jean-Michel Cousteau, 2002[1]

THE SEA IS A SITE of metaphor and romance, of fear and joy; it is there to be sailed conquered, battled against and swum in. It is a repository of dreams.

Perhaps it is the contrasts, the dualities, the infinite possibilities of the sea that are so captivating. Both seducer and careless destroyer of life, the sea simultaneously beguiles and terrifies us. Its immense power and capricious unpredictability remind us of our humanity, of our insignificance and powerlessness in the face of nature; of our finite existence on an earth that continues long after we are gone. It can be whipped by gales into huge pounding waves, and rise to catastrophic heights when disturbed by underwater eruptions. Its vast expanse can cause the loss of both orientation and time. It can be ominously becalmed, or it can glitter seductively under a cloudless blue sky.

Waves foam, furl and crash against rocks, hiss and suck over sand. The tides ebb and flow with the moon. Children splash joyfully in the shallows, creating happy childhood memories, whilst holidaymakers lounge on deckchairs gazing idly at the horizon. Fisherman brave the waves to bring home food which sustains us. Families are reunited by sea voyages, whilst others are forever separated. Desperate refugees brave the sea's treacherous waters in vessels ill-equipped for its tempestuous moods, often tragically losing their lives. Lighthouses signal or boom out warnings of sandbanks or rocks. Super-tankers, cargo ships, cruise liners, ferries and sailing boats navigate the sea lanes. There are racing yachts with one lone sailor, and ships with thousands of passengers. The lure of the sea provides eternal inspiration for poets and artists.

Depictions of sailing vessels have been found on the walls of caves dating back thousands of years; navigational charts were pioneered during the 13th Century; and Leonardo da Vinci made drawings of seas and storms, including his *Bird's Eye View of the Sea Coast* (*c.* 1515). The physical power of the ocean to inspire artists, witnessed by the interviews in this book, remains undiminished: its drama, colour, atmosphere, edges, trade routes and the invisible geographical boundaries and mysteries contained within it excite a myriad of artistic responses in many different media. As the contemporary photographer Thomas Joshua Cooper comments in his interview in this book, 'There is this compulsion towards the sea. It attracts because it appears to be so generous, but it's also just brutally neutral.'

In Homer's epic poem *The Odyssey* (*c.* 800 BC), the mythical Odysseus is not only blown off course by a terrible storm, but also resists the fatal songs of the Sirens by lashing himself to the mast. Allegedly, Joseph Mallord William Turner also had himself tied to a mast to experience the full brunt of a storm (at 67 years old) in order to authentically paint his *Snow Storm – Steam-Boat off a Harbour's Mouth Making Signals in Shallow Water, and Going by the Lead. The Author was in this Storm on the Night the "Ariel" left Harwich* (1842). Turner's almost certainly mythologised experience has been the subject of much debate, as has his use of the word 'author' in the inscription. Nevertheless, reflecting on the composition in his 1846 work *Modern Painters II,* the critic John Ruskin suggested that it was 'one of the very grandest statements of sea-motion, mist and light that has ever been put on canvas'.[2] Whether or not he was physically battered by the storm, Turner's ability to evoke a tempestuous atmosphere set new standards for artists wishing to capture the elemental forces of nature by combining emotion and memory with innovative technique.

Painted in the tradition of the Romantic painters of the 18th and 19th century, Charles Frederick Williams' watercolour *Waves Breaking on a Rocky Shore* (1864) also conjures up instantly the mood of a storm,

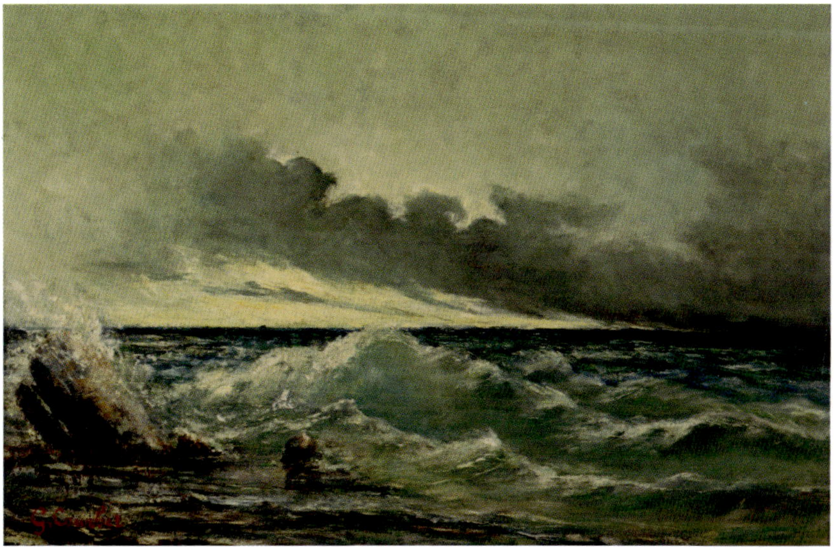

Gustave Courbet, *La Vague*, *c.* 1869. Oil on canvas
© Southampton City Art Gallery

the sea pounding against the chalk cliffs in the fishing village of Beer, South-East Devon, a steamer in the background valiantly pitching and ploughing through the English Channel. Delighting in observing the effect of changing light and weather on the sea, Williams would make quick sketches of storms or incidents that he witnessed or heard about, returning to his studio to complete them using a small brush and washes.

Painting a different coastline and working in oils, Gustave Courbet's *La Vague* (The Wave) (*c.* 1869) also shows the sea smashing against the rocks, on the French coast at Étretat. Returning many times to the area, Courbet enjoyed the savage natural force of violent storms and the changing cloud formations in extreme weather, finding something mesmerizing about a stormy sea and its relentless power. There is something inevitable about each wave cresting, to break with spumes of spray on the rocks, and it is easy to imagine Courbet watching the rhythm of the storm and capturing it with his brush. Writing in *Gil Blas* in 1886, the author Guy de Maupassant recounted a visit to Courbet, where he observed the artist painting: 'From time to time he would press his face against the window and look out at the storm. The sea came so close that it seemed to batter the house and completely envelop it in its foam and roar. The salty water beat against the windowpanes like hail, and ran down the walls'.[3]

In addition to artists striving to capture the intense physicality of seething seawater, there is also a tradition of portraiture associated with the sea – intrepid emigrants embarking on long voyages, or those left watching and waiting on the shoreline or harbour's edge. Ford Madox Brown's *The Last of England* (1855) was inspired by the departure for Australia of his friend, the Pre-Raphaelite sculptor Thomas Woolner, the canvas dominated by an emigrating couple, modelled by Brown and his second wife Emma [Hill]. With the couple's backs turned to the White Cliffs of Dover the evocative perspective, constrained by the roundel design, is further enhanced by the trepidation on the couple's faces. In his interview for this book, Humphrey Ocean describes how Brown's *The Last of England* inspired the title for his work *The First of England* (1999), an enormous canvas which, in contrast to Brown's painting, shows tourists returning from a day trip across the Channel to stock up on duty-free goods, the very antithesis of those departing from Dover often never to return.

James Tissot presented a different vision of the sea in *The Captain's Daughter (The Last Evening)* (1873): Having fled to London in 1871 after the fall of the Paris Commune, and finding success as an illustrator

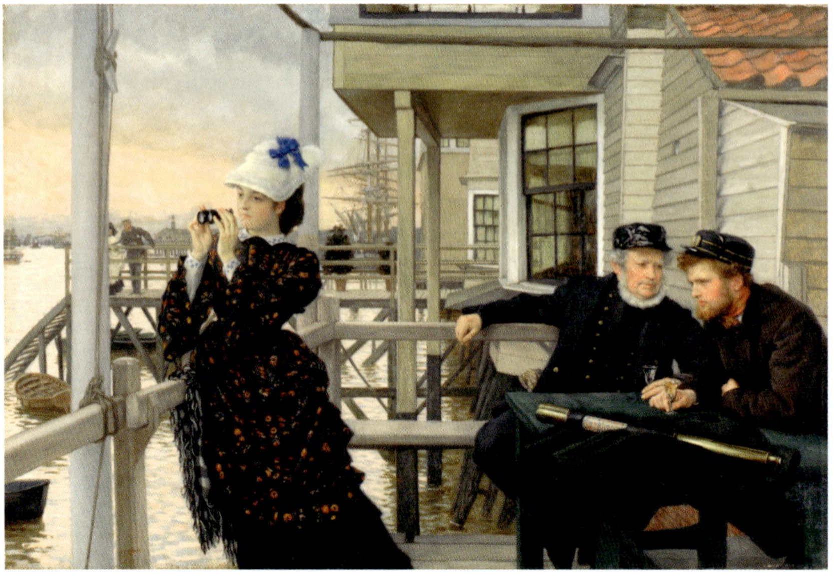

James Tissot, *The Captains Daughter (The Last Evening)*, 1873. Oil on canvas
© Southampton City Art Gallery

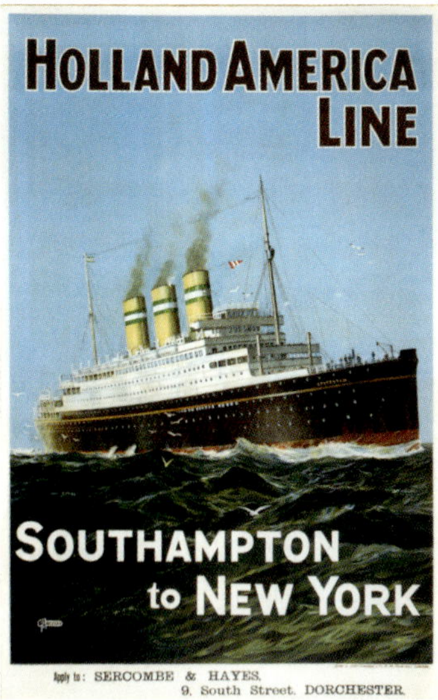

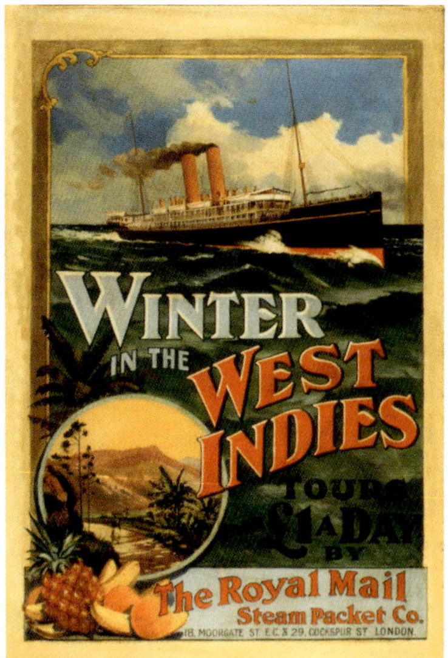

Holland America Line and Royal Mail Steam Packet Company posters
© SeaCity Museum, Southampton

and painter of contemporary life, Tissot's observations of people and his attention to detail, particularly in terms of the fashions of the day, add a frisson and ambiguity to his painting, set on the balcony of the *Falcon Tavern* in Gravesend, Kent. The expression on the model's [Margaret Kennedy, wife of his friend Captain John Freebody] face as she lingers, opera glasses in hands, gazing out over the harbour, presents an enigmatic narrative that is both romantic and poignant.

The romantic and adventurous aspect of the sea also became a marketing tool with the advent of posters and postcards promoting ocean-going voyages. The rise of cruise lines such as P&O – who from 1841 began to carry passengers for leisure as well as those emigrating and immigrating – and the introduction of Atlantic crossings and more European routes, brought adverts on full-colour posters. Some of these were hand-painted, capturing the imagination of potential travellers and persuading generations to 'take to the high seas' for an adventurous voyage, winter sun or a few days of bracing sea air. The beautiful lines of the ships were emphasized by artists and were often set against exotic locations coupled with smiling faces, waving hands and lists of tempting destinations. Postcards would be available on board on the writing desks in the cabins, and began to be collected in albums as reminders of voyages, or sent to give news from abroad. The way that the crew and passengers lived, ate and behaved on board is reflected in archives and collections of menus, artefacts and souvenirs. Daily news sheets were produced for the passengers, which included highlights of international news events as well as stories relating to the ship and information on ports of call. A news sheet from the *Queen Mary's* maiden voyage in 1936 carries hints of impending crisis. She was later to play a key role in the outcome of World War II, bravely carrying thousands of American GIs across the Atlantic to Europe, painted grey and travelling at full-speed, unescorted.

Archival recordings such as *Southampton Speaks – Sea Voices*[4] re-animate the past of the great ocean liners from the 1930s to the 1960s. Listening to the cabin boy or stewardess, the telephonist in the pre-satellite telephone exchange, the nanny, officers, or the captain, whole strata of society are revealed with their class mores and intricate lines of authority, as well as the rules and duties of each employee. Coming from a shipping family, I have many memories of sailing the oceans, including gala meals on Ellerman Line's *City of Exeter*, whose menus I kept from voyages as a child in the 1960s, with exotic choices like 'Canapé Charlemange', 'Paysandu Ox-Tongue' and 'Chateaubriande Lombardie' [*sic*]. I crave the excitement of stormy sea crossings, of steel trollies laden with food careering and crashing across the dining room – I loved being on Cunard's *Queen Mary 2* on her maiden transatlantic voyage to New York in a Force 10 gale – or of sitting on the prow of smaller boats being whipped by the wind and spray.

Richard Long's works *Ocean to River, France, 2005*, (2005) and *Tide Walk, Weston-super-Mare, England, 1992*, (1992) returns me to the land and to walking along the shore. In *Ocean to River* Long is exploring not only the relationships between time, distance, geography and measurement but also the differences in water – the vastness of the salty Atlantic Ocean and the freshwater and flow of the River Rhône. Long walked across France carrying water from the Atlantic at Pointe Espagnole to Pougny-Gare, where he poured it in the Rhone, leaving no trace. His actions work on the viewer's imagination, as they see Long's words printed in Gill Sans typeface and imagine his physical journey. In *Tide Walk*, Long pondered on the idea that his walk could be measured in lunar time, and that he could use the tides to do this, since tides are governed by the moon. The words 'relative to the walker' in Long's text work are important, since tides are affected

OPPOSITE: Excerpts from *Southampton Speaks – Sea Stories*, 2005
© Southampton City Council

She stood 60 feet from the water line to the bow, and of course she was more than a quarter-of-a-mile long, and she stood the height of a 20-storey block of flats. An enormous thing... And I said, 'My goodness, Geoffrey, how do you ever learn to drive anything quite as big as this?'
Captain

Well, we looked astern and we saw the lights of the *United States* - which sailed about three hours later than we did - coming up behind us. Eventually, she came steaming past and blew a blast on her whistle, to which we replied. Then we had a little signal from Commodore Manning, which said, 'Sorry to have to pass you like this', to which Harry Grattidge made what I though was a marvellous reply: He sent another signal back. He said, 'It's quite all right. A real lady never likes to be seen in fast company.'
Unidentified Male

I think the first day I joined the ship was rather a frightening experience... I got directed to the telephone exchange and I took one look in there and I thought, 'Oh, I don't know if I've done the right thing...' And this lady just glared at me and said, 'You must be the new telephonist', and gave me the once-over from head to toe. She was the Chief Telephonist.
Telephonist

Well, the *Comito* was a very happy ship. It was like one big family. There was always parties in the crew, you know. I used to go ashore and get the Jamaican rum and that. The parties until two in the morning, three o'clock - fantastic! I used to love it. But it was flat-bottomed and it used to roll if another ship passed... One trip, we had just left Bermuda and we hit the tail of a hurricane. Oh, I thought the ship was going to turn over! And you had to put the lifelines up in the galley to hang on to; and lifelines in the restaurant to hang on to when you were serving.
Steward

The *Ocean Times* used to get printed, you know, and you used to deliver them. But I remember one trip we had Lord Beaverbrook and Lady Astor, and they both had to get their paper at exactly the same time, apparently. For some reason, Lady Astor had got her paper early, and something in there was interesting, so she phoned Beaverbrook and told him. And he hadn't had his paper, so there was a big noise made about it.
Bellboy

You didn't go into a gentleman's cabin. The steward always did that... Of course you had quite a number of cabins to look after... Well, it was quite heavy work when it was all what they call 'silver service', and it was very heavy and hard work to do. And then you tidied up the room, re-made beds that needed it, turned them all down, put all the covers away. Get that all ready for them. Sometimes they'd want cocktails, which the steward usually got. You'd be on and really never finish till about 10 o'clock at night.
Stewardess

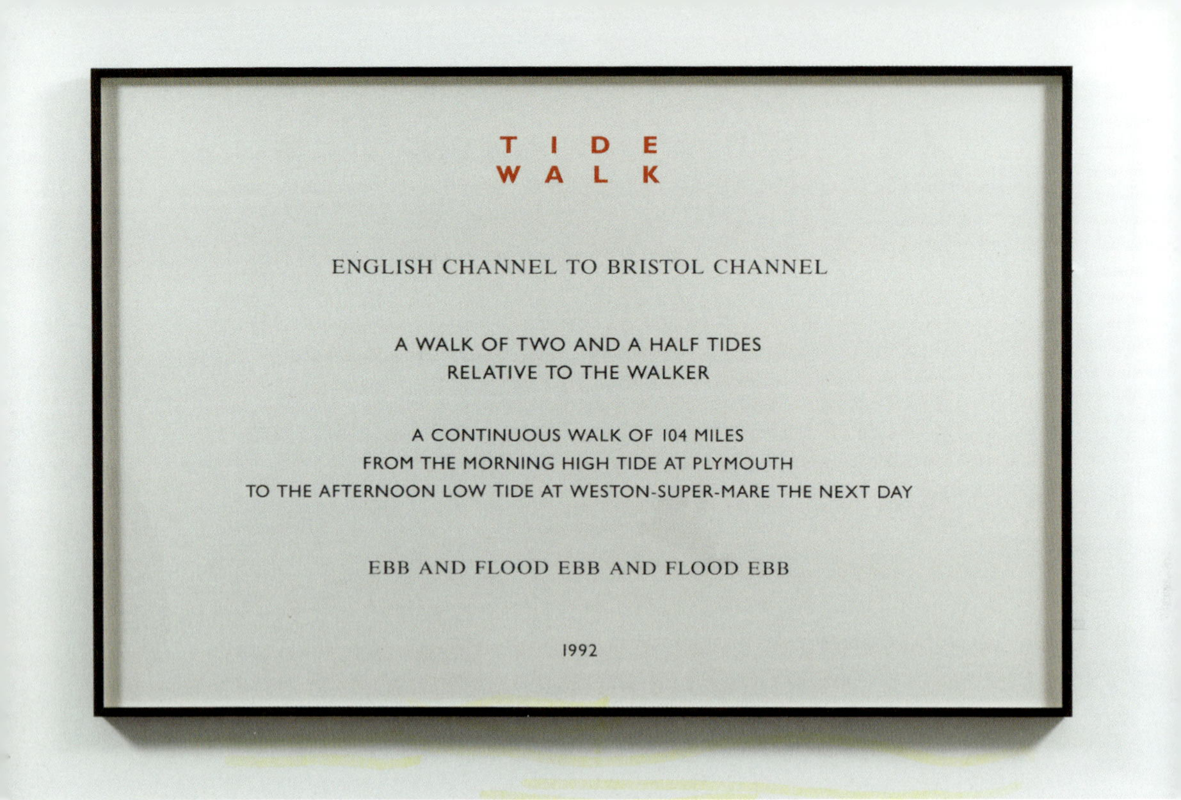

Richard Long, *Tide Walk, Weston-super-Mare, England*, 1992
Text work, framed, 106 × 157 × 4 cm

by the coastline shape and characteristics of the sea bed, so the tide times on his journey would vary as he moved around the coast from the English Channel to the Bristol Channel. Thus his walk was very much about relativity, as the tide would always be in a different state in the place he had started the walk, to where he would end it. Southampton has double tides with prolonged periods of high water making it an ideal seaport.

The exhibition *Ship to Shore: Art and the Lure of the Sea* (2014) included works by seventeen internationally renowned contemporary artists. Through painting, film, photography, sculpture, prints and archival objects they evoked the beauty and power of the sea, the romance and poignancy of sea travel, and the link to significant others through ship-to-shore communication. As sixteen of the artists shared their memories, experiences and thoughts with me for this book a rhythm developed – an ebb and flow between the very different interviews. Tantalisingly, themes began to emerge which weave together the different artworks and artists' personal histories and passions.

For some artists such as CLAIRE KERR, the connections between history of art and the present are very specific. Kerr's *Surface* (2013) is an oil painting on a gesso panel, based on a section of Claude Lorrain's *Harbour Scene at Sunset* (1643) which she had originally seen in an exhibition at the Queen's Galley in Buckingham Palace. Lorrain's canvas is a romantic, picturesque and classically balanced composition, seemingly based on the Neapolitan coastline, though in reality the location of the featured Roman ruins was a 'squalid corner of Rome, not an idealized harbour'.[5] However, in Kerr's small composition the architectural detail in Lorrain's painting – and the figures loading and unloading at the harbourside – are banished. Kerr explains that she focused on just one aspect of Lorrain's painting – a section of the clipper as if sailing into view, the small figure on the lookout gazing out to sea and the setting sun reflected on the water. Kerr talks about her almost fetishistic attention to detail and about how she created an atmosphere of distance, the scene portrayed 'as if seen through a telescope'. She suggests that when looking at the sea and looking at paintings, '…our eyes and our minds switch between this idea of surface and depth, unity and complexity, detail and panorama – both actually and metaphorically.'

DOROTHY CROSS is also interested in history, though her connection is to Ireland and the Atlantic Ocean, which she can see from the window of her studio. A core theme in her work is the link between cultural traditions and the wild Atlantic seascapes off the West Coast of Ireland. Like Kerr, Cross based her three-minute video, *Teacup* (1997), on an isolated part of a historical work – the 1934 film *Man of Aran*[6], directed by Robert J. Flaherty. She describes how she used a scene from the film where three rowers in a currach (a small boat made of wood and animal skins) battle against a raging sea. Flaherty had put the men he was filming in danger by asking them to row out in their fragile vessel in bad weather. In her interview, Cross describes the immediacy of the experience brought about by the currach's size and physical closeness to the water, and discusses how she came to use a delicate teacup to 'contain the storm', projecting the struggling rowers onto its liquid surface. Somehow the contained scale of the video heightens the tension of not knowing whether the men will live or drown, ironically drawing the viewer into the experience rather than simply being a distant observer.

TACITA DEAN describes a very different struggle with the sea. Her image *Teignmouth Electron, Cayman Brac* (1999) is part of a series of artworks she began in 1996, collectively entitled *Disappearance at Sea*, which were inspired by the story of Donald Crowhurst. A businessman and amateur sailor, Crowhurst entered the 1968–69 *Sunday Times* Golden Globe Race with his trimaran the *Teignmouth Electron*, aiming to be the first person to sail solo non-stop around the world. His hope was to claim the prize money to save his failing business. Dean talks about her fascination with Crowhurst, whose boat had not undergone proper sea testing: With failing instruments and increasingly desperate as he realised that he had no chance of winning, he began to fake his progress around the world. Falsifying his position and logbook, and showing increasing signs of 'sea madness', he eventually ceased radio contact. His yacht was subsequently found floating in the Atlantic, deserted. In her interview Dean retraces her journey to find Crowhurst's diary, trying to understand his psychological state – and presumed decision to jump overboard clutching his chronometer – from its poignant entries. She also searched for his abandoned boat, which she finally located on the Caribbean island Cayman Brac, and describes her reaction to the boat's abject, haunting presence when photographing it.

In contrast, when commissioned to make a work to coincide with the Tall Ships Race of 2005, the American artist CHRIS BURDEN decided to challenge himself by developing and constructing a crewless self-navigating sailing boat, *Ghost Ship* (2005). In his interview, he describes his installation *Ghost Ship* (2005/2014), which documents the journey of the crewless boat as it attempts the complex feat of navigating the wind and the waves on its 2005 maiden voyage between Fair Isle, Scotland and Newcastle upon Tyne. He recalls that when his father explained to him about sailing as a child, 'It seemed very improbable that one could sail *against* the wind, using the wind's force to zigzag back and forth whilst heading into the wind, towards its source. It's a little bit like magic, or perpetual motion'. He discusses his deceptively simple drawings, which powerfully illustrate the gap between desire and reality since the *Ghost Ship* could not fully tack, jibe, change course, sail trim or furl sails autonomously so needed input from a mother ship, the *Bernicia*, which made adjustments via remote control. Burden's installation in the John Hansard Gallery in 2014 showed the hand-crafted, traditional, single-masted ship mastering the waves, its fluttering pennant now an object fixed to the gallery wall. The complex hydraulics and integration of the off-the-shelf computer systems, the time taken to sail, the different heights of the waves and the weather conditions remain now as photographs, objects, a film and an archival website. In his interview, Burden describes how *Ghost Ship* succeeded as a partially failed but heroic endeavour, despite severe weather, commenting that such frustrations were just 'part of the daily struggle' when creating his works.

Charts are part of any seafarer's equipment, and SIMON PATTERSON used 18th and 19th century Admiralty charts from the National Maritime Museum's hydrography collection – principally of the Aegean and Mediterranean Seas – as the basis for the hanging fabric charts in his installation *Cousteau in the Underworld* (2008). Patterson describes how as a boy in the 1970s, whilst his friends were 'preoccupied with outer space', he would watch the highly popular television series *The Undersea World of Jacques Cousteau*, marvelling at the underwater footage. So he empathises with Cousteau's son, Jean-Michel, who, when recalling diving trips with his father, talks of having been '...awash in a new world. And as children do, I imagined fantastical monsters around the crags and corners... I now realize that I was engaged in one of humankind's oldest avocations: spinning myths about the sea'.[7] Talking about the inception of his 2008 installation, Patterson describes how he could only find 'fragmentary and often-inaccurate information' when researching the life of this great French oceanaut, and it suddenly struck him 'how rapid the slide is from life to history and into myth.' He explains that his artwork is partly about narratives which amplify Cousteau's status, blurring the lines between fact and fiction; narratives that occur in the oral tradition of history and find a parallel in the workings of the internet. Patterson describes how surprised he was, when researching his subject, by the number of parallels between Cousteau's life and the story of Odysseus, as told in Homer's *Odyssey*. These connections have brought new life and narratives to the historic Admiralty charts in his installation, where each features an aspect of, or exploit in, the epic life of Cousteau interspersed by excerpts from the *Odyssey*.

Myths and danger also surround the subject of lighthouses, and these are the theme of works by two artists interviewed in this book – Steffi Klenz and Catherine Yass – who talk about their fascination for these distinctively-designed buildings. Standing proudly on promontories above the sea, or situated in the sea itself, historically they present a romantic vision, evoking lighthouse keepers living in isolation surrounded by rocks endlessly pummelled by the sea (in the UK at least, they are now wholly automated).

STEFFI KLENZ has made many works about the sea. In her interview she talks about how her practice is concerned with challenging conventional conceptions of architecture and about her research for the twelve diamond-shaped photographic images of a lighthouse Fresnel lens. In *Concert for Maison Sirène* (2014), Klenz wanted to evoke the rhythmic and repeating pulse of the lighthouse signal, and her abstracted images are coupled with a seductive musical score alluding to the mythological Sirens who lured sailors to their death. Klenz was particularly interested in the sound, composed specifically for her by Neil Codling of the group *Suede* and based on Arnold Schoenberg's twelve-tone musical theory, its atonal principles translated into a piece for piano and violin. She talks in detail about her sequenced photographs with their refracted colours ascending and descending on the wall; how they need to be hung in a particular way like notes on a musical sheet, a carefully composed progression of aural as well as visual 'voices'. As she explains, 'The last thing standing between us and the unremitting sea, which can create a disorientating psychological state, is the lighthouse. So I like to think of my colourful images as abstractions that can hint at that'.

CATHERINE YASS' response to the Royal Sovereign lighthouse also presents a psychological and disorienting portrait. Yass photographed the extraordinary modernist structure – completed in 1971 and lying five miles out to sea off Eastbourne on England's south coast – for her series of Duratrans transparencies on light boxes, *Lighthouse* (2011). Somehow both monumental and precarious, the lighthouse provided a fascinating subject for Yass, who in her interview discusses her interest in the psychological effects of architectural space set against the power and unpredictable nature of the sea. She describes how she used her analogue medium format plate camera to explore time and space through manipulated film stock, inversion and reversal. Her images are produced using a unique method of overlaying a positive photographic transparency with a negative transparency taken moments after the first. The *Lighthouse* series captures the sun as it moves behind the north-eastern face of the structure, and the motion of the sea. Yass' process turns the image inside out, inverting the sun into a deep blue-black blind spot, a poetically altered reflection of reality which she finds seductively fascinating. Linked to the photographic series is Yass' film *Lighthouse* (2011), in which she filmed the Royal Sovereign Lighthouse's square platform resting on a circular pillar, from a helicopter, a boat and underwater. In her interview Yass remembers dreams which were 'both fantasies and fears, of falling, or the desire to fly, or drowning – all of those very physical extreme acts and emotions'. It is these extremes that she exploits in her film, disorienting the viewer. Describing her work as 'a temporal drawing', Yass' camera is always moving as it follows a trajectory around the lighthouse, turning, circling, spiralling, inverting, and submerging. In a dizzying array of shots the sea swirls in constant motion as Yass lures us around the lighthouse and in her interview she talks of her emotional and physical engagement with the power of dangerous waters.

TRACEY EMIN's *She Lay down Deep Beneath The Sea* (2012) is also a work where personal thoughts are transformed into a public statement, through the hand-blown neon that has become a crucial medium in her sculptural practice since she first used it in 1995. Emin is fascinated by the sea, and brightly lit neon signs form part of her visual sensibility, something she saw every day on Margate seafront when she was growing up, luring people into the amusement arcades and fish and chip shops. In her interview she talks about her handwriting and how its transformation into sculpture seductively challenges us, communicating her personal desires, her thoughts on death and her relationship with her father, Enver Emin, through a very public medium. Her interview responses weave her personal story from past to present, speaking of sadness and ultimately peace. Reading Emin's words makes us contemplate what it might mean to lie down deep beneath the sea, as we are reminded of her understanding of the moods of the oceans and her thoughts on the forces of nature, longing and loss.

ISAAC JULIEN speaks of a different loss in his conversation about *The Leopard (Western Union: small boats)* (2007) the final part of his compelling trilogy of audiovisual film installations which also include *True North* (2004) and *Fantôme Afrique* (2005). The film considers the stories of so-called 'clandestines', traversing the Mediterranean Sea from Libya to escape war and famine. Julien explains how *Western Union: small boats* is also a personal film: the Italian island of Lampedusa, the location for the film is just a few hundred miles off the North African coast, and while making trips to Italy with his mother he had observed how that part of the Mediterranean had become the front line for migrants trying to enter Europe without papers. Ten years later the work is still relevant, as Julien suggests in his interview, since the tide of desperate migrants fleeing war and poverty across the sea remains unstemmed. The boats in *Western Union: small boats* survived the journey intact, but were later found abandoned by Julien in a junkyard. Julien also describes how his film references Luchino Visconti's 1963 film *Il Gattopardo (The Leopard)*[8], and how he set part of it in the Palazzo Valguarnera–Gangi, a key location in Visconti's film. In his interview he discusses the complexities of filming, his use of metaphor and the deeply troubling circumstances of migrants and diaspora. The balletic underwater sequences, the man tossing and turning on the floor or adrift on his boat, and the extraordinary singing, all speak of exploitation and death by drowning, and of beauty and loss. There is a metaphorical undertow in this work as Julien questions the circulation of human lives and the role that the sea plays in migration from one country to another.

The underlying theme of ZINEB SEDIRA's *MiddleSea* (2008) is also migration, displacement and the sea Parisian-born Sedira, whose parents were Algerian freedom fighters who emigrated to France only to return in 1988, talks of identity, tension and the Algerian civil war, as she explains how *MiddleSea* developed from her earlier work *Saphir* (2006). *Saphir* was inspired by the tension between her happy feelings on returning to contemporary Algiers, and an awareness of the more ambivalent feelings of those left behind during the civil war, some of whom still long to escape across the sea to France. She describes how the maritime channel between Algeria and France symbolizes the strong ties that still exist between the two countries, despite the 50-plus years since Algeria was decolonised. Sedira describes how *MiddleSea* – the mesmeric film of a journey across the Mediterranean between Marseilles and Algiers (though the direction is never actually specified) – traces the somnambulant movements of a lone male as he wanders around the deserted corridors of the *Tariq Ibn Ziyad* ferry. The soundscape, created in collaboration with artist Mikhail Karikis, has a dreamlike quality, interweaving, distorting and intensifying sound recorded on location – a radio attempting to tune in, the rumbling of the engine, the hints of voices. Sedira explains how she wanted her audience to be disoriented and displaced, to have the sensation of being alone on a ship ploughing its course through the sea. She made the journey between Marseilles and Algiers many times, and the film is also a personal meditation on her own history and family. She wanted to give the film a hypnotic style and to linger on elements that might appear trivial.

When HUMPHREY OCEAN was commissioned to paint a vision of modern maritime Britain he also decided to set the scene on the deck of a cross-channel ferry, but *The First of England* (1999) is a very different vision from that of Zineb Sedira. He recounts how, when painting his canvas, he thought of England's maritime past and of Philip Larkin's poem *MCMXIV*[9], which describes men lining up to enlist in the First World War, eager to be shipped to France. With the Dover ferry's floating duty-free store, the day trippers returning to the White Cliffs are neither shattered, nor shell-shocked, nor dead, fortunately, but arrive bearing trollies of duty-free lager. In his interview he discusses his family background, his determination to study painting and his influences. He explains how the scale and flatness of his work reference Pop Art and the Abstract Expressionism, whilst its subject portrays an unromantic image of the relationship of the British with their coastline, and an eclectic group of people sharing a common experience.

YINKA SHONIBARE MBE also references cultural identity and maritime history in his work *Nelson's Ship in a Bottle* (2010) which contains a replica of Nelson's flagship, HMS *Victory*, on which he died during the Battle of Trafalgar, on 21 October 1805. The richly-patterned sails on the ship were inspired by Indonesian batik, which was mass-produced by Dutch traders and sold to the colonies in West Africa. In his interview, Shonibare discusses how today these designs are associated with African dress and identity. Shonibare explains that the way he looks at fabrics is 'a sort of cultural study really, almost anthropological, in that I'm trying to actually understand human culture and material culture and the relation of that to history'. The legacy of Dutch Wax fabric assumes a distinctly maritime significance when used as the sails of his ship in a bottle, and its characteristic bright colours and abstract symmetries add complex layers to the work, suggesting ambivalent associations with colonialism, industrialisation, emigration, cultural appropriation, and the invention (and reinvention) of tradition.

LANGLANDS & BELL's multi-channel digital animation, *Into the Blue* (2014), has a different focus, continuing a theme that has fascinated them for a number of years: the structures that we inhabit and the networks that permeate and connect them. The two artists have been collaborating since 1978, and in their interview they describe their meticulous working methods and discuss the philosophy behind their work. They explain how *Into the Blue* reflects the way in which ships and their registered names become encoded as social, political and economic phenomena: In the installation the complex networks linking liners and cargo ships, trade routes and names become intertwined, rising and falling on the screens as combinations of the world's seas and international ocean liners appear and disappear at random, their identities surging, exchanging and dissolving into each other, the registered names of the vessels speaking of history, geography and enterprise, the mysteries of stray ships and lost regions supplanting one another in a restless search across the world.

THOMAS JOSHUA COOPER often spends years preparing the journeys to locate and photograph his seascapes. Cooper is a traveller, a nomadic artist whose extraordinary black-and-white images are made in series at significant points around the globe, most often at its extremities. In his interview he describes how he uses an 1898 Agfa Field Camera, and hand-prints all his works using 19th Century techniques. Inspired by photographers such as Ansel Adams, his silver gelatin prints have a meditative, almost philosophical quality. If he completes his project, begun in 1990, he will be 'the first person in the world to have circumnavigated the Atlantic basin from all five continents and both poles by land', to photograph where the land meets the seas and oceans. He explains that he gives his photographs titles that reference their exact location, but which also suggest 'the physicality of the time, the place, the nature of the light'. He also describes the often difficult and arduous treks to 'find' his images, and his fascination with the different formations and moods of coastal areas, seas and oceans.

MARK POWER's *The Shipping Forecast* (1993–1996) was also a long-term photographic project. Over a period of four years, he visited each of the 31 sea areas whose weather conditions were broadcast four times a day on BBC Radio 4's Shipping Forecast, taking an image from the nearest landmass or coastal town and captioning the photographs by the 0600hrs forecast on the day they were taken. Power's interest in the sea began at a young age: his father was in the Merchant Navy and built him his first dinghy – an Optimist – in the garden, fostering a life-long love of sailing. But it was curiosity that inspired him to visit every region in the Shipping Forecast to see if the reality of what he found 'bore any relation to the imaginary landscapes that had developed in my head'. He was intrigued by the difference between what the disembodied voice reciting the forecast conjured up, and the actual reality of both location and weather. Power's desire was to produce pictures 'which looked like the forecast sounded', and the resulting images are both fact and fiction, a navigation between photographic truth and disembodied reports and predictions.

One of SUSAN HILLER's first memories is of being roughly tumbled in the surf when she was a child, and of her father coming to her rescue. Perhaps it was then that a fascination for the wildness of the sea was lodged in her unconscious, an interest which led to her collection of 'Rough Sea' postcards, which has become an archival typology of English coastal resorts. In her interview Hiller discusses how the sea is a metaphor for the unconscious. She describes the postcards she has worked with as a 'miniature domestication of the sublime', likening people in them standing looking at the (rough) sea to 'voyeurs watching a sexual act. These images are miniature evocations, or reminders, of the sublime elements in a seaside holiday.' Ultimately she suggests that what the 'Rough Sea' postcard images are saying 'is paradoxical and contradictory, as I believe our notions are'. Hiller's methods and strategies have been described as an 'examination of real and imagined phenomena, probing the unseen and the unheard in order to create art that evokes absences, memories and ghosts'.[10] It is this 'probing' that she suggests created her compulsion to reanimate the seaside scenes in *Nightwatch* (2009), a series of nine enlarged giclée prints which, with their glowing colours, compellingly denaturalise nature.

In this book each artist has a story to tell, but it is the meaning, power and lure of the sea which link the sixteen artists and their very different practices. As the words and images unfold, we are reminded how the sea has enticed us across the centuries, capturing our imagination and thrilling us with its seductive vitality.

I must go down to the seas again, for the call of the running tide
Is a wild call and a clear call that may not be denied;
And all I ask is a windy day with the white clouds flying,
And the flung spray and the blown spume, and the sea-gulls crying.
Sea Fever, John Masefield, 1902

NOTES

1. Cousteau, Jean-Michel. "Introduction: A World of Wonder". *Oceans*, by Sue Hostetler, Rizzoli International, 2002, p. 15.
2. Ruskin, John. *Modern Painters* I-VI. John Wiley & Son, 1866, p. 376.
3. Maupassant, Guy de. "La Vie d'un Paysagiste". *Gil Blas (periodical), 28th September 1886*, p.1.
4. *Southampton Speaks*, 2005, www.plimsoll.org/StartHere/PartnersAndCollections/SCCOralHistory/SotonSpeaks.asp#1
5. Filippo Baldinucci. *Notizie de' Professori del Disegno, da Cimabue in Qua*, 1681–1728. Stamperia di S.A.R., 1728, p. 356.
6. *Man of Aran*. Dir. Robert J. Flaherty. Gaumont-British Corporation, 1934. Film.
7. Cousteau, Jean Michel. "Introduction: A World of Wonder". *Oceans*, by Sue Hostetler, Rizzoli International, 2002, p. 12.
8. *Il Gattopardo* (The Leopard). Dir. Luchino Visconti. Titanus, 1963. Film.
9. Larkin, Philip. 'MCMXIV'. *The Whitsun Weddings*. 1964. Faber & Faber, 2001, pp. 25–26.
10. "The Collective Conscience, Susan Hiller." *Aesthetica Magazine*, 16th November 2015, www.aestheticamagazine.com/susan-hiller-lisson-gallery-london/

THE DARK AND DEEP BLUE OCEAN

Philip Hoare

Consider all this; and then turn to this green, gentle, and most docile earth; consider them both, the sea and the land; and do you not find a strange analogy to something in yourself? For as this appalling ocean surrounds the verdant land, so in the soul of man there lies one insular Tahiti, full of peace and joy, but encompassed by all the horrors of the half known life. God keep thee! Push not off from that isle, thou canst never return.

Herman Melville, *Moby-Dick*[1]

WHENEVER TEMPESTUOUS WEATHER hits the British Isles, members of the public are warned not to walk near the sea, let alone approach it any more closely. It's as if mere sight of it might prove fatal, posing a malign, preternatural threat. Such a draconian warning – to stay clear of waves which are rising up like spumy, punitive dragons – is necessary partly because we have lost an ancient, instinctual awareness of its power. Yet even as we are disconnected from its meaning, we are discovering new and astounding revelations about the sea that surrounds and belts our world, forming far more of the planet's surface than our paltry slivers of land.

Scientists recently released new information about the gigantic, internal waves, hundreds of feet high, that move through the oceans unseen. From above – from our perspective – their effect on the surface is barely detected, rising to only a few inches. But these waves – which can travel vast distances – have as-yet immeasurable effects on the planet's climate and its ocean's ecosystems. Defined by differing densities – cold and salty below, warmer and less salty above – they mix the oceanic waters, drawing heat from the atmosphere, and creating the cyclical conditions that feed their own perpetual momentum.

Reaching up to 550 feet in height, such waves are 'the lumbering giants of the ocean', says Professor Thomas Peacock, Professor of Mechanical Engineering at the Massachusetts Institute of Technology.[2] They are animate, watery monsters, conjured up by a subaquatic climate. The fact that such phenomena have lain undetected until now is another reminder of our paradoxical removal from the sea.

The ocean is never the same. Look at it, then look at it again – it has changed in that moment of witness. What we see is a liquid gas; something and nothing. Its colour is defined by the sky above and sea bed below, rather than by itself. It is a shifting, fugitive element – yet it is estimated that nearly half of all life is found in the sea, and most of those species have yet to be scientifically identified.

The sea is where we came from, and it is what sustains us. It provides us with the oxygen we breathe, and the food we eat. It brings to Britain ninety per cent of the goods that we consume and use, many of them in container ships travelling up and down Southampton Water. We have long considered ourselves to have conquered the sea, an inexorable process which began when the first watercraft was made in prehistory. Through trade and warfare, from dugout to skin canoe, to trireme and galleon, steamship and nuclear submarine, we assume our ascendancy over the ocean.

Although the Romans had proclaimed the Mediterranean as *Mare Nostrum*, and despite the Renaissance extensions of European power via exploration, exploitation and trade, up until the eighteenth century the ocean was *Mare Liberum*, unsubjected to the assertions of sovereignty which had already carved up much of the terrestrial globe. In 1812 Byron could still write in *Childe Herod's Pilgrimage* that 'Man marks the earth with ruin – his control / stops with the shore…'.[3]

But then the world's latest and greatest maritime power, Britain, declared a three-mile nautical extension – the distance which a cannon ball could be shot – asserting its imperial rights. By the twentieth century, a new empire, the United States, had extended that limit to two hundred miles off its shores.

Now even the waters under the Arctic ice cap are staked out by Russian flags, while European fishing fleets pillage the coastal waters of African countries. Piracy and slavery flourish; plans are made to mine newly-discovered abyssal volcanic vents, on the deepest ocean beds, for rare earth metals; and off the British coast, four thousand year-old spires of coral on cold-water reefs are casually destroyed by trawlers.

As Joel Found notes in his essay *The Sea and the Desert*[4], 'We constantly place ourselves at the centre of a world we perceive to be furnished for our own experience'. And yet, as we make these arrogant extensions of our supposed dominion, we physically and psychically turn our backs on the sea, perhaps out of fear that it will rise up against us.

✧

More than a century before Professor Peacock's contemporary investigations into unseen waves, other attempts had been made to encompass the restless potency of the sea. In the nineteenth century, the Stevenson family of Scotland were renowned as lighthouse builders, celebrated in the slogan, 'Battered by storms, ravaged by waves, built by Mr Stevenson'.[5] Thomas Stevenson – whose father, Robert, had built the famous Bell Rock Lighthouse in 1807, and whose son, Robert Louis, would spurn engineering in favour of writing – continued in the family tradition.

From the Whalsay Skerries in 1854 to Ailsa Craig in 1886, Thomas Stevenson's towers were rearing emblems of Victorian engineering, constructed by a technocratic pioneer who devoted his life to defending an empire's ships against the treacherous rocks of its own mother country. But Thomas was not content to build buttresses against the sea as his father had. As he grew older, he became obsessed with waves, a force that haunted his dreams.

Stevenson seemed to see their power as bordering on the supernatural, 'as proof of the existence of something far greater than straightforward science', as Robert Louis wrote in his memoir of his father, composed when he was living in Bournemouth (in a house he named Skerryvore after a lighthouse his uncle had designed).[6] Thomas had measured waves, assessed their height and length and volume using a wave pole and a dynamometer, and asked lighthouse keepers to record wind speed, height of spray and water pressure per square foot. He even sought to weigh waves, and published his findings in the journal of the Royal Society of Edinburgh.

But his studies of waves 'were only descriptive', as Rosalind Williams, contemporary historian of technology, concludes in her book, *The Triumph of Human Empire*:[7] 'He was not able to reduce their tumult to a scientific understanding robust enough to make predictions'. Quite simply, the sea was beyond Stevenson and beyond science, infused with infinite power. He could not have predicted a world in which human actions would cause those waves to rise even further, wreaking their revenge.

✧

My father spent all his working life at Pirelli General's cable works, a factory built on land reclaimed from the sea at the feet of Southampton's medieval walls, not far from the mythic point at which Canute was said to have commanded the tide to turn back, to 'Let all men know how empty and worthless is the power of Kings'.[8] When he arrived in Southampton in the 1930s, fleeing the Great Depression of Bradford, the landlocked town in which he had been born and bred, my father stepped out onto a platform made of concrete mixed with shingle from the beach; you can still see the shells embedded in it. On the other side of the road (a site now occupied by acres of soulless retail sheds, incrementally defying Canute's declaration) lay the sea itself.

In Pirelli's sprawling brick edifice, an industrial replacement for the town's medieval sea buttresses, giant cables were manufactured, the thickness of a man's waist. Strands of bundled copper and wire encased in shiny black rubber, they were wound onto huge wooden drums, or played out over a gantry that straddled the street, directly into the hulls of cable-laying ships. Unrolled across the Atlantic, they represented a physical tethering of the fallen maritime power to its new imperial master, for all that Southampton still proclaimed itself as the 'Gateway to the Empire'.

At that time Southampton was still a place which lived and traded by the sea. Nowadays visitors come to Southampton and never even see the sea. Pirelli's has long since been demolished; and the wave-lapped medieval walls which Turner drew, from where Georgian bathers dipped, and which were once hymned as a romantic seascape, look out onto dual carriageways and multi-storey car parks.

As a boy, the docks scared me. They seemed to be strange, no-man's-lands where ships unloaded crates of bananas which concealed, so it was said, hairy tarantulas carried here inadvertently from the Caribbean.

The docks took away my friends, the school mates whose families emigrated to Australia, carried off down the water and out to the unknown.

I remember being taken on a school trip to the docks; it felt like we were entering forbidden territory, not part of England at all. After our bus drove past dinosaurian cranes and dark warehouses, we disembarked at the furthest end to find a gigantic dry dock, like a Roman amphitheatre constructed from stepped granite, big enough to contain the largest known liner; to hoick it out of the water like a salmon, and leave it stranded there, rusted and dripping. Its yawning space evoked the negative absence of some unknown leviathan, a monumental tomb awaiting an impossibly huge whale.

✦

Up in Tudor House, one of Southampton's oldest surviving domestic buildings, a graffiti-covered wall was recently restored during renovations of the museum there. Among the marks and names scratched into the plaster, some of them dating back to the building's origins, is a crude sketch of a wading bird – to my eyes at least the shape of an oystercatcher, which then as now, and perhaps for many of thousands of years, has made its living from these muddy shores. It is another emblem of the connection from shore to sea, of the liminal meeting of land and water.

Southampton stands for many ports around the British coast. In fact, it was England's first naval base and shipbuilding site, established in 1420 and briefly pre-empting its rival, Portsmouth. It bore witness to a rapid expansion of trade in the medieval period. In 1439, for instance, a Venetian great galley sailed from Southampton carrying 2,783 cloths and 14,000 tons of tin. Yet as Lincoln Paine notes in *The Sea and Civilisation*, each container ship that slips down Southampton Water today contains more cargo than the total volume of trade carried to Venice during an entire year of the fifteenth century.[9]

Today, as I swim in that water with the grebes and the cormorants, I watch those monstrous vessels slide in and out of port. In tonnage and technical achievement, they far surpass the *Titanic* which made that same journey down this estuarine sea a century ago. But no-one stands on the quay to wave these maritime juggernauts off; there are no cheering crowds or brass bands to bid them goodbye. They are the anonymous facilitators of our global world, the complicit mechanism of our voracious consumption.

A contemporary container ship, which can carry 50,000 tons of cargo, is a barometer of macroeconomics, a plimsoll line of success. The lower it sits in the water, the better things are; the higher it rides, the worse off its exporting nation. Neither it nor its car-carrying cousins, which also push out from these quays like laden, upended skyscrapers, would ever fit in any dry dock. Their dimensions are themselves a measure of their global role, built, as they are, to accommodate their breadth to the width of the Panama Canal.

Their routes stitch an incessant network, sewing the world together in a remorseless and oddly senseless exchange. In his book, *Down the Sea in Ships*,[10] Horatio Clare, sailing on the *Maersk Pembroke* from Holland to Canada, records the ship's manifest on its arrival in Montreal: 'Indian spices, twenty-five tonnes of Greek wine, Danish yeast, British malt, Latvian clothing, Estonian chemicals, German tools, thirty-four tonnes of Belgian chocolate, twenty-four tonnes of Sri Lankan tea…'

'But why ninety tonnes of Argentinean milk, and why send it via Europe? What is so desirable, in this land of forests, about the three hundred tonnes of sawn timber from Germany, and the eighty more from Russia?' To Clare, it is clear that this is an unsustainable industry which depends 'on people's appetites for stuff, on our inability to produce it where it is wanted, and the readiness with which we throw it away'. Little wonder that we ignore these ships. They are too painful a reminder, a shameful reflection of the actions from which we turn away.

✧

In 'Loomings', the evocative opening chapter of *Moby-Dick*,[11] which begins with the unreliable narrator, Ishmael, despairing suicidally of his land-bound life and longing for the escape of the sea, the author Herman Melville sees the ocean as a mirror of the human condition: 'And still deeper the meaning of that story of Narcissus, who because he could not grasp the tormenting, mild image he saw in the fountain, plunged into it and was drowned. But that same image, we ourselves see in all rivers and oceans. It is the image of the ungraspable phantom of life; and this is the key to it all'.

Writing in 1850, Melville was torn between the brutal physical reality of the whaling industry that he had experienced at first-hand, and which he recorded in his book, and the numinous, meditative and awful greater meanings of the oceans he had sailed. He had been to the farthest ends of the earth, into the remotest seas. But like Thomas Stevenson, he could not reconcile himself to their immensities; and like Professor Peacock, he was faced with extraordinary new revelations.

Yet Melville had one advantage over Victorian engineers and twenty-first century scientists. He was an artist; and he could ask questions without having to supply answers. He was like a sailor dropping his plumb line over the side in order to gauge the depth of the sea, waiting for his lead weight to come to a stop, only to discover that the line would play out forever.

NOTES

1. Melville, Herman. "Brit." *Moby-Dick; or, the Whale*. 1851. University of California Press, 1983, p. 281.
2. Massachusetts Institute of Technology. "Ocean's hidden waves show their power: Origins of giant underwater waves explained." *ScienceDaily*, 8 Jan. 2014. www.sciencedaily.com/releases/2014/01/140108102453.htm
3. Byron, George G. [Lord]. *Childe Harold's Pilgrimage: Canto* IV. 1818. Echo Library, 2007, p. 143.
4. Found, Joel. *The Sea and the Desert in the works of Cormac McCarthy and Tim Winton*. Dissertation, University of Southampton, p. 10.
5. *The Museum of Scottish Lighthouses*, 2017, www.lighthousemuseum.org.uk
6. Williams, Rosalind. *The Triumph of Human Empire: Verne, Morris, and Stevenson at the End of the World*. University of Chicago Press, 2013, p. 255.
7. Ibid., pp. 255–256.
8. Holliday, James A. "Three Encounters with King Canute." *As is the Sea: An Anthology*. Critical Writing in Art and Design, Royal College of Art, 2014, p.77.
9. Paine, Lincoln. *The Sea and Civilisation*. Atlantic Books, 2014, pp. 337; 341, 345.
10. Clare, Horatio. *Down to the Sea in Ships*. Chatto & Windus, 2014, p. 267.
11. Melville, Herman. "Loomings". *Moby-Dick; or, the Whale*. 1851. University of California Press, 1983, p. 4.

PHILIP HOARE is Professor of Creative Writing at the University of Southampton. An award-winning author, broadcaster and filmmaker, Hoare's prolific work includes the books *Leviathan or, The Whale* (2008), which won the 2009 BBC Samuel Johnson Prize for non-fiction, *The Sea Inside* (2013), and RISINGTIDEFALLINGSTAR (2017), and the BBC Arena film *The Hunt for Moby-Dick* (2008), which he wrote and presented. With artist Angela Cockayne, he also co-curated the *Moby-Dick Big Read* (2012), a free-to-access online reading of Melville's classic novel, delivered by celebrities including Tilda Swinton, Sir David Attenborough and former Prime Minister David Cameron and accompanied by images from contemporary artists such as Anish Kapoor, Antony Gormley and Susan Hiller.

THE ARTISTS

INTERVIEWS WITH JEAN WAINWRIGHT

CLAIRE KERR

SURFACE, 2013

What was the genesis of your painting, Surface?

I've always been drawn to images of the sea and marine paintings, and I found Claude Lorrain's painting *Harbour Scene at Sunset* (1643) – which I saw in an exhibition of Dutch landscapes at the Queen's Galley in Buckingham Palace, in 2011 – particularly evocative. What I have done is taken a small detail of the scene as if seen through a telescope. The subject matter is a harbour scene, and the surface of the original painting, which was made so tangible with the brush strokes and cracks, seemed to me like an allegory of painting.

So when did you first realise that you wanted to use the Lorrain painting as your subject matter?

It was something that came to me very suddenly when I saw it. It was odd, because I was walking along, looking at these very beautiful landscapes and seascapes, works by Jacob van Ruisdael, for example, and then suddenly *Harbour Scene at Sunset* was rather different. In fact of course it's not really a Dutch landscape at all, but an Italianate one, though Claude was certainly influenced by Dutch painters. The Dutch landscapes and seascapes had a real sense of the weather, and the Claude Lorrain was obviously an imaginative scene of an idealised harbour, so it has a very different feel.

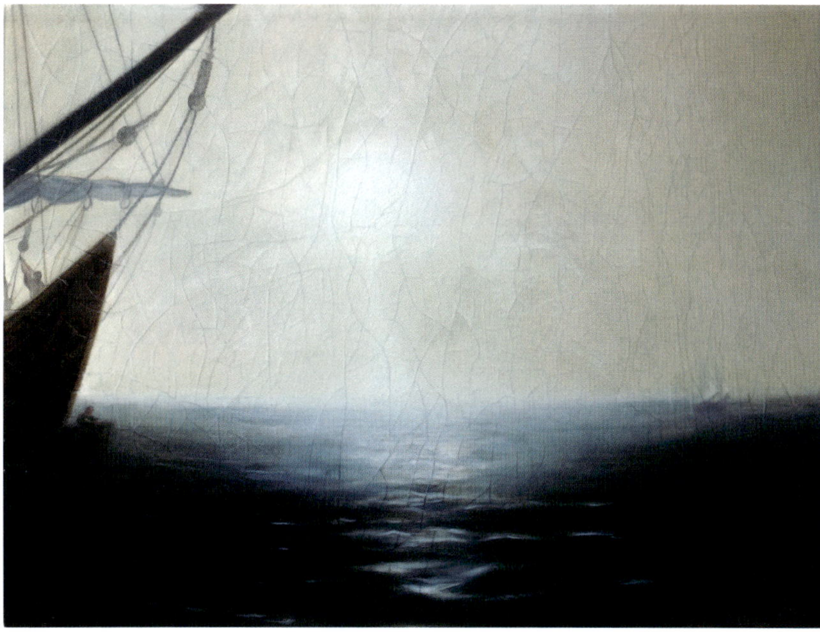

Claire Kerr, *Surface*, 2013
Oil on gesso panel, 12 × 16 cm. Private collection, London

So you took a section and painted it with meticulous attention to detail, particularly on the surface of the work: You focused on a certain area right in the centre of the painting.

Well, I'd been reading about longitude and John Harrison's chronometers, and thinking about time passing and navigation at sea. This made me think about the cracks in the surface of the paint in the Lorrain work. You have an idea of time passing which you get from the cracked surface, and then you have the horizon and the sun which were the vital elements for taking sextant readings for latitude. People talk about photography in the context of time, but I think you get this incredible sense of time with paintings because you have an idea of duration, the very direct link with the past (Lorrain finished the painting in 1643), and the signs of ageing, which are very tangible. The irony is that I've painted this by spending *time* reproducing the signs of time passing – it's like a circle.

Can you tell me about your working methods? You use almost obsolete methods.

There is something about the contemporary world which is so complex, so fleeting. One way to counter that is to focus on something which is ridiculously time-consuming and requires a high degree of concentration, which is like an antidote in a way. And I focus on apparently obsolete ways of working, partly because in the contemporary world things become obsolete extremely quickly. It's a bit of a risk, I feel like I'm experimenting on myself. I have adopted a method of painting with oil on gesso which is very time-consuming, but it gives me time to think very exhaustively about what I'm doing. I used to do huge paintings at college, and gradually they got smaller and smaller. The problems are actually to do with time, there are absolutely no short cuts. You have to start at the beginning and you have to just keep going until you've finished and there's nothing you can do about the fact that it just takes forever. You have to accept that. You have wait for your paint to dry so I tend to work on a lot of paintings at the same time.

There's a lot of gradation in the light, I would imagine it was quite challenging to get that exact colour.

You can become too obsessed with the detail of what you're doing. On the other hand, there's also something fascinating about making a decision about every single brushstroke, every single colour that you mix. I remember when I was doing *Surface,* the light changed and I thought I'd mixed the colour I was using before, but it came out wrong, so I had to repaint it. I think one of the problems that that situation creates is that you have to remain true to the ideas that were in your head, and not let them get drowned out by the technical aspects of what you're doing. I think in this kind of painting there's a particularly important relationship between the wider aspects of the idea and the very absorbing, technical aspects.

The scale, it's really small, and like a precious object.

I do like working on a small scale and I've always enjoyed contemplation as part of the experience of looking at all kinds of art. I want to somehow

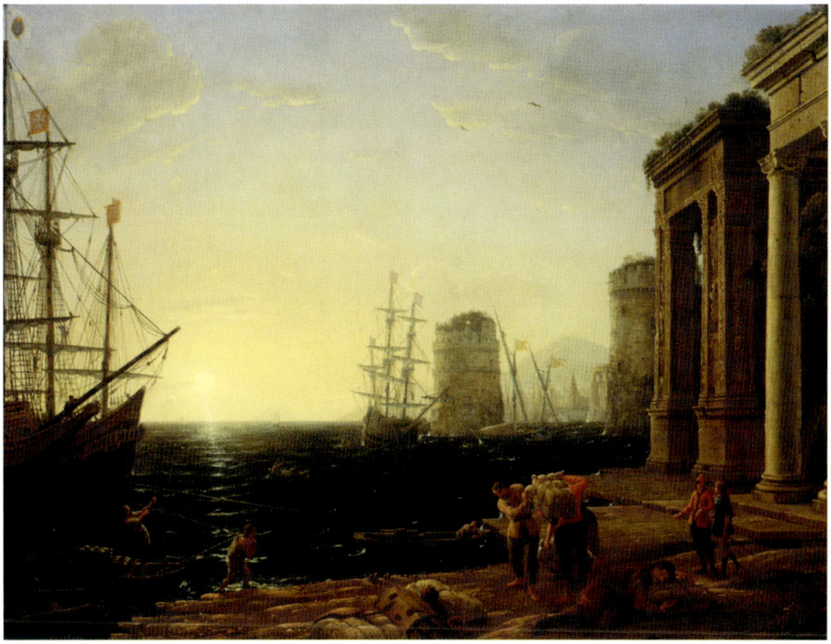

Claude Lorrain, *Harbour Scene at Sunset*, 1643. Oil on canvas
Royal Collection Trust/ © Her Majesty Queen Elizabeth II 2014

draw people in to look at a surface. One way to do that is to make your paintings very large, or else you can make them very small and perhaps encourage people to walk up and look very closely.

Ideally you like your works to float on the wall with their edges exposed. Can we talk about that, because when you saw the Claude Lorrain, the painting would have been in a big gilt frame and rather magnificent?

Yes. One really good thing about that exhibition was that you were allowed to go up very close. There were no barriers at the Queen's Picture Gallery, which I loved because I always go up dangerously close to paintings to look at them in order to really stare at the surface. If I go to an exhibition I want to look at the sides and underneath, to go up close, then stand back. I want to think about how the painting was made technically. I think when paintings are framed you do lose that, there is a sense of the surface becoming unified. When you are looking at a painting you are looking at thousands of brushstrokes.

For me, paintings are very complicated objects, and that's why people are, I think, still interested in them. It's a surface but it's also an object, whether surrounded by a frame or by a wall.

Can you tell me about the cracks in the surface? They look so authentic. Are they?

Yes and no! The actual cracks were less apparent than the ones that I painted and they were also slightly different. I conducted a certain amount of research about cracks on paintings and in oil paint, and paint cracks differently according to the atmosphere, or the way the paint was applied. I have actually painted some of the cracks as if they are cracks in the varnish and some as if they are cracks in the actual paint. But the cracks are not all faithfully reproduced. I have more of them and I wanted to make them more evident.

Can you tell me about your interest in the sea?

I now live in Dublin, so latterly the sea is very present. In Ireland you're never far from the sea. So now I can't imagine not living by the sea. But for many years I was about as far as it was possible to be in the British Isles from the sea, I think.

The sea has a beautifully reflective surface which is shown in your painting. Is that difficult to paint?

It's so fascinating to paint. You have this surface which is completely ephemeral, it changes thousands of times a second, particularly when you have light of any kind. On the other hand, when you look out to sea sometimes it's a solid mass, and I think that's why it's so fascinating. But whether looking at the sea itself or at a painting of the sea, our eyes and our minds switch between this idea of surface and depth, unity and complexity, detail and panorama – both actually and metaphorically. And of course *Surface* is a painting of a *painting* of the sea...

What first attracted you to wanting to paint, or become an artist?

I think what originally made me want to paint was not actually the idea of reproducing things that I saw, it was looking at other paintings. I was fascinated from very early on by paintings of things, rather than things to paint. So, when I first started to paint, many years ago, I wanted to paint paintings, as opposed to *things*. I thought, 'How do people think about reproducing something on a two-dimensional surface?' So rather than, 'Oh, I want to paint the sea', it was, "I want to paint a *painting* of the sea."

And were you interested in particular genres of paintings?

It's interesting you use the word 'genre', because it's something that fascinates me. In literature there are very particular genres, like marine literature, and I'm interested in marine paintings as a genre, for example, or particular kinds of landscape painting. I think I often look at things as part of a genre rather than individually. My paintings are part of a genre as well, and you can't get away from that. In the same way, art is always of its time: you can always tell when something was painted, pretty much. It reflects a particular way of thinking about the world. That is what really interests me: how art reflects over time a certain idea of thinking about the world, rather than, you know, an idea of representing something.

Are there any particular works of art or galleries that have inspired you?

When I was living in Paris I used to go to the Louvre almost every day, and I think that was the first time I had ever really looked at how paintings were made. I remember going to a *Nabis* exhibition and seeing Pierre Bonnard's work. I remember quite suddenly realising, or rather being aware of, technical aspects of how these paintings were made. There are so many art galleries in Paris: I used to go to them all, and I think that's why I became so interested in this way of looking at paintings from the past. I'm always interested in how meaning in an image is built up from the tangible material aspects of an object such as a painting, and then all the other less tangible aspects, particularly where these relate to the history of art, or culture. There's a sort of strange recipe which involves all these very physical aspects of a surface and an object, and then the imagination and our cultural viewpoint and our relationship with the history of art together create meaning. In *Surface* there's an object and a surface, which is also on another surface. It taps into art history or cultural history and the powerful place that the sea has in our imagination.

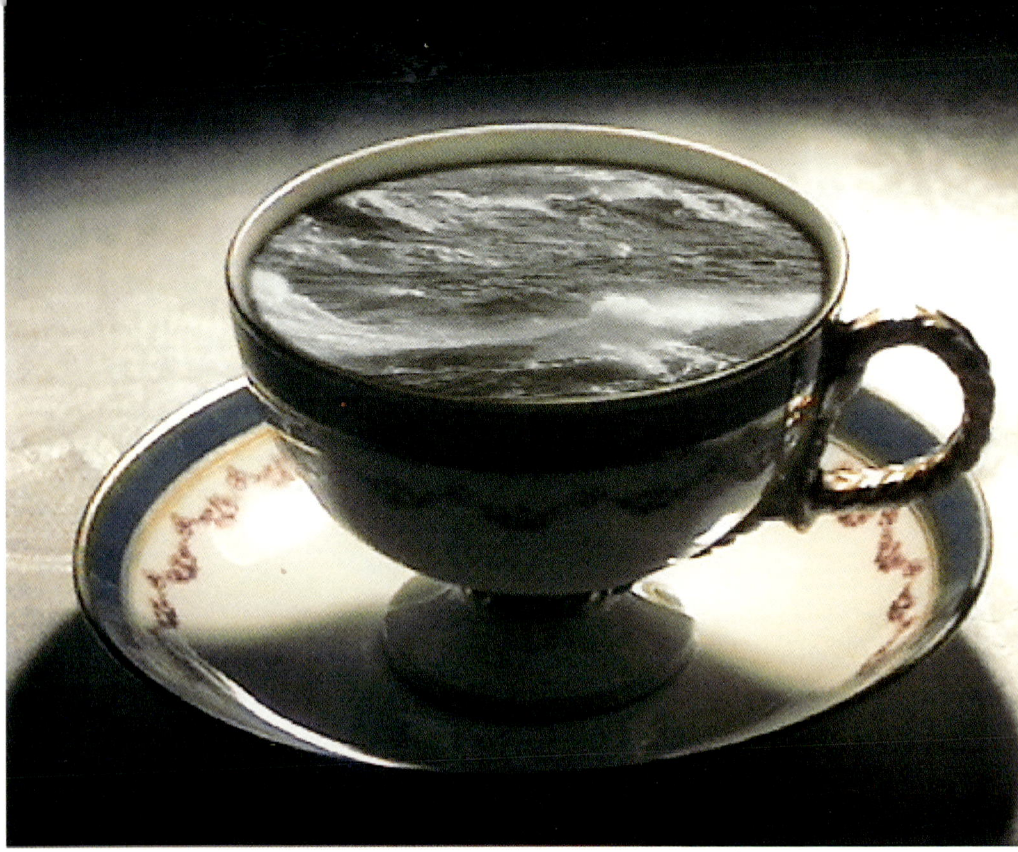

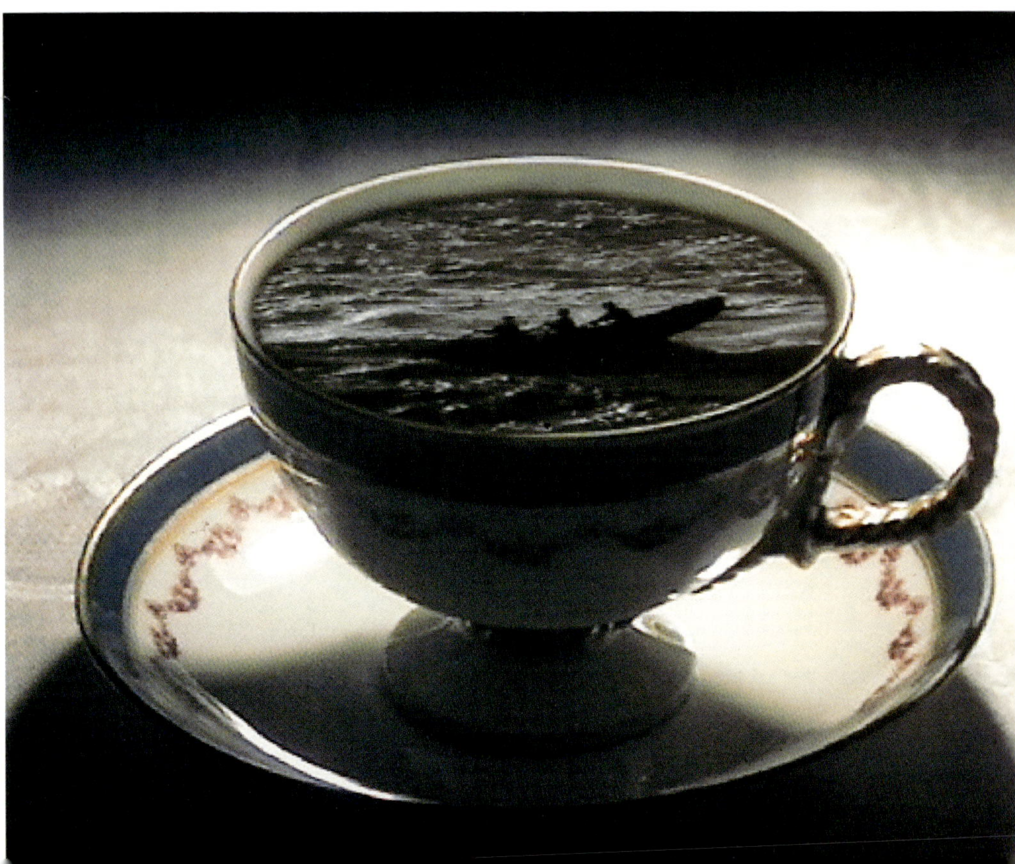

DOROTHY CROSS

TEACUP, 1997

Can we begin by talking about the circumstances that led to you making Teacup?

Well, in 1997, about ten artists were used as guinea pigs to make a piece of work using technology. I was a complete novice when it came to editing, or anything on a computer, but I had a perfect, simple idea, so I worked with a technician to resolve it. The genesis was that I had been fascinated by the 1934 film *Man of Aran*[1] directed by Robert Flaherty, the Irish-American film maker, which I saw as a teenager. I then spent time camping on the Aran Islands and wrote an essay in my early art education about the islands and the traditions there. The opening credits of the film roll with, 'In this desperate environment, the Man of Aran, because his independence is the most precious privilege he can win from life, fights for his existence, bare though it might be. It is a fight from which he will have no respite, until the end of his indomitable days or until he meets his master – the sea'. The film is very much about the romanticised essence of a traditional family on the island of Aran, for example, the little boy fishing with a string over a cliff, and it was all a little bit too perfect. What it did do for me was to emphasise the

OPPOSITE: Dorothy Cross, *Teacup*, 1997. Video transferred to DVD (3 minute loop)
Courtesy the artist and Frith Street Gallery, London

exaggeration of the domestic life and the sea, because I'm interested in pitching things against each other. So I was interested in the union of the family, and the chickens, cows and seaweed, and the scene where they hunt a basking shark, particularly since I have had a basking shark in my studio in order to make work. There is also a very beautiful scene in the film where fishermen are out in a currach, a traditional Irish rowing boat. Flaherty asked the men to set out in a wild sea, which they wouldn't normally do, and the currach crashed against the rocks on the shoreline when returning to shore. I remember even as a young person thinking, 'Goodness, how extraordinary that these men are pulling their tiny oars through these massive seas.' Those snowstorm globes that you shake came to mind, and remembering the storm scene I thought I would attempt to make a little storm held in a beautiful teacup. I didn't know whether or not to project it into the teacup, or what to do technically. What we ended up doing was creating a vignette inside the teacup, then photoshopping in a three minute loop of the storm scene.

So one centre of passion for me was the ocean, and the risk involved in those men rowing in that storm. The other concern was the teacup. I spent a long time trying to find the right cup, because it had to be perfect; it had to be civilised; it had to represent a certain class of tea drinking, not just a workman's mug, or a chipped old cottage teacup. My mother had very beautiful things, so I searched her house and found the bone china teacup, then shot it on a piece of white Irish linen. The technical people helped me place the storm inside the teacup. Occasionally people are disappointed that you don't come across an actual teacup on a table and see the storm projected inside, but I think it works as a complete projection because of the intimacy of the scale. It's projected the *size* of the teacup; the video being small presents an intimacy, almost shrine-like.

For me, *Teacup* is a mixture of a toy-like fascination and the risk involved with the fishermen out in nature, combined with the comfort of tea drinking. In the video loop you don't actually know whether the men drowned or not. You see the currach crashing up in the waves, and then just foam before the currach appears again. So if you don't know the film you actually wouldn't know what occurred. I wanted that quality of the wildness of the stormy sea really exaggerated in relation to the tame quality of the cup.

I love the conflation of the Atlantic Ocean that you're so familiar with, and the domestic teacup. It has always struck me there's something very beautiful about that cup of tea – that delicate and feminine teacup, and the men struggling against the ocean.

For me, there is also the Englishness of the cup of tea: the idea of the British aristocrat with this very delicate china, the "civilisation" of afternoon tea in English society. It was also about colonisation, and the fact that the west coast of Ireland remained relatively untainted by colonisation because it didn't have any wealth for the British. It was popularly thought that the English said, 'To hell or to Connaught', and Cromwell's general, Edmund Ludlow, said that the west coast was 'a country where there is not water enough to drown a man, wood enough to hang one, nor earth enough to bury him...'[2]. So it was a really savage territory – *sauvage* – you know, wild. It is important in the work that you have this culture of tea drinking which is in some ways labelled as English, and inside that is this manic attempt to live in nature. It is a very simple piece: people can relate to it on any level.

Can you talk about your fascination with the sea?

Well, as kids, we grew up with the sea. We were lucky enough that our father had a small house in Fountainstown by the sea, and we went there for three months of the year. My mother met my father in West Cork on her brother's yacht, and my father had a yearning for the sea: he always wanted to go to sea, but inherited a job and had children. So he imbued us with that love of water. As kids we were always out in boats, swimming and catching fish.

When did you start really being interested in swimming?

I was a bit of a scaredy-cat actually. I wasn't as brave as my sister or my cousins. We used to swim in a cove called Shell Hole near our house by the sea. I only learnt to swim properly when I was about eight, which was quite old. I nearly drowned once, when I was trying to follow my sister out to a rock. I remember sinking into the deep green water, and my head coming up and hearing laughing and shouting, then going down again into silence and then coming up again, and, you know, kind of knowing I was drowning; then my sister grabbing me and dragging me back to the shore. She was probably ten or eleven and I was mortified. I said, 'Please don't tell Mum and Dad', because I thought it was shameful that I nearly drowned. Then my brother started training me as a swimmer, and from the age of eleven I swam internationally for six years. For seven years we trained every day for hours.

I think of being in water as a kind of suspension; the fact that we can't fly, but when you're in water it's the closest thing to flying. And it also removes you from language, so it's a wordless place. For me, swimming is also something to do with a sense of another membrane: it's about an extension of your body, that you become part of the water, your skin merging with something else. I hate wearing a wetsuit, as you lose that contact. It's also a very beautiful sensation when you're gently diving or when you can swim very well, because it's effortless – an area of desire.

Did you ever have your own currach?

Yes. I had a beautiful traditional currach, which I bought when I first moved to Connemara. I had it for four years, and then it broke its moorings in a storm and broke up against rocks north of here. I was in bed when I heard the gale and I said, 'Oh no, oh no, my boat!'. And in the morning it had gone. Originally, currachs were covered with cow skin, and later with tarred canvas. Travelling in one on the sea, it feels almost like it's an extension of your own body, as the taut canvas membrane is so thin and is the only thing separating you from the ocean. When currachs got a hole, the fishermen sometimes used to repair them with bits of old socks, and things that they could stick in the hole so it wouldn't sink. Currachs never feel permanent: they are constantly being repaired and reskinned. The modern world is so much about trying to make everything permanent, which in itself holds its own destruction. There is a life cycle of destruction and repair with the currach. I've used some broken currachs in my practice, to bring in the notion of that cycle, of the perilous quality of materials, including our own material, physical bodies. I believe we should not lock ourselves away from the experience of nature, from the violence or the calm.

Here on the West Coast where my studio is, I swim at the edge of my land. Sometimes the sea's aquamarine turquoise, and when you dive through it, it's like diving through glass. Yet today the same ocean is churning: white, grey, full of kelp, sucking up through the cracks in the rocks. It's incredible, that shift of weather, from calmness to wildness. It's very beautiful.

NOTES

1. *Man of Aran*. Dir. Robert J. Flaherty. Gaumont-British Corporation, 1934. Film.
2. Ludlow, Edmund. *The Memoirs of Edmund Ludlow, Lieutenant-General of the Horse in the Army of the Commonwealth of England, 1625–1672*. Vol. 2. Clarendon Press, 1894, p. 292.

TACITA DEAN

TEIGNMOUTH ELECTRON, CAYMAN BRAC, 1999

In 1968 Donald Crowhurst was one of nine competitors who entered the Sunday Times *Golden Globe Race, attempting to be the first person to sail single-handedly around the world without stopping. I wanted to start by talking specifically about his abandoned boat* Teignmouth Electron, *which you photographed on Cayman Brac in the Caribbean in 1999.*

I learned about the location of Crowhurst's trimaran from a local newspaper article in the tiny museum in Teignmouth, Devon. A local man, who was in the navy, had seen it when out in the Cayman Islands. I eventually tracked down Winston McDermot, who had bought *Teignmouth Electron*, and decided to go to Cayman Brac to photograph it, with the support of the National Maritime Museum.

When you saw the boat, it was rather dilapidated, and had quite a history after being found floating in the Atlantic Ocean, on 10th July 1969.

Yes, after his boat was found abandoned at sea, it was acquired by someone called Bunny Francis in the West Indies. With a few adjustments, they made the trimaran work well. Crowhurst had not had the time to do proper sea tests, so it's particularly sad that he so nearly built a good racing boat, but for a few relatively minor adjustments. Later, it was bought by Winston McDermot, who knew the story, and it ended up on Cayman Brac. Subsequently it got damaged in a hurricane. McDermot believed it was haunted. When I found it, it was quite beaten up but it was still complete. Now it's really destroyed – I've seen photographs of it recently.

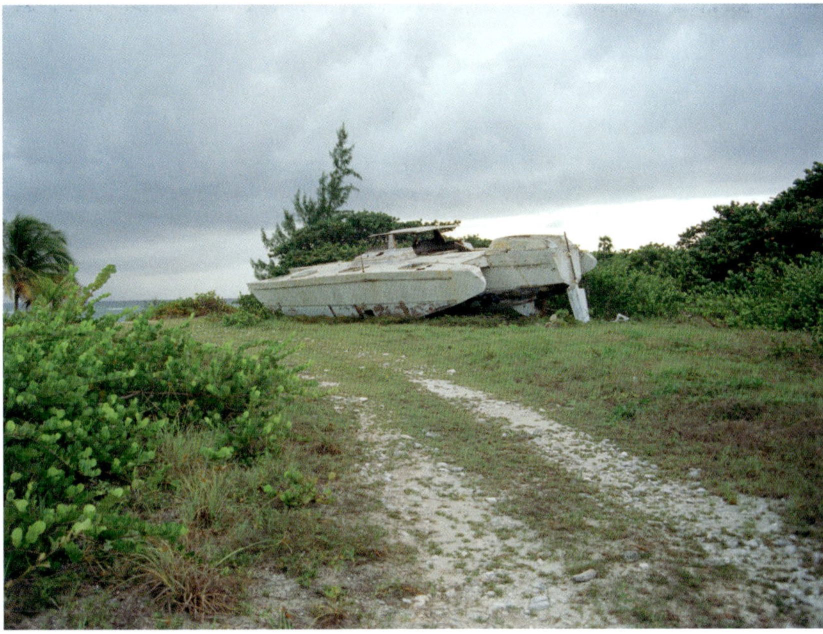

Tacita Dean, *Teignmouth Electron, Cayman Brac*, 1999 (also detail on p.53)
Colour Photograph, 68 × 89 cm / 112 × 130 cm
Courtesy the artist, Frith Street Gallery, London and Marian Goodman, Paris/New York

I wonder if you can cast your mind back to when you first came across it, and how you felt finally finding it?

I remember it was like the reward of a pilgrimage. It was incredible. We arrived in the evening and then we had to try and find it. And we *found* it! Seeing it in the evening light was amazing, because things become mythical in your own narrative, so to actually find its tangible form, to know it's not a spectre, was quite incredible. I was on the island for a week, the weather was terrible, and we were always ducking the storms. I remember the filming well, because I also had my 16mm film camera with me, but only ten rolls of film. There were two roads on the island and one day we decided to explore the other one, which was a cul-de-sac, and found the *Bubble House*, a [then, in 1999] deserted and half-completed house built by a Frenchman. So then I had to eke out my film stock in order to film both *Bubble* and *Teignmouth.*

You also explored beneath the boat.

I knew Crowhurst had this storage facility in case he capsized. On a trimaran this is a real fear, because you can't right yourself like you can with a monohull. So he had made this emergency set-up – a concealed, screwed-up compartment underneath the boat, between the floats, but over the years the wood had become rotten. I remember I put my hand in and felt something. I pulled out food and lozenge wrappings from the sixties, and other quite amazing things, but then I felt his boat flares, which were called, rather appropriately, 'Pains Boat Flares'. I brought them back with me on an aeroplane, which I see now was rather irresponsible. I mean, now I would have been put in prison for that, but it didn't cross my mind at the time. I gave them to the National Maritime Museum for safekeeping, and they blew them up in a controlled explosion a little while later.

You were fascinated with Crowhurst's logbooks, and also wrote to J. G. Ballard, the author, about him.

Yes, I remember thinking Crowhurst was such a Ballardian name, and at the time I'd just begun a correspondence with Ballard, so wondered what he thought about him because there were elements of Crowhurst's adventure that might have appealed to him. Ballard remembered the story, but he thought Crowhurst was foolhardy. He did write a beautiful piece comparing *Teignmouth Electron* to one of those Second World War planes that are still being found in the jungles of the South Pacific. It was the anachronism and the de-contextualisation which fascinated Ballard: this strange beached boat with a single palm tree near by, which was poignant. I had also previously held Crowhurst's logbooks in my hands, and read them. What's interesting is that even within one logbook, one can see the very strained fictional version of his journey, in very neat handwriting, where he was trying to maintain his faked journey – which didn't last for very long. And then, at the other end of the logbook, you see his whole real journey: his genuine log where everything is unravelling. Crowhurst's chronometer, which is now an obsolete instrument, was extremely important in terms of trying to locate oneself at sea, but it had to be kept accurate to Greenwich Mean Time. Even a minute out is a lot, several *miles* out at certain points in the Equator. So if the chronometer has an error, the sailor has to keep the error in mind in all their calculations. But Crowhurst lost track of his chronometer's time and its error, so in the logbook you see him counting down chronometer time, but then at a certain point, you realise he doesn't even know whether it's day or night. He then obsesses about the error, and writes 'MAX POSS ERROR'. He counts down to his decision, which I think he took deliberately, to jump overboard with his chronometer, which has always been deeply existential for me, but I remember his son thought it was very practical, to weigh him down. By the end, you can tell from the logbook that there was total affinity between Crowhurst and his chronometer in terms of time. He began to suffer from 'time madness', which is when you no longer know the time at sea, therefore you no longer know where you are: you are lost in time and space, which is what often used to happen at sea before the invention of the Harrison clock and the ability to keep Greenwich Mean Time on board ship. If you are in London and don't know the time, you're not lost anywhere – you're still in the street. But at sea it must be terrifying when you don't know where you are anymore. Crowhurst also invented an instrument called the 'navicator', which also didn't work accurately. I remember reading about it in the *Strange Last Voyage of Donald Crowhurst.*[1] That would have been one of the first of many failures, I think, after he set off. What is so extraordinary about this story is the small-worldness of it. I remember reading all the Teignmouth Council minutes, and it was unbelievable how local the whole thing was, as against this massive existential crisis that Crowhurst had. It was all about bravado, and the man next door, and the caravan park owner who gave him the money to build the trimaran. It's a particularly English story in a way. Actually there's another tragic story related to the race, about Nigel Tetley, one of the other competitors. In the lead, he learned mid-Atlantic that Crowhurst was supposedly very close on his tail, so he pushed his boat too fast and it sank, and he had to be rescued. He would have genuinely won the *Golden Globe*. He later hanged himself from a tree. So this story has more than one tragedy.

Were you able to trace Crowhurst's increasing engagement with a strange parallel universe through the logbooks?

Well, the thing is that Crowhurst took as his reading Einstein's *Theories of Relativity*, whereas Robin Knox-Johnston, the winner, got the scouts to choose his books, and I think you've got the whole thing there in a nutshell. Crowhurst starts reading the theories of relativity and becomes, in his insanity and because he was clearly losing his grip, part of this cosmic game. He really thought he was playing chess with God in the end, and with fate.

Was he a religious man?

No, but I think he called fate 'God'. I don't think he was a religious man but, you know, in that generation everyone was passively religious. He was a great chess player. I remember his son, Simon Crowhurst, explaining the relationship with chess to me because I'm not a chess player, and he had studied his father's last writings about chess and then his words, 'It is finished, IT IS THE MERCY... I will resign the game'. I think in the end he chose to confess, to reveal his lie. They found a paintbrush balanced on top of a cup, so there can't have been any jolting of the boat. He was in the Sargasso Sea, a legendary calm part of the Atlantic, and I believe he chose the truth in the end, and laid out his confession for it to be found. He left the logbooks, he didn't jump over with them... I don't think he was in a devious situation any more, I think he had come through that, and deliberately chose to leave the logbooks.

And the final resting place of the trimaran?

Cayman Brac. It is a tiny island, and *Teignmouth Electron* sits on a beach right by the little airport where you take the small plane back to Grand Cayman. I filmed out of the plane window, because you see the boat from above. It seems like an appropriate resting place.

NOTES

1. Tomalin, Nicholas, and Ron Hall. *The Strange Last Voyage of Donald Crowhurst*. Hodder and Stoughton, 1970.

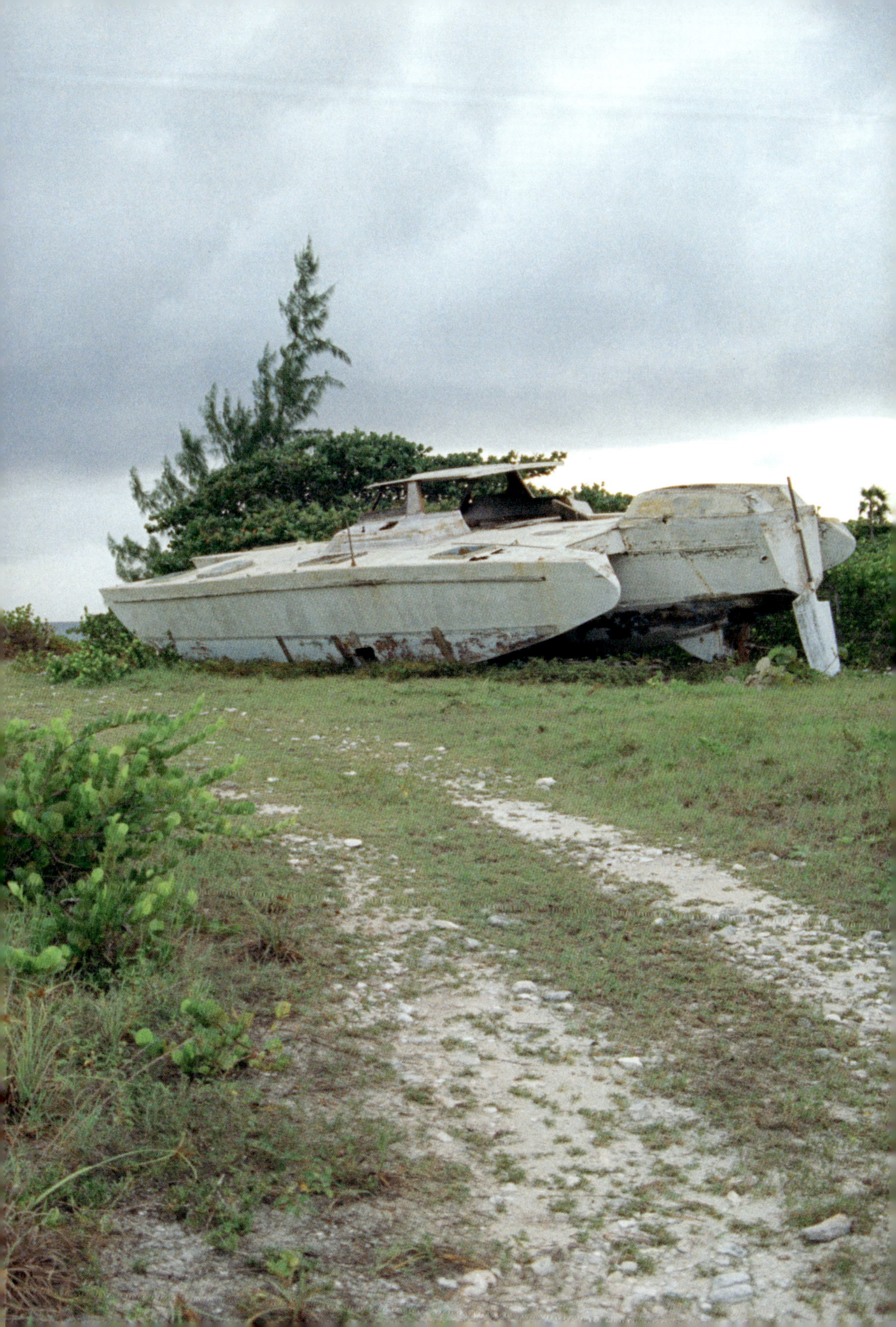

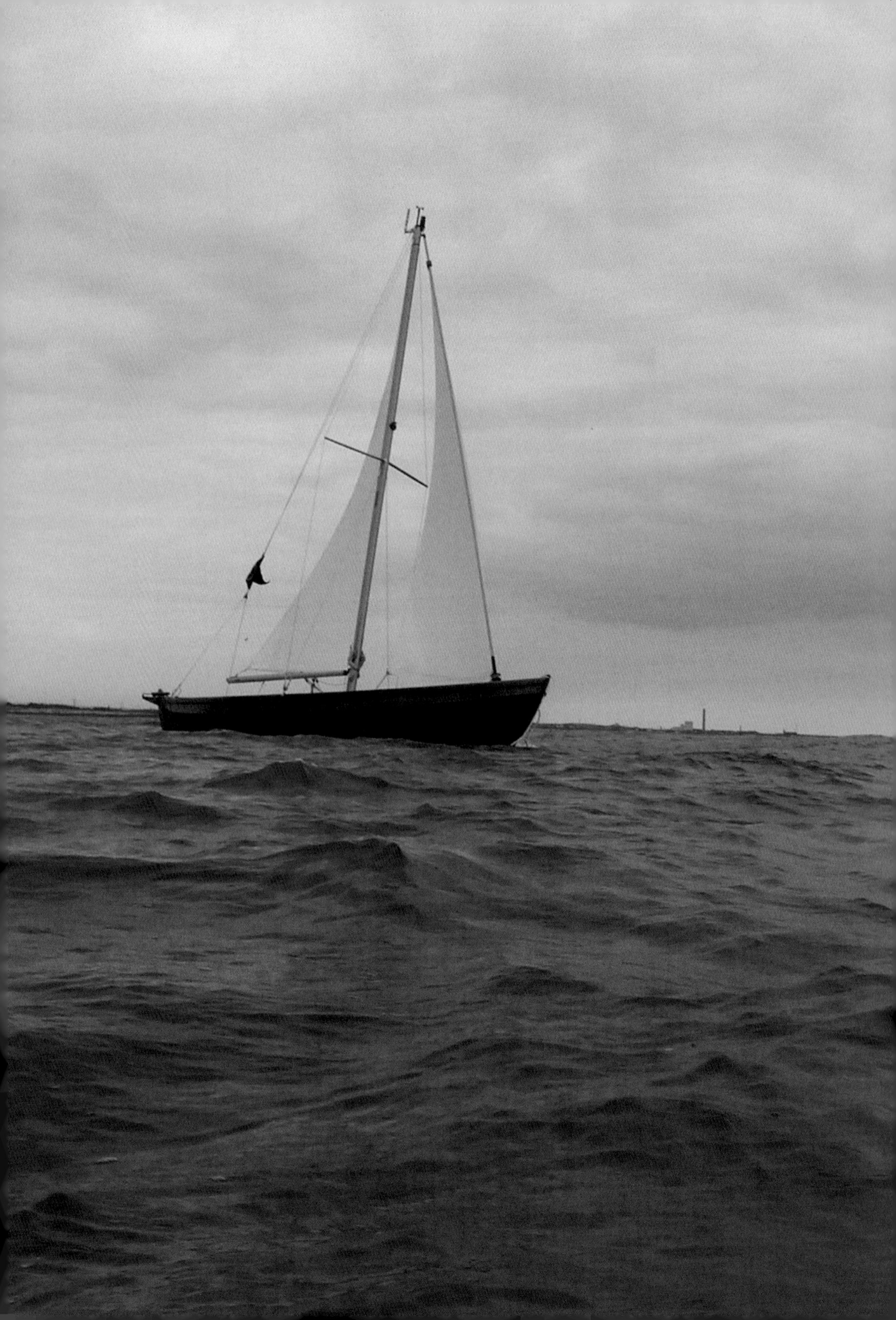

CHRIS BURDEN

GHOST SHIP, 2005[1]

Can I start by asking what the lure of the sea means to you? I know, for example, that you sail.

I have a sailboat here in Los Angeles on dry land, but I used to sail with a friend of mine off the coast of Oxnard, California around the Channel Islands a little north of Los Angeles.

And are you a competent sailor?

Well, I guess. I always sail without a motor, and I make it back.

Because what interested me, looking at Ghost Ship, *was your understanding of what the sea can do to a small sailing vessel, the necessity to tack and navigate.*

Well I remember, as a twelve-year-old living in Connecticut, that we had a big pond, and my dad explained to me about sailing. It seemed very improbable that one could sail *against* the wind, using the wind's force to zigzag back and forth whilst heading into the wind, towards its source. It's a little bit like magic, or perpetual motion. It's counter-intuitive, because if you look out of the window leaves blow with the wind, not against the wind.

OPPOSITE
Chris Burden, *Ghost Ship*, 2005. Digital photograph
Courtesy the artist / Locus+ Archive. Photo: Jonty Tarbuck

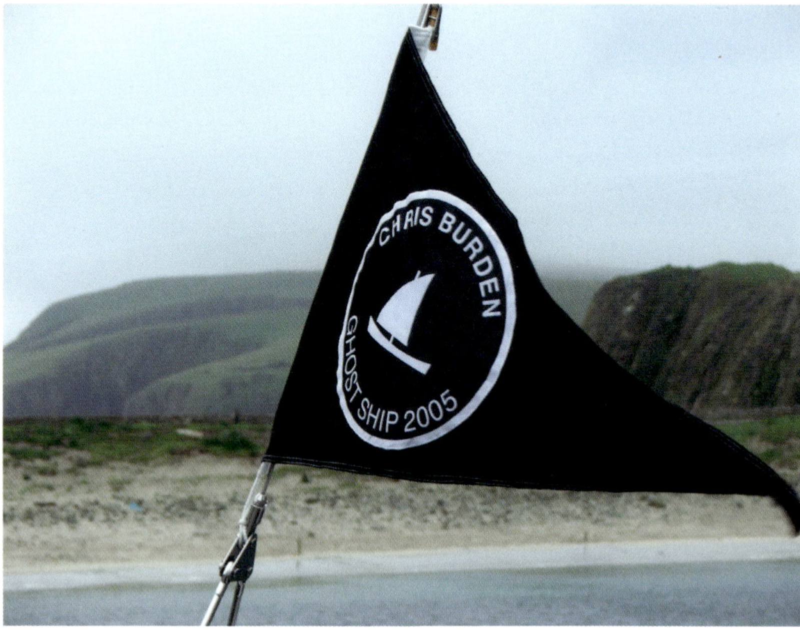

Chris Burden, *Ghost Ship*, 2005. Ghost Ship's ensign flag. Digital photograph
Courtesy the artist / Locus+ Archive. Photo: Jonty Tarbuck

So was your first sailing experience on freshwater then?

Well, sort of. I went to high school in the Boston area, and the Charles River flows by Harvard University growing wider and wider until it becomes part of a big bay, where it meets the sea. In their wisdom, the city of Boston had a fleet of forty or fifty 16-foot open sailboats, and for a very small fee of ten or fifteen dollars any child could sign up and learn how to sail. That's how I learned. You could sail back and forth across the bay under the eye of an instructor. When you got good enough they would let you take the boats out alone. It was a wonderful thing. These small boats didn't have engines. The 20-foot boat that my friend and I sailed out of Oxnard [California], was also engineless.

Tell me how your work Ghost Ship *began its journey in 2005.*

The *Ghost Ship* was built on Fair Isle, in the Shetlands. It was supposed to sail from there to the Tall Ships festival in Newcastle upon Tyne. The tall ships were coming into the harbour in Newcastle on a very specific time and date, and the idea was to link up. I was in Peterhead [Scotland] with Jon Bewley of Locus+ [visual arts agency]. The crew was ready to launch from Fair Isle when a huge storm hit, and we kept waiting and waiting for the storm to clear. We realised that unless *Ghost Ship* sailed, it wouldn't make it to Newcastle on time. So the *Ghost Ship* was launched in a huge North Sea storm with ten foot seas; it ended up having to be towed by the mother ship *Bernicia* through the night because the seas were so strong. There was a young French sailor who was part of the crew on the *Bernicia*. At some point during the middle of the night the tow rope broke and the *Ghost Ship* was basically adrift in the dark, in tumultuous seas. The Frenchman jumped from the *Bernicia* onto the Plexiglas deck of the *Ghost Ship* and secured the rope to the mother ship, which was just an insane thing to do because basically if he'd gone overboard, they weren't going to be finding him any time soon. I recall a conversation I had in a taxicab in New York, in which the taxi driver said, 'You know, I was in the US Navy and the thing that destroyed most of the US Navy was the Typhoon Cobra in 1944, off the Philippines'.

Chris Burden, *Ghost Ship*, 2005. Digital photograph
Courtesy the artist / Locus+ Archive. Photo: Jonty Tarbuck

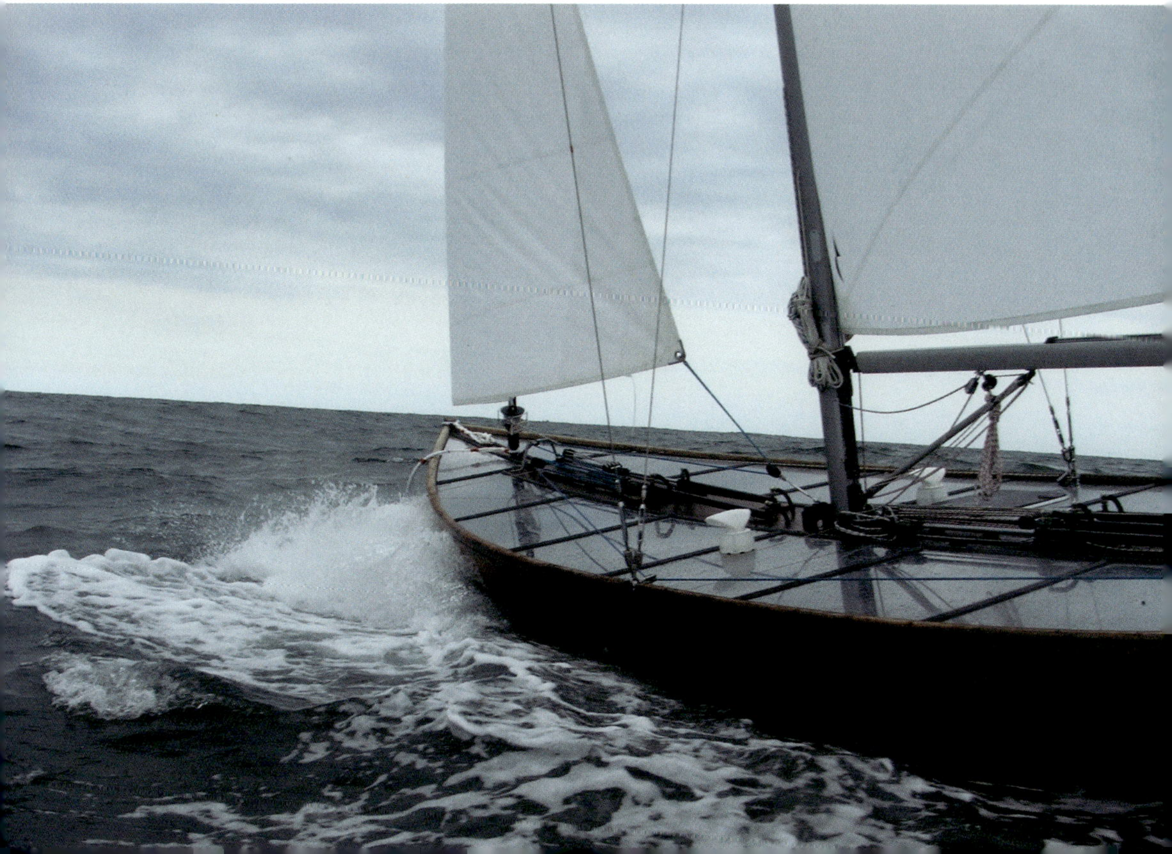

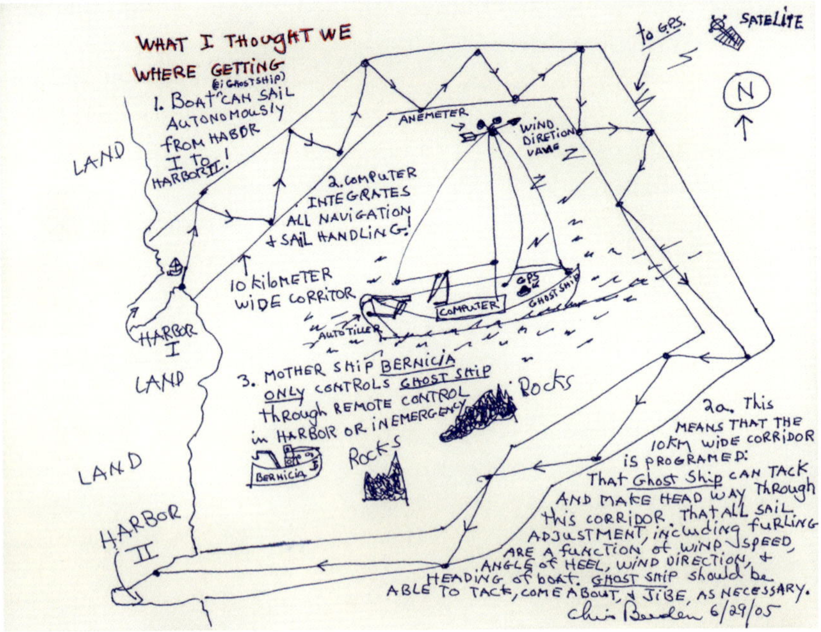

Chris Burden, *Ghost Ship (What I thought we were getting)*, 2005
8.5 x 11 inches – framed. Ink on paper (Giclée print)

Ghost Ship *was an ambitious idea – a self-navigating vessel programmed to understand all the dynamics of longitude and latitude and the sea and weather systems – all computer-controlled. What inspired you to make this work?*

The technology for a self-navigating vessel exists in theory, but to be able to realise it is still a daunting challenge. There is a maritime tradition of ghost ships, both actual and legendary, and they are very scary things. If you are at sea in the Pacific and you come upon a ship with no sailors on board, that's a very spooky thing. But the idea that you could send something across an ocean autonomously using the very ancient method of being able to sail against the wind was a compelling concept.

I am much taken with the mysteries of crewless ships found at sea, such as the Mary Celeste, *but also with the idea of the new driverless cars, tube trains*

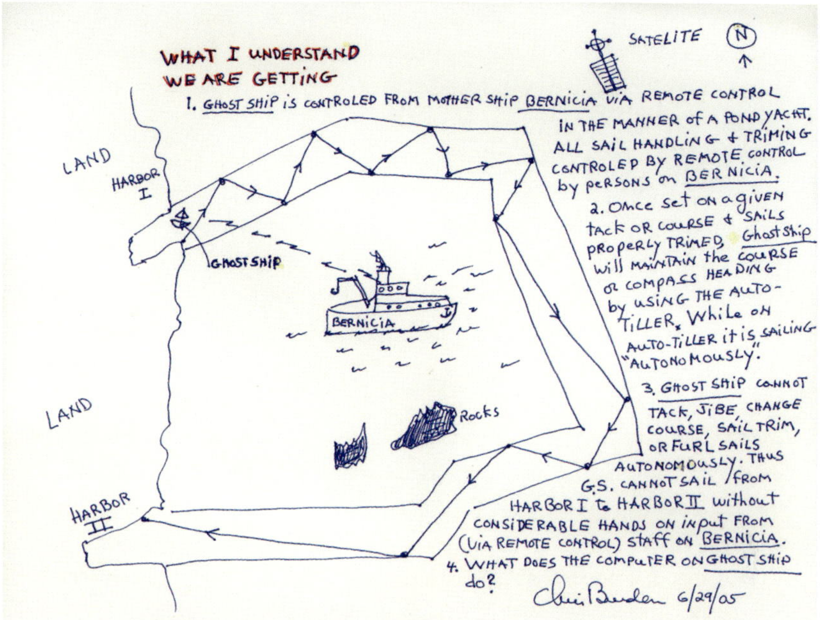

Chris Burden, *Ghost Ship (What I understand we are getting)*, 2005
8.5 x 11 inches – framed. Ink on paper (Giclée print)

and drones. You were able to use the technology to make that leap with shipping. When you started designing the Ghost Ship *and working with Southampton University, were there any surprises in terms of things you found that were problematic or difficult to programme?*

Well let's be clear, the *Ghost Ship* was conceived to do one thing, which in the final analysis it was not capable of doing. You could not be in Portsmouth and dial in the longitude and latitude of Liverpool and expect the ship to find its way there. There are two drawings which explain what I *thought* we were getting and what we were *actually* getting: I thought we would get a boat that could be self-navigating with sails that could furl and tack. What we ended up getting was a sailboat which we had to control and navigate on some occasions from the mother ship – which was not exactly what I had envisioned. It wasn't a complete failure though, it was a step in the right direction. I think what surprised me was that the scientists and marine professors at the University of Southampton said that to write the code for a program using all this information – i.e. location, current, wind speed, tacking, furling the sails – and trying to figure out how to stay on course, would be a very complex program requiring a couple of years to write.

I was trying to get an autonomously-sailing vessel realised and would probably have gone down a different track, but I understand the organisers' reasoning. The money that was raised to do this project was tied in with the Tall Ships' Race. I think Locus+, the organisers, felt they should somehow celebrate the tradition of British seafaring. They commissioned the boat to be made by Ian Best, who lives on remote Fair Isle, where the weather is stormy most of the year and the kids have to be flown off the island to school. The vessel was built in the traditional manner. But the sailing rig was not traditional because the Sixareens [traditional fishing boats used most commonly around the Shetland Islands] were rowed to a destination, then sailed with the wind on the return trip, using a square sail. They weren't designed to tack.

The Locus+ people decided that they should spend a portion of the money on having a replica of this traditional boat built to celebrate British seafaring. We had planned that the boat would stop in a series of smaller towns on the way from Fair Isle to Newcastle upon Tyne. These small towns had boat museums or fishing museums and we were going to put the boat on display for a day or two, but we ran out of time. So that didn't happen. If I'd done the project myself I'd have bought a cheap sailboat and spent the bulk of the moneys on the electronics, but that's not what happened.

I was really fascinated with the drawings, and the wonderful photographs and video of the Ghost Ship *sailing in the different weather conditions. But the sculptural installation kind of took over, didn't it?*

Well I think there was a need on the part of the organisers to fulfil the heritage aspect.

I loved the way that chance and frustration played a role, and it reminded me of your previous practice, and works such as When Robots Rule: The Two Minute Airplane Factory *(1999).*

Yes, that's part of the daily struggle.

Ghost Ship is a continuing sculpture...

Yes, it is. I had made a work previously that related directly to *Ghost Ship*. I was invited to create a sculpture in Charleston, South Carolina, an art component of a music festival. I admired a boat builder and designer named Phil Bolgers, who lived in Maine. He had an anti-yachting aesthetic: He didn't believe in brass and teak decks, he believed in instant boats that could be nailed together using plywood, and that were exceptionally seaworthy. The boats would be *consumed* in their use. In other words you could make a boat cheaply and quickly that would be used. When it wore out you could just make a new one. I really liked his aesthetic, and he designed this little 16-foot boat that was blue-water capable. My idea in Charleston was to build three of these boats, and they would be called individually the U, the S and the A. At the time I considered the boats to be an art object titled *Three Ghost Ships* (1991). The concept was to do a reverse Boston Tea Party. We were going to sail tea, robotically or autonomously, from Charleston to Southampton, England. I would fly from America to Southampton and be at the docks to greet my tea coming in. However, there wasn't money to fully equip the boats electronically, and my vision of three small sailboats electronically rigged to be able to sail without a human sailor from America's Atlantic coast to England was not fulfilled. *Ghost Ship* is a sculpture and a sailing vessel. Unfortunately it still needs considerable hands-on input from the mother ship *Bernicia*, but in the future this could change.

✦

Chris Burden died on 10th May 2015, shortly after this interview with Jean Wainwright.

NOTES

1. *Ghost Ship* Installation, *Ship to Shore: Art and the Lure of the Sea*, John Hansard Gallery, Southampton, 2014

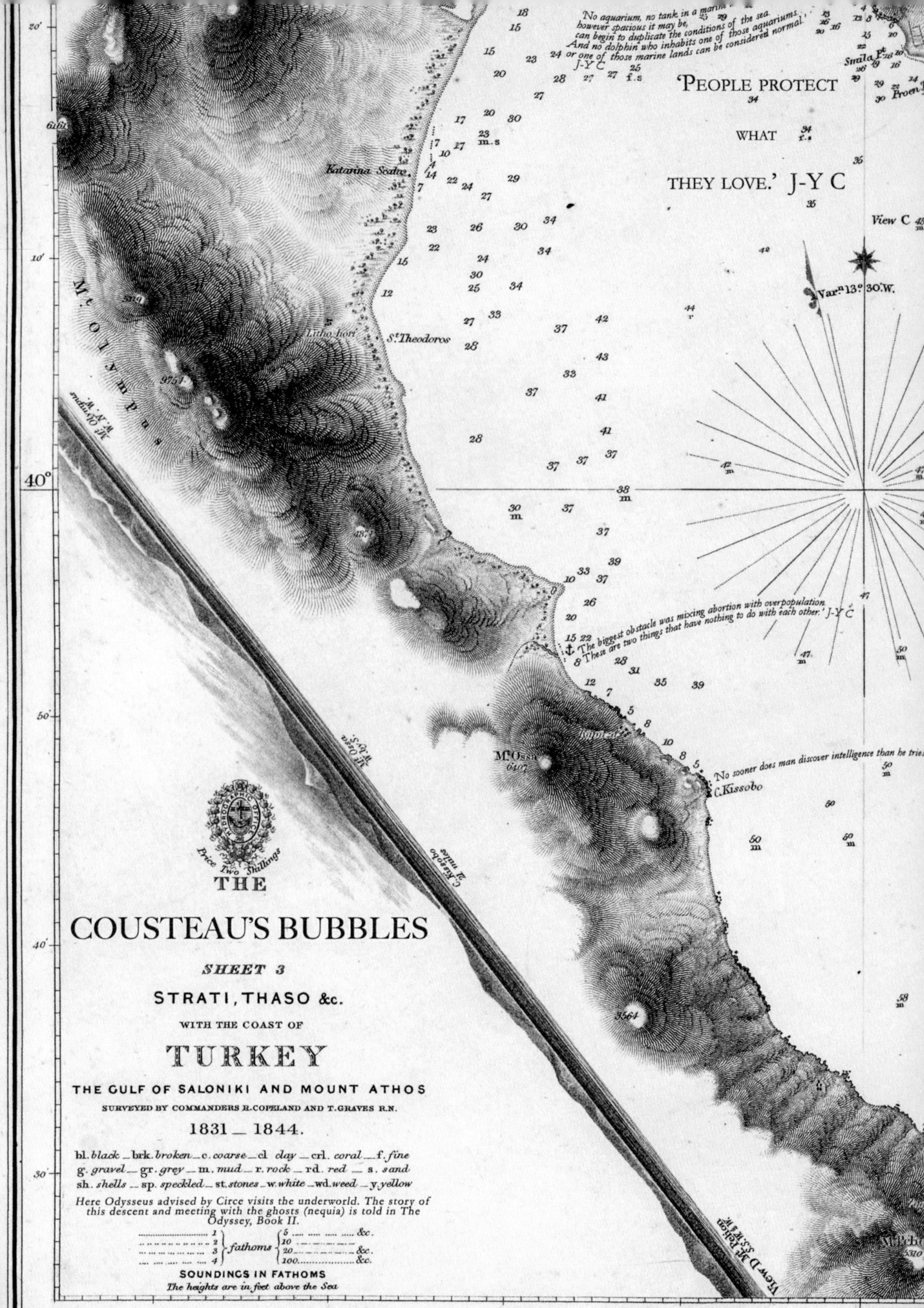
No aquarium, no tank in a marine
however spacious it may be,
can begin to duplicate the conditions of the sea.
And no dolphin who inhabits one of those aquariums
or one of those marine lands can be considered normal.'
J-Y C
'PEOPLE PROTECT
WHAT
THEY LOVE.' J-Y C
Katarina Scala
St. Theodoros
Mt. Olympus
Var.n 13° 30'W.
View C
The biggest obstacle was mixing abortion with overpopulation.
These are two things that have nothing to do with each other.' J-Y C
No sooner does man discover intelligence than he tries
C. Kissobo
Mt. Ossa
Price Two Shillings
THE
COUSTEAU'S BUBBLES
SHEET 3
STRATI, THASO &c.
WITH THE COAST OF
TURKEY
THE GULF OF SALONIKI AND MOUNT ATHOS
SURVEYED BY COMMANDERS R.COPELAND AND T.GRAVES R.N.
1831 _ 1844.
bl. black _ brk. broken _ c. coarse _ cl. clay _ crl. coral _ f. fine
g. gravel _ gr. grey _ m. mud _ r. rock _ rd. red _ s. sand
sh. shells _ sp. speckled _ st. stones _ w. white _ wd. weed _ y. yellow
Here Odysseus advised by Circe visits the underworld. The story of this descent and meeting with the ghosts (nequia) is told in The Odyssey, Book II.
1 2 3 4 fathoms 5 &c. 10 20 &c. 100 &c.
SOUNDINGS IN FATHOMS
The heights are in feet above the Sea
20' 30' 40' 50' 23° Longi

SIMON PATTERSON

COUSTEAU IN THE UNDERWORLD, 2008

Simon, can I take you back to your initial idea for Cousteau in the Underworld?

Well, I was commissioned by Lisa Le Feuvre to make the work for a show at the National Maritime Museum, London, in 2008, called *The Undersea World and Other Stories* – and was given carte blanche. I decided to base it around a childhood hero of mine, Jacques-Yves Cousteau, oceanographer and self-styled oceanaut. After talking to the curator of hydrography, I decided that I wanted to make a work based on admiralty charts from the 18th and 19th centuries. What appealed to me about them was that they were in a large heavy atlas, each sheet compiled by a different cartographer. Sometimes the cartographer had added magnificent illustrations of views of the coastline, so that they were almost like illuminated manuscripts where the margins might show beautiful pictures, or, in some cases, where a monk might have doodled. Others were just very dry, with outlines of the coastline and numbers for fathoms, depth soundings and various navigational points. Another thing that appealed to me was that the charts were made by different hands and, because the information is about the sea, they are the opposite of terrestrial maps because the land is represented as negative space – it is the sea that is the interesting part.

OPPOSITE AND FOLLOWING PAGES:
Simon Patterson, *Cousteau in the Underworld*, 2008
25 Fabric charts. Courtesy the artist

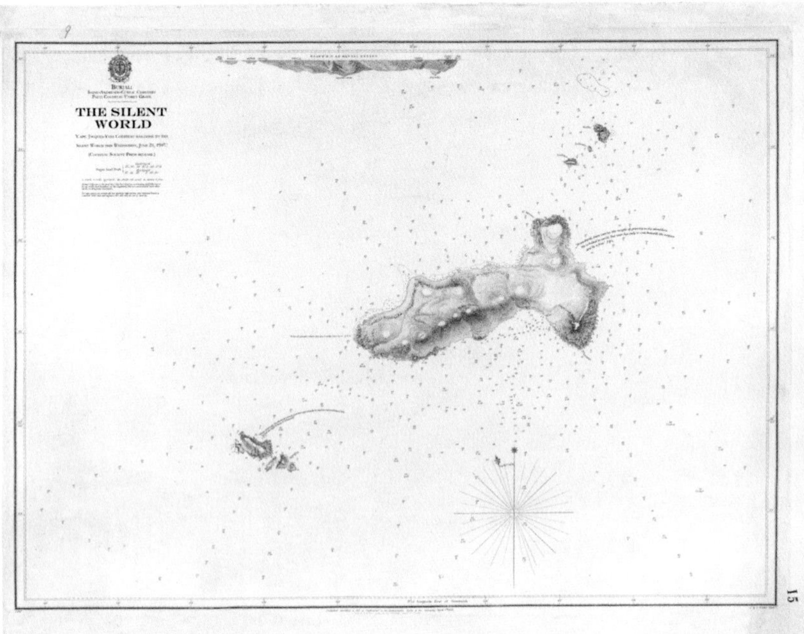

What was it about Jacques Cousteau that made him your hero?

Firstly, as a child in the 1970s, when everyone at that time was preoccupied with outer space, I watched his highly popular television series *The Undersea World of Jacques Cousteau* and marvelled at the underwater footage. Now, with TV series like *The Blue Planet,* we are used to those kinds of programmes, but then it was genuinely new, and people were fascinated. I had also been shown various old *National Geographic* magazines from about 1958, just before the space race, with images of Cousteau's undersea laboratory, like a space station – like Mir – under the Mediterranean.

Cousteau did so many things. He won various medals for gallantry in the war, during which he had been a navy diver whilst secretly working for the Resistance – he had wanted to be a navy flier, but a car accident in his youth made that impossible. Among other things, he co-invented the aqualung and was a pioneer of environmentalism. He persuaded a rich patron to purchase an old Royal Navy minesweeper for him, which became, after conversion, the *Calypso.* He also dived the wreck of the *Britannic*, sister ship of the *Titanic*, in 1975, taking down with him in his submersible an 80- year old nurse who had survived the sinking in the Aegean of the converted hospital ship (there was speculation about whether the *Britannic* had been hit by a German torpedo or had hit a British mine).

Part of Cousteau's appeal was the idea of being in your living room with the television – the porthole into the sea.

Cousteau's approach was not necessarily scientific. He was a populariser – they had a film and sound studio and processing lab on board the *Calypso*, so they were able to edit their films on board this small vessel. But what I found fascinating was that Cousteau, who had been a household name – a film and TV star – is now largely forgotten. I was fascinated by the way in which you pass from life into history, and ultimately into myth. I found that the only way that I could get the information I needed, apart from finding a few books in France in second-hand stores, or in Oxfam shops, was to surf the internet, where of course the information is often inaccurate. I liked the idea of this slippage between fact and fiction, so I decided to embrace that in the work. I transferred 25 charts onto sailcloth, which hang on battens like school maps and charts, each one charting a different aspect of Cousteau's life. So, in the same way that there are many different hands at work in the original charts, I've taken those same charts and had a friend insert photoshopped text using 18th and 19th century style calligraphy. Some of the texts carry factual information about Cousteau's life, much of it contradictory. Others might be a sample from a song about Cousteau found on the Internet, or information about his controversial brother.

Can we talk about the placing of the text on the charts?

Each text was specific to each chart. The legend, or key, at the top of each chart is printed in different fonts – all derived from the original chart – to indicate different sources: the original information about the chart and its compiler, excerpts from Homer's *Odyssey* and parallel narratives from the life of Cousteau culled from Internet. It was that very rapid slippage from fact to myth that interested me. I thought of the work as a sort of atlas of a person's life.

Was there significance in the number of charts?

No, there wasn't. In the *Ship to Shore* exhibition it was installed to look like a room. There are 25 fabric charts in total, but there could have been 250 – there was so much that could have been included. You are meant to read them rather than look at them. The work is meant to be incomplete and open-ended. The installation includes a boat hook that leans against the wall so that, notionally, the charts can be moved, the order altered, which is partly why I printed them on sailcloth rather than on paper.

Although ships have the latest technology, there are still officers with binoculars, sextants and charts, and your work reflects that layering and history.

Until they were acquired by the museum they were working documents. So the corners are dog-eared or torn, and, because of the way they were folded, ink has transferred from one chart to another. In order to make the work, the charts were taken out to be photographed by the Maritime Museum. The slight show-through left a ghost image, so it looked as though they had been photographed with another chart behind them. My charts are digitally printed, and I liked the idea of using contemporary technology. If you look closely, you can see the pixelation.

Why did you want that?

To be clear that the work is not about fakery, it's true to what it is. Though the work refers to something from the 18th or 19th century, it is mediated by a contemporary process – it is not about replication. Part of my process involved good old-fashioned cut-and-paste – which was then translated into the digital version.

You must have had fun finding all the facts and the cross-references. Were there any surprises?

I was surprised by the number of parallels and connections between the *Odyssey* and Cousteau's life. The chart titled *Cousteau and the Bomb*, for example, relates Cousteau's heroic fight to prevent France, under de

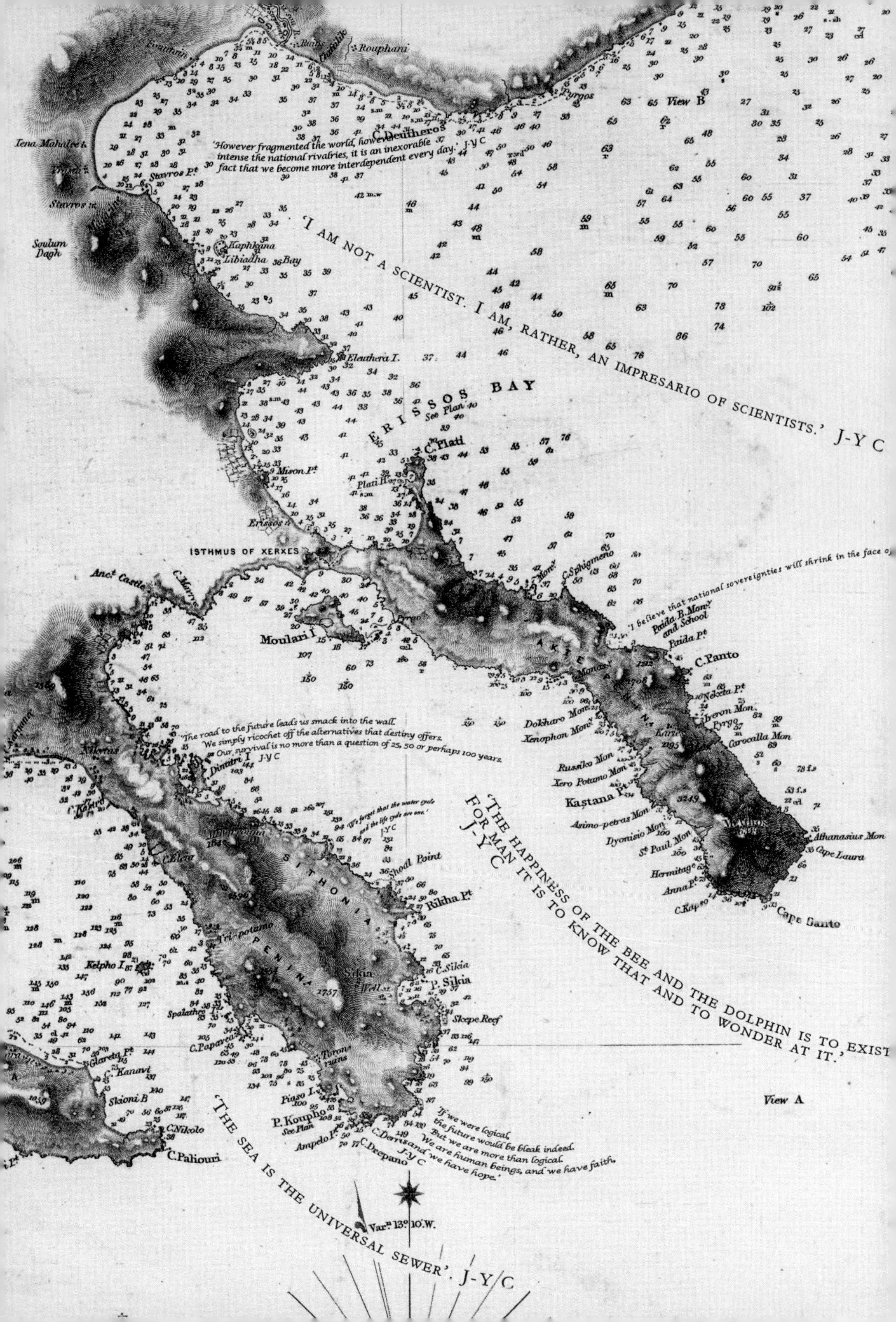
'However fragmented the world, however intense the national rivalries, it is an inexorable fact that we become more interdependent every day.' J-Y C
'I AM NOT A SCIENTIST. I AM, RATHER, AN IMPRESARIO OF SCIENTISTS.' J-Y C
'I believe that national sovereignties will shrink in the face of
The road to the future leads us smack into the wall. We simply ricochet off the alternatives that destiny offers. Our survival is no more than a question of 25, 50 or perhaps 100 years. J-Y C
'We forget that the water cycle and the life cycle are one.' J-Y C
'THE HAPPINESS OF THE BEE AND THE DOLPHIN IS TO EXIST. FOR MAN IT IS TO KNOW THAT AND TO WONDER AT IT.' J-Y C
'If we were logical, the future would be bleak indeed. But we are more than logical. We are human beings, and we have faith. We have hope.' J-Y C
'THE SEA IS THE UNIVERSAL SEWER'. J-Y C
ERISSOS BAY
See Plan
ISTHMUS OF XERXES
View A
View B
C. Deutheros
Pyrgos
Roupharu
Stavros Pt
Kaphkana
Libiadha Bay
Eleuthera I.
C. Plati
Plati H.
Mison Pt
Erissos
Anct Castle
Moulari I.
AKTE PENINA
C. Sphigmeno
Paida Pt
C. Panto
Nekeia Pt
Iberon Mon.
Carocalla Mon
Dokharo Mon
Xenophon Mon
Russiko Mon
Xero Potamo Mon
Kastana Pt
Asimo-petras Mon
Dyonisio Mon
St Paul Mon
Hermitage
Anna Pt
C. Kapso
Mt Athos
Athanasius Mon
Cape Laura
Cape Santo
SITHONIA PENINA
Dimitri I.
C. Elaia
Shoal Point
Rikha Pt
Tripotamo
Kelpho I.
C. Sikia
P. Sikia
Skepe Reef
Spalathro
C. Paparea
Toron ruins
Piaso I.
P. Koupho
See Plan
Ampelo Pt
C. Dervisand
C. Deepano
Glareta Pt
C. Kanavi
Skioni B
C. Nikolo
C. Paliouri
Varn 13° 10' W.

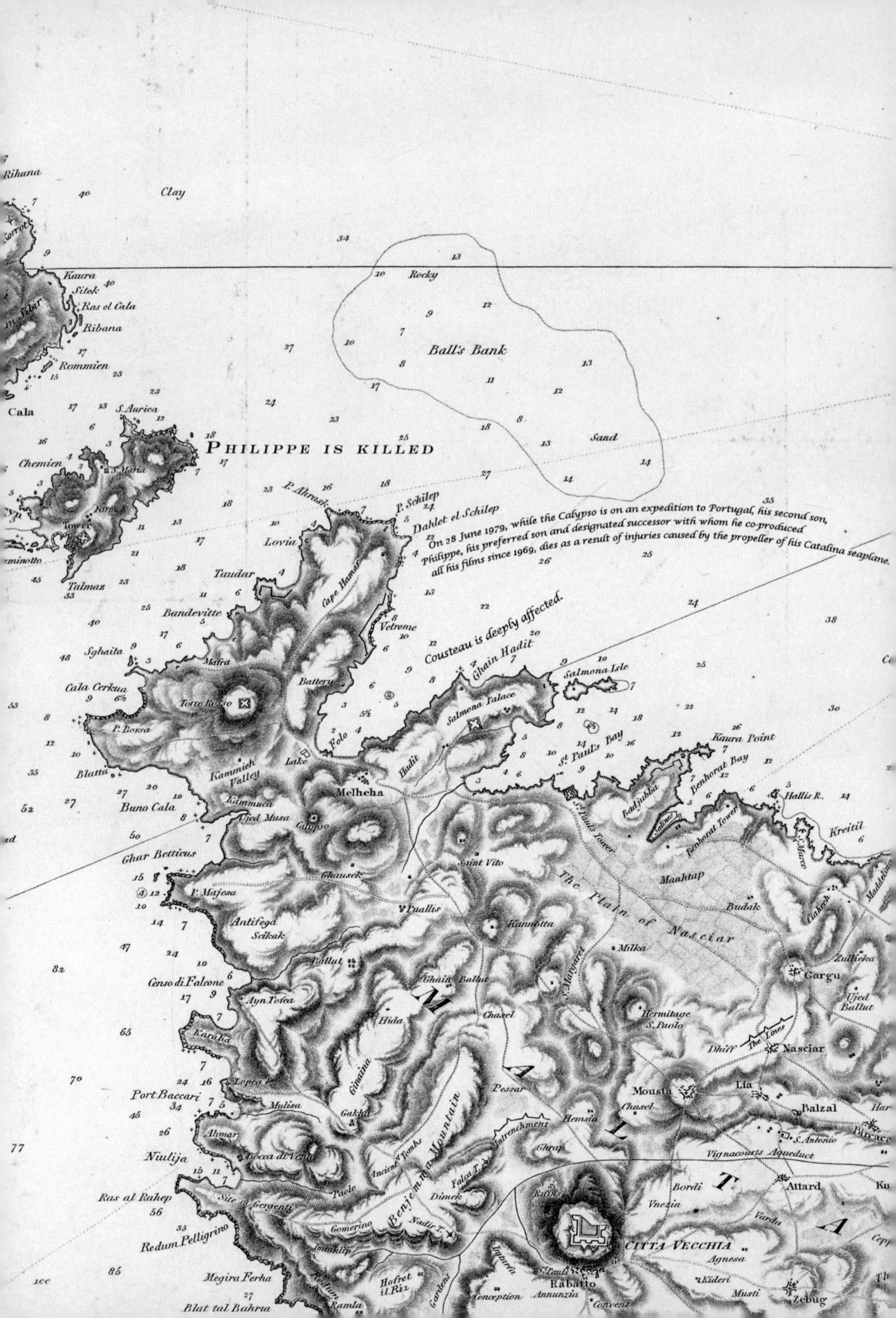

PHILIPPE IS KILLED
On 28 June 1979, while the Calypso is on an expedition to Portugal, his second son, Philippe, his preferred son and designated successor with whom he co-produced all his films since 1969, dies as a result of injuries caused by the propeller of his Catalina seaplane.
Cousteau is deeply affected.
Ball's Bank
Rocky
Sand
Clay
Rihana
Kaura
Sitek
Ras el Cala
Ribana
Rommien
Cala
S. Aurica
Chemien
S. Maria
Tower
Talmaz
P. Ahrash
P. Schilep
Dahlet el Schilep
Lovia
Taudar
Cape Hamar
Bandevitte
Vetreme
Sghaita
Maira
Cala Cerkua
Torre Rosso
Battery
Ghain Hadit
Salmona Isle
Salmona Palace
P. Borza
Folo
Lake
Kammieh Valley
Hadit
St. Paul's Bay
Kaura Point
Benhorat Bay
Blatta
Melheha
Buno Cala
Kammuca
Ujed Musa
Calypso
St. Paul's Tower
Badjubba
Benhorat Tower
Hallis R.
Kreitil
S. Marco
Ghar Betticus
Saint Vito
Maahtap
Ghausek
P. Majesa
The Plain of Nasciar
Puallis
Antifega
Scikak
Kannotta
Budak
Milka
Ballut
Ghain Ballut
Censo di Falcone
Ayn Tofca
Gargu
Zullieka
Ujed Ballut
M A L T A
Hida
Chasel
S. Margaret
Hermitage S. Paolo
Karaba
Ginaina
Dhiff
The Lines
Nasciar
Port Baccari
Mulisa
Gakha
Pessar
Mousta
Lia
Balzal
Benjemma Mountain
Hemsia
Ahmar
Intrenchment
S. Antonio
Niulija
Bocca di Venti
Ancient Tombs
Ghrap
Vignacourts Aqueduct
Ras al Rahep
Paolo
Falca T.
Dimek
Bordi
Attard
Vnezia
Varda
Redum Pelligrino
Gomerino
Nadir T.
CITTA VECCHIA
Agnesa
Megira Ferha
Hofret il Riz
Gardens
St. Pauls
Rabatto
Kideri
Musti
Zebug
Blat tal Bahria
Ramla
Conception
Annunzia
Convent

Gaulle, from dumping waste from its nuclear weapons programme into the sea. The parallel is with the story of Odysseus and his battle with the Cyclops, whom he overcomes by guile rather than force.

I love the idea of the journey. When you are on a sea voyage you can't see what's on the land – you often only have a vague impression of even the outline of it.

That's a really nice way of thinking about it. It's to do with the idea of incompletion. All maps are abstract and subjective, though maritime charts seem particularly rational in a way, as they are strictly to do with currents and other vital information.

Yes, they're very practical things, to help ships navigate and avoid hazards. But what I love about the Odyssey *is the different kind of mapping, because you have things like the sirens on the rocks and it seems that everywhere Odysseus goes has a physical effect on him. Of course with Cousteau as well there's that physicality of the exploration of the* Undersea World.

For me the myth is important. Cousteau was a great self-mythologiser. He had to be a self-promoter in order to finance his expeditions. But in a way his stories are classic mariners' tales. Like all heroes, however, he had feet of clay – he was human after all. All heroes have some kind of Achilles' heel.

Were you interested in books that included mythical maps as a child?

I wasn't really into fiction as a child. I was not a great reader. I grew up with television – most of my early knowledge was from watching, for example, nature documentaries. At the time of making it, I wasn't quite sure where *Cousteau in the Underworld* fitted with the rest of my work, but after a time you begin to see it more clearly in terms of other works that may be formally quite different. I hope it is an affectionate portrait of Cousteau – a partial biography. From now on every time I show *Cousteau in the Underworld* in a different venue, it will be different. Time changes things.

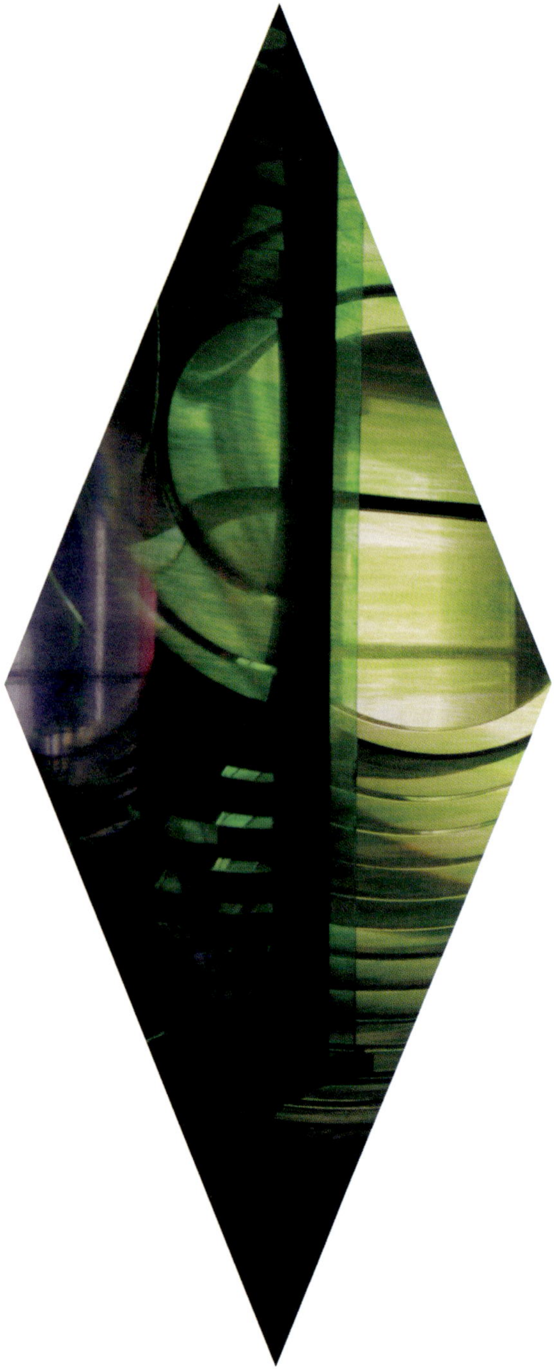

STEFFI KLENZ

CONCERT FOR MAISON SIRÈNE, 2014

Can we talk about how you conceived this piece, and about the process you went through to achieve the luminosity of the diamond-shaped images? They appear like pieces of stained glass window...

Well, from the start I wanted the individual diamond shapes to create a desire in the viewer, and I needed to translate this technically into imagery that draws the viewer in. I used very specific metallic paper that increases the highlights and also the contrast level of the photograph, and makes the individual images appear to glow when lit in the gallery. I wanted people to step back and see how luminous the photographs are, as if the images had caught the light and held it.

Yes, I find Concert for Maison Sirène *captivating. You can see it's images of a lens in abstracted form, but the work also has several components, layering it with meanings. Can we talk about the way you work, because this piece is very characteristic of your practice in general?*

My practice is fundamentally concerned with challenging conventional conceptions of architecture, engaging with the space in question as a location for transition and transformation. I have made work previously, such as *Ariadne's Thread* (2012), which is composed of six individual aluminium panels and therefore questions photography's relationship to serialism, rather than photography 'in a series'. Equally, *Concert for Maison Sirène* explores the question of photography as a specific medium, and challenges the notion of the photographic series – producing a sequence of images that are different yet similar.

OPPOSITE: Steffi Klenz, *Concert for Maison Sirène*, 2014 (detail)
12 individual metallic C-Type Prints, framed in brushed steel tray frames
Courtesy the artist

I like the fact that the piece doesn't provide a focal point. It doesn't give you an indication of where to look: you have to find yourself in relation to it. In a way it's a refusal to make a 'whole image', and rather offers the viewer a relation of parts to parts. In a way the ordering of the individual images provides an experience of looking: a form of unfolding.

You have previously mentioned Virginia Woolf's novel, To the Lighthouse[1] *in relation to this work. How did it contribute towards your thinking about the piece?*

I think you're referring to my interest in how Woolf's novel investigates the means of perception, attempting to understand people in the act of looking. There's no direct link between the novel and my piece in terms of the narrative, nor am I interested in Woolf's weight as a historical figure, *but* the plot unfolds through shifting perspectives of each character's stream of consciousness. These shifts can occur even mid-sentence, and in some sense they resemble the rotating beam of the lighthouse itself.

Yes, I can see a connection to the notion of fragmentation which is integral to your piece. There's also a huge amount of colour in your work – from vibrant red to blues – and each image is very different from the other, yet they share similarities. Where is the colour coming from? Is it the different refractions and reflections of the lens in the lighthouse lamp?

The last thing standing between us and the unremitting sea, which can create a disorientating psychological state, is the lighthouse. So I like to think of my colourful images as abstractions that can hint at that. But my piece is particularly engaged with the rhythmic and repeating pulse of the light signal inside the lighthouse lamp. The French engineer Augustine-Jean Fresnel developed the multi-part Fresnel lens, which is much thinner than a comparable conventional lens, taking the form of flat sheets of glass. This Fresnel lens reflects and refracts the light, also allowing the beam to be sharper, and visible over greater distances. I was fortunate enough to be able to work with a Fresnel lighthouse lamp that had coloured sheets of glass inside it. The repeating light pulse hits these different sheets of glass and creates these wonderful varying colours. But for me repetition is not about repeating the same

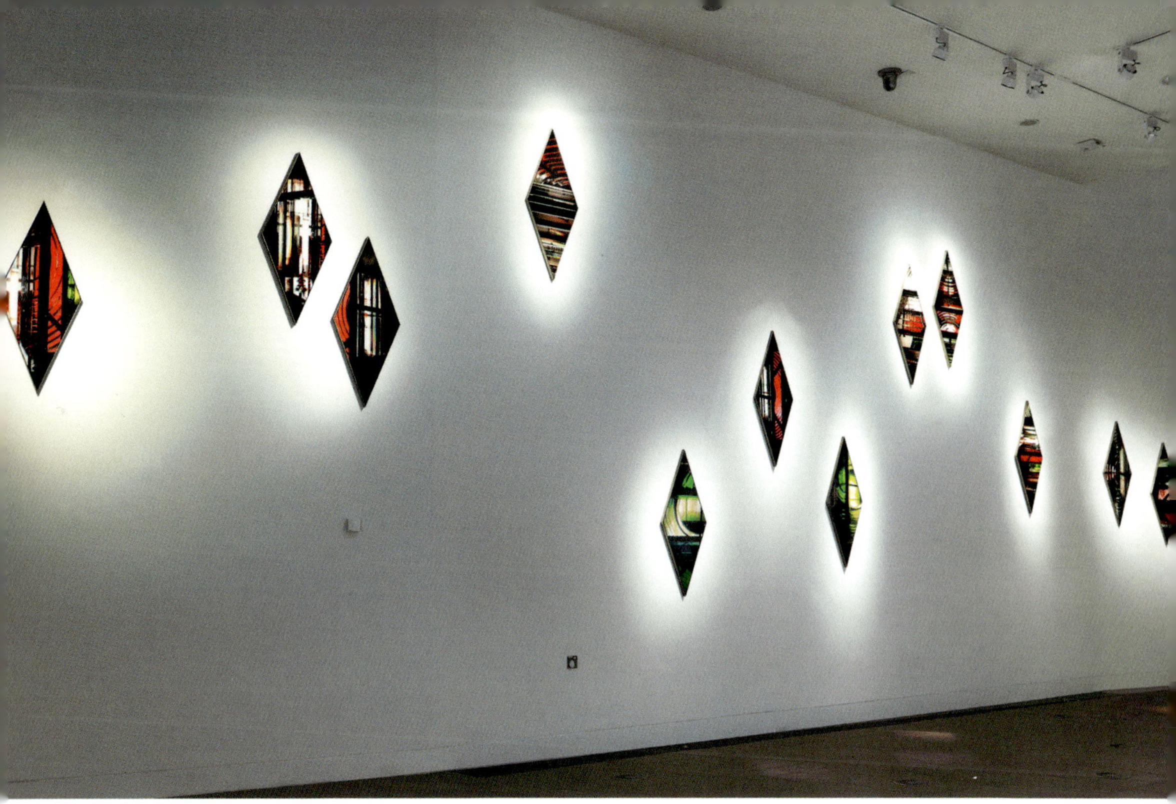

Steffi Klenz, *Concert for Maison Sirène*, 2014
12 individual metallic C-Type Prints, framed in brushed steel tray frames
(installation view, *Ship to Shore: Art and the Lure of the Sea*,
SeaCity Museum, Southampton, 2014) Courtesy the artist

thing. It's about small differences – between each moment, each image, each colour, and also each sound.

Is this lens also related to the photography itself?

Yes, it's related to the large-format camera that I use. The camera's back element has a Fresnel screen added to the ground glass to direct the light entering from the front element through the lens. The light travels from the lens through the ground glass and Fresnel screen towards the expected location of the viewer's eyes. The Fresnel screen is a focusing screen: it bends slanted rays of lights toward your eyes so that the corners of the ground glass appear as bright as the centre of the field. So my camera and a lighthouse are used in very similar ways: to increase the apparent brightness by focusing the light toward the viewer.

Your images are also accompanied by a sound work.

Yes, the sound comes from speakers situated beneath the structure of the floor, and directs the viewers towards the images, the sound getting stronger or louder the closer you get to the images and fading as you leave it. I collaborated with Neil Codling, who is a songwriter and keyboard player for the alternative rock group *Suede*. Neil has extensive knowledge of Arnold Schoenberg's musical theories, and I commissioned him to translate my visual piece into a musical piece for the piano and violin applying Arnold Schoenberg's twelve-tone technique. Schoenberg was an Austrian composer who was interested in creating serial music, and created the twelve-tone technique in 1923. He consciously used an ordered series of twelve notes in the chromatic scale for a structural purpose to give equal importance to all notes, so, as such, twelve-tone music is atonal.

Why is Schoenberg's twelve-tone technique so relevant to this piece?

Well, Schoenberg indicated in his music theory that only atonal music represents a system of composition which can truly describe serialism, as a means of organizing and structuring more coherently modes of repetition. For me this was integral to the piece in that the light signal of the lighthouse is continuous and I needed to think about modes of repetition. I also focus on the repeating light signal as a visual voice of the siren. The musical seduction of the siren's luring voice is validated in my piece through the use of enchanting light. So my piece becomes a play between visual and oral structural modes of repetition and movement. It becomes a carefully composed display of visual voices: sequenced photographs ascending and descending on the wall like notes on a musical sheet.

Concert for Maison Sirène *also has another visual layer in its exploration of fragmentation.*

Well I'm interested in notions of fragmentation, not 'merely' the fragmentation of the light signal in the lamp, but also fragmentation in relation to time. There is the lens that in one moment provides all these fragmentations and refractions, so in a way I play with the moment it produces the sequence. I am interested in trying to work with models of association, like a lyrical abstraction in a moment as well as across time. The other thing that's very relevant to the piece is the distance and height and the grouping of the notes. A lighthouse never reflects onto the sea: it throws the light out.

Yes, into the distance, sweeping out to sea. And the way the piece incorporates both links and breaks between each image reminds me of the way a lighthouse signal is continuous but its beam rotates – so if you stayed in the same position, you would have to wait before the beam hit you again. Almost like communicative interruptions.

I like that. Almost a threat of the failure of communication. This evokes the translation of the siren as an ambiguous figure of the sea, not only seducing the sailor but also luring them into danger. When I did research around the Kent coastline, I learned that relying on the lamp of the lighthouse as the only navigational device – or rather being lured by its light without checking characteristics of the particular sea terrain – can be detrimental. Nearly 2,000 boats have followed the repeating beams of the lighthouses in the English Channel and become stranded or wrecked upon the Goodwin Sands, which are these massive sandbanks whose outlines are constantly altering and shifting.

Your work creates an illusion, producing imagery that is confusing and disorientating, but very beautiful. As you draw close, the music of the sirens soars and the images soar – enticing the viewer into the work, through the desire to influence it. And in Greek mythology it was this that enticed the sailors into danger – they misunderstood what they were seeing and hearing, driven only by desire.

Yes, it's all about illusion and delusion – and desire.

NOTES

1. Woolf, Virginia. *To the Lighthouse*. 1927. Penguin Classics, 2011.

OVERLEAF: Steffi Klenz, *Concert for Maison Seirén*, 2014 (detail)
12 individual metallic C-Type Prints, framed in brushed steel tray frames

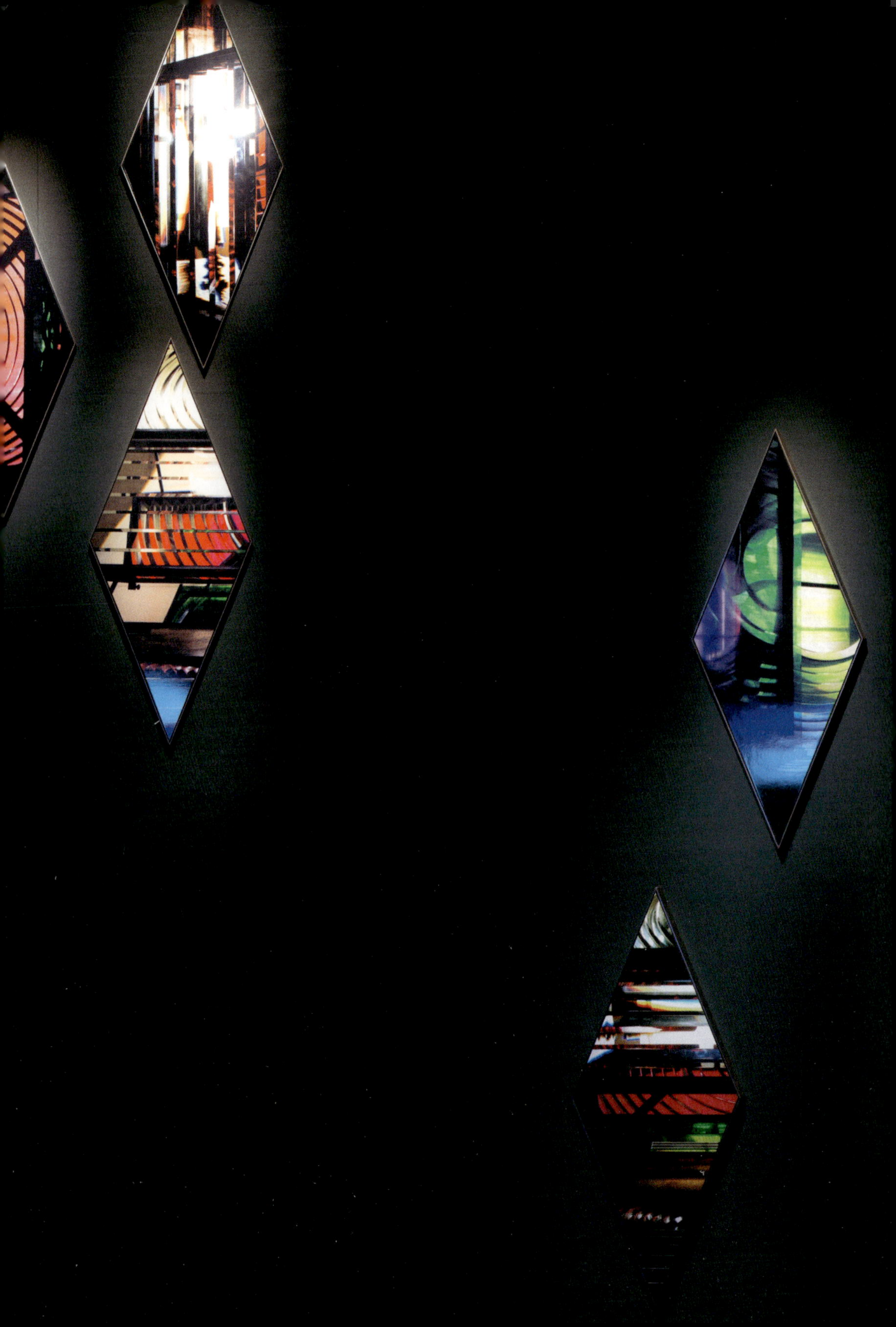

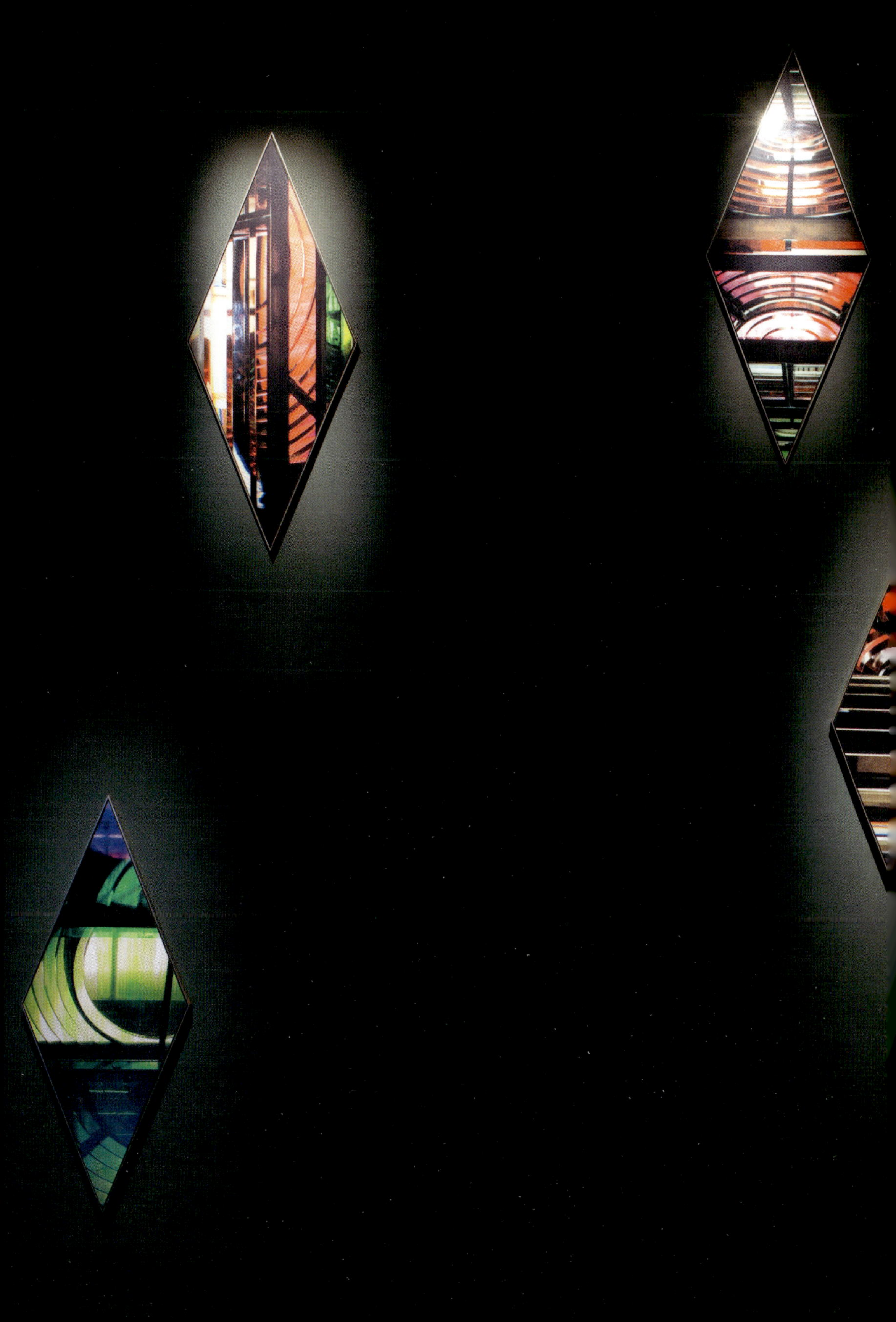

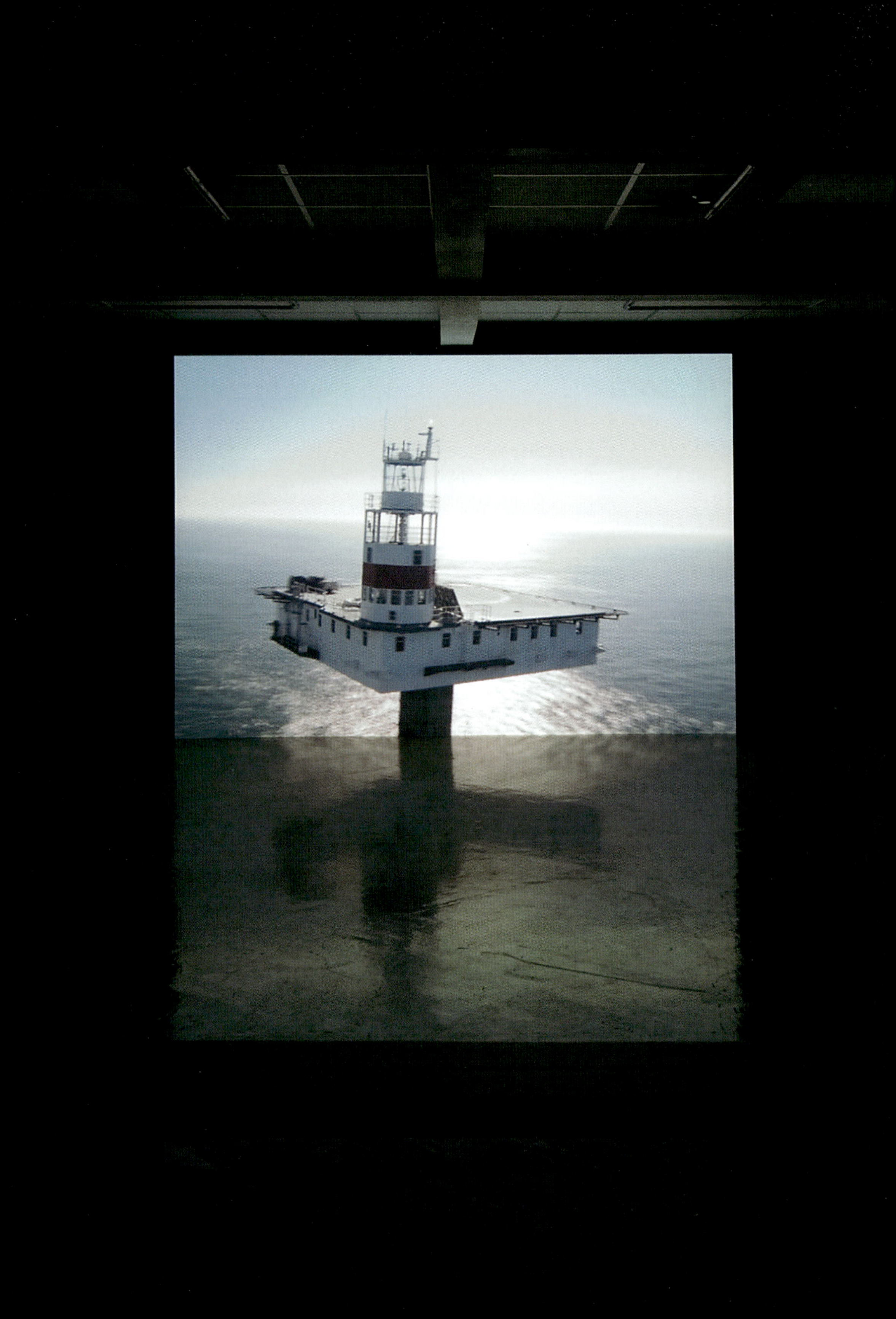

CATHERINE YASS

LIGHTHOUSE, 2011

How did your film Lighthouse*, and the light boxes that are part of that body of work, come about?*

Well, I was at the De La Warr Pavilion planning an exhibition, and I asked if there were any wrecks or interesting things off the coast, because I had always wanted to do a film underwater. I've done one film about falling, which is *Descent* (2002), one in the air – *High Wire* (2008) – and it seemed like the next one should be underwater and about drowning.

Why drowning?

When I originally thought of my *Descent* work, I was thinking about certain dreams, which are both fantasies and fears, of falling, or the desire to fly, or drowning – all of those very physical extreme acts and emotions. Sometimes when you dream you lose gravity, so I was thinking about those strange scenarios you can get into in a dream. There seemed to me to be a trio of work, so *Lighthouse* was the third. But as soon as I saw the Royal Sovereign Lighthouse, I knew that it wasn't going to be just about drowning any more.

Because it's an unusual-looking structure, isn't it?

Yes. It was completed in 1971. It has a square base on top of the post, with the lighthouse on one corner of the post. It looks really precarious – as though it's going to tip over. Around that area of the Royal Sovereign shoal – which lies in the Eastern part of the English

OPPOSITE: Catherine Yass, *Lighthouse*, 2011.
35mm and HD film transferred to ProRes QuickTime (12 minutes 42 seconds) (installation view, *Ship to Shore: Art and the Lure of the Sea*, John Hansard Gallery, Southampton, 2014). Photo: Steve Shrimpton

Channel – there are shallow waters with dangerous currents, and it was a complex engineering task to bore down into the sea bed and build the post to put the structure on. They concertinaed it up – one part was pushed up through the other. I'm very interested in modernist concrete structures. They represent a kind of aspiration, or Utopia, on a kind of community or social level. I'm also interested in people's personal dreams or fears, what their parallels might be in a social context. So I was very attracted to the way that the lighthouse standing in the sea was supposedly saving people's lives, which is aspirational but it is not always going to work – it's almost like it's some desperate attempt to control the waves. What I do find interesting is that it's supposed to represent a symbol for safety, and yet it looks so dangerous: the water is quite shallow and the lighthouse itself creates dangerous whirlpools of current.

Which you show in your film Lighthouse.

Yes. A boat would normally never get that close or be endangered by the currents, but actually if you are in thick fog, which we once were, you actually don't see the lighthouse. So for me it symbolises danger and safety at the same time, which I find interesting. I worked with Franz Pagot, a cinematographer skilled in underwater and stunt filming. The most complicated part was the helicopter, because you had to have excellent weather as you can't clean the camera lens on the nose of the helicopter. We didn't end up filming till the end of April, having waited since February. Then there was algae on the sea and so you couldn't film underneath the structure. Eventually we did the aerial filming on a sunny day, which I didn't really want but in the grading that's evened out, as we filmed from the boat later on a very grey and quite stormy day. We had an underwater motorbike that went in circles round the base of the lighthouse: the divers had to have knives because there are fishing nets in the water and you can get your feet trapped; also the currents are very strong.

Once you got the footage and edited the film, you then made a decision to disorient your viewer: there are dramatic differences in perspective.

I was thinking about the film in terms of a temporal drawing, and how I would describe the lighthouse, and it seemed to be all about turning. Because the top is square, it actually faces east, south, north and west

– it's like a clock. Then obviously there are the currents going round it at the bottom; and the post is round. So I thought that the circling helicopter would be on one level above the structure, then there would be a close-up also circling round the lighthouse, but this time with the image itself turning on the plane of the screen. The turning theme is taken up when the camera goes onto the boat, and although the image isn't spiralling any more the confusion is continued, because rather than doing a straight spiral I opened it out going down the post, so it was as though the spiral was losing its own logic and coming undone. When the camera goes underwater there's another spiral: it goes around the post again, but upside down. You don't notice it at first, but there's light coming from the bottom of the image which gives a sense of having lost your balance or orientation. Most of the shots were pre-planned, but I only thought of being upside down underwater when I saw the light coming through the surface of the sea and thought it would look good coming up from underneath.

You really evoke the feeling of the power of the sea, and what happens when you fall in.

I was thinking about the way the film starts off being quite controlled and in order, and gradually breaks down. If you were drowning, or you were thrown off-balance and fell into the sea, your bearings would disintegrate. And for me, it's like a parallel with if you were dying: you would maybe forget the logic of things and maybe time and language would start to get all jumbled up, or come undone. You know, if you have a flat spiral made out of paper and you cut it and you pull the bottom out and it goes into another dimension – I was thinking in that direction.

You also made a series of duratrans of the lighthouse from different vantage points. For a number of years you've used a very distinctive technique, which you discovered at art college.

I keep on testing myself and thinking I should only be making light boxes if there's a real reason to, and not as a signature. I try every other way – I try to do straight images, and I try turning them upside down, or making them a different colour – and nothing else works. So the process began when I was given a 5 x 4 camera, and loaded the film the wrong way round. When I got the results I realised that they were interesting, so then I put through lots of different types of film to see what would work, resulting in yellow, turquoise or red. At that time I was interested in the negativity and the underside of photography, and sort of undoing its apparent veracity, yet I didn't want to just be negative and make a kind of dogmatic statement about it, because I also recognise that there's something very seductive about the medium. So, to me, the blue negative combined with the positive transparency seemed to set up a kind of ambiguity about the image, which both seduced you and made you doubt it. There's also a gap between the images – the time it takes to turn the dark slide as one image is taken after the other. This little sliver of time is very important for me, because it prevents the photograph from being one moment of truth, and it sets up a short gap of uncertainty when actually nothing was captured and something elided the camera – which happens when you blink, and when you click the shutter. So often the two images don't quite register when they're laid on top of each other – for example, if there's been a little movement in between. There's also a kind of white halo, where the blue negative is always slightly smaller than the positive, because the negative process is done at a different temperature and it slightly shrinks the film. Which is why you can't really simulate it very easily on a computer.

Are you still working with an analogue camera?

Yes, it's a 1950s Graflex film camera with analogue film. People around me often say, 'Surely you can do this digitally?', because it's such a hassle to do it analogue – the translation to digital when you print onto duratrans, which is a digital process, is agony. But every time anyone's ever tried, they can't simulate it – it's not like you can just press a button and put blue, because there are very strange things that happen to the reds and the greens and everything. However, I once bought another camera thinking I needed a back-up: With my Graflex camera there's an area in the corner that's always very slightly out-of-focus, and I thought, 'I really shouldn't be doing this. I really should have a proper camera, and it should have a proper ground glass with proper measurements on the back'. But I hated the other camera – the image was too good. So I went back to my original camera. Now I have to use a magnifying glass at the back to see if it's in focus, so people I'm photographing, or situations, take ages.

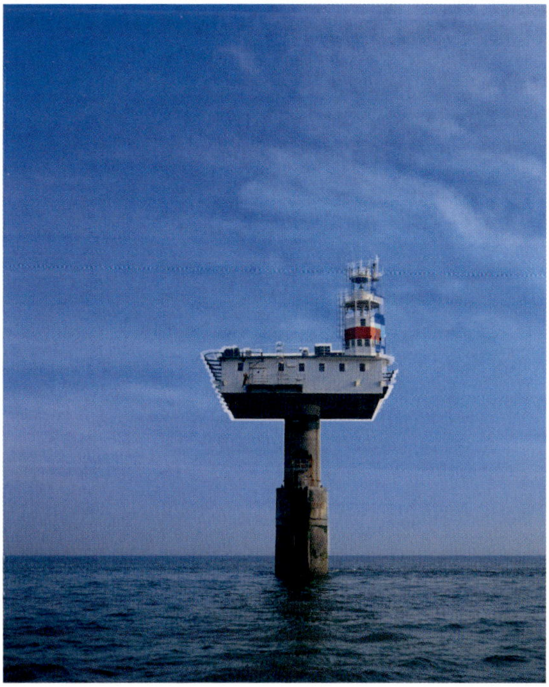

Catherine Yass, *Lighthouse (North North West)*, 2011. Duratrans transparency, lightbox. Copyright the artist. Courtesy Alison Jacques Gallery, London

When you took the Lighthouse *series of still images, you were actually on the deck of the boat?*

Yes. The thing with a Graflex film camera is that you can't see through the lens when you put the dark slide in. That's quite a few seconds, and if you're bobbing up and down on a boat you have to keep the lighthouse in the centre – twice, because you're doing the overlay. You have to get them to match.

I wonder how you managed to get any *images, Catherine!*

Well I understood that you had to feel what the wave was doing. I did it by looking at the back of the camera – if the lighthouse was framed and coming just above the back of the camera, I could predict. So I just took pot luck. So obviously I have a lot of photographs with a

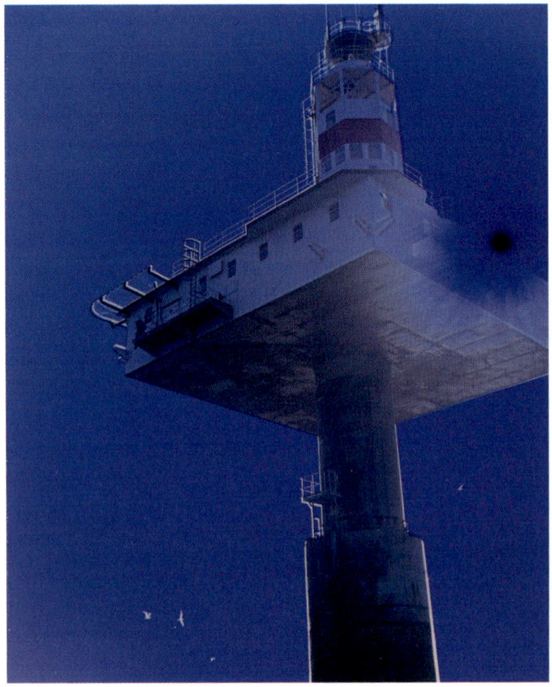

Catherine Yass, *Lighthouse (North)*, 2011. Duratrans transparency, lightbox. Copyright the artist. Courtesy Alison Jacques Gallery, London

lighthouse in the corner, or off, not even appearing. The boat can't stay still, it's being pushed by the tidal currents, so when you see the light boxes and they have different types of halo around them it's because there's more-or-less of a discrepancy between the positive and negative.

And then of course the blues change with each of the works according to the light.

In this case I did north, south, east and west so that I got each face of the lighthouse. When you see the images in a row, or in a square, you get a sense of temporality, and also spatial direction. Then I went back and did different views closer up. But one thing I got very interested in was photographing into the sun, because it goes very, very deep blue, almost black, which reminded me of a book *Black Sun*, by Julia Kristeva[1], and also of the concept of black holes. So I was trying to capture the way that if things are going wrong under that lighthouse everything inverts itself, and there's the sort of pulling in of the sea and then the sun being like a black hole sucking you in, light turning to darkness. But I also took the decision to work in portrait format because I wanted it to be like a portrait of a lighthouse, because for me the lighthouse is almost like a protagonist or a person, as well as offering something to people.

The lighthouse is now unmanned, and the light automated. It's maintained, but you can no longer gain access to the structure. So perhaps that's a link to other series you have done?

Yes, in *High Wire* they demolished the Red Road housing scheme in Glasgow soon after I filmed it. I think that lighthouse is on the cusp of being used and not used, so it's quite an important moment for it – like a swansong.

It's definitely a link with your interest in structures that have a meaning or history.

Yes. There's also almost an attraction to the edge, so I think it *is* a fear, but it's like an attachment to it.

Do you fear drowning?

I do fear it, but at the same time I'm absolutely fascinated by it. I love leaning over boats and looking at the suck and wake behind the boat. I get incredibly travel sick as well, in a boat or car or a helicopter or aeroplane, so I'm very aware of motion. I think it's because something in my body is resisting the disorientation, and it's very physical, I think. Maybe the sickness comes out of a fear of displacement perhaps, or disorientation.

Can we also talk about the fact that for a number of years you've used light boxes? How they illuminate the image and also leave a trace when the light box is turned off.

The reason I started using them was again this mistrust of photography. I wanted to show the fact that the photograph began as a negative, that it's light-dependent and vulnerable to change. Also, if you put the image in a box, the viewer can't just accept it unquestioningly as being a window onto the world, because actually it's a protrusion into the gallery space – it becomes an object as well. As a viewer you have to negotiate it in the space, and immediately your relationship to it becomes a question, rather than something you can take for granted. The light box has its own internal space, the effect of the blue negative pulls you in. I often put the focus at the edge and not in the middle, as though a person's been taken out and you could fall into it and lose yourself – again a sense of falling. The blue works against the perspectival space of the positive: it actually throws you back on yourself but also sucks you in, though via a different kind of space, so it brings in a conflicting language of spatial understanding which is through colour – and the two are set up against each other. The internal space of the light box is also a metaphor for a psychological space.

What is your interest in the psychology of space?

I suppose you live most of your life with quite automatic references: you know where your keys are hopefully, or the front door, or the edge of the windows. Then there can be moments when that seems to disappear – there's always a subtext to what you're doing on the surface. Like when you're doing something quite automatic and something crops up that you don't expect, some little thought or memory that wells up and erupts, sometimes quite violently. So I'm talking about that. I'm also talking about when there's a conflict set up between the different kinds of space and the two moments that don't match: It's almost like… yes, it *is* like this falling, maybe into this space beneath yourself that doesn't have language, or that sort of falls between all the stools and can't be quite defined, and there's nothing to hold you.

You mentioned Kristeva's Black Sun[1] *earlier. I was wondering what attracted you to that book, and when you first came across it?*

Well the first book of hers I read was *Desire in Language*,[2] which talks about the nature and structure of language, and how we communicate; how grammar is a kind of a structure that holds us together, which we need, but at the same time there's always a sort of crumbling underneath it, where there's a collapse or it's not enough. You can't say everything through the language that we have, there are limits to it. So

Kristeva is taking a sort of a dance around these structures I suppose, which maybe connects to my interest in these sort of quite brutalist structures in architecture – they are like a sort of visual grammar.

One thing that strikes me is how different the lighthouse in your images is from the more stereotypical lighthouse that we think of. It's almost surreal, and also it is *brutal. Were you attracted to lighthouses as a child?*

Well I'd read *To the Lighthouse* by Virginia Woolf[3] when I was a teenager, which had a big effect on me. I think I found it quite disturbing. But I re-read it, and it's an amazing book actually, because there is the very firm structure in the Ramsey family and they only get to the lighthouse once the matriarchal figure has died and the family has experienced various tragedies. The lighthouse holds a particular meaning for James Ramsey which is a psychological desire. It is that desire that perhaps caught me.

> 'It will rain', he remembered his father saying. 'You won't be able to go to the Lighthouse.'
> The Lighthouse was then a silvery, misty-looking tower with a yellow eye, that opened suddenly and softly in the evening...
> Virginia Woolf, *To the Lighthouse*

NOTES

1. Kristeva, Julia. *Black Sun: Depression and Melancholia*. Translated by Leon S. Roudiez, Columbia University Press, 1989.
2. Kristeva, Julia. *Desire in Language: A Semiotic Approach to Literature and Art*. Translated by Thomas Gora, Alice Jardine and Leon S. Roudiez, Columbia University Press, 1980.
3. Woolf, Virginia. *To the Lighthouse*. 1927. Penguin Classics, 2011.

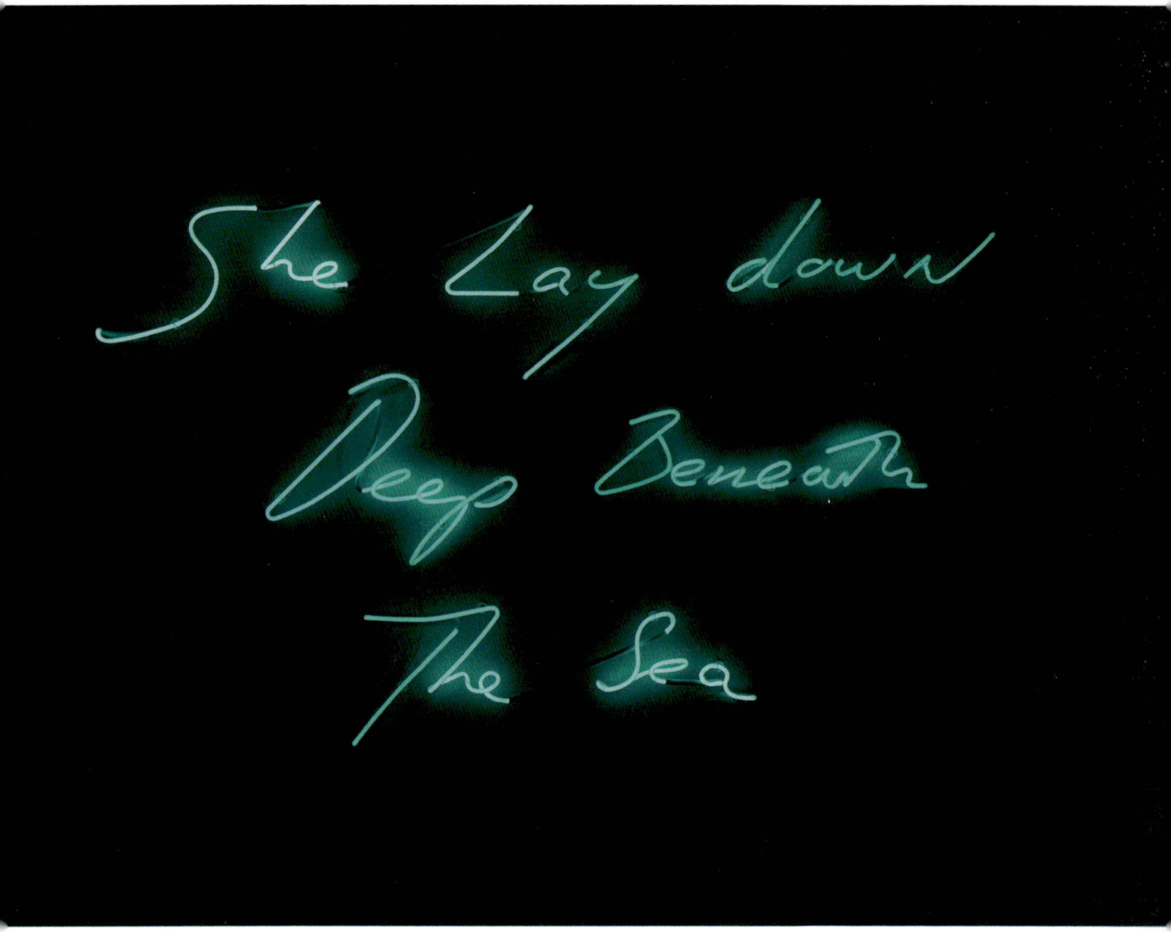

Tracey Emin
She Lay down Deep Beneath The Sea, 2012
Neon

TRACEY EMIN

SHE LAY DOWN DEEP BENEATH THE SEA, 2012

What was the first neon you saw?

It was in Margate, it would have been The Flamingo, Dreamland, or The Lido. In the 1960s or 70s, the whole seafront was neon lights, strobe lights, just a complete light show. And now there's hardly any neon lights. I would like to campaign to get the neon back, because it's a really beautiful thing, it makes people happy. The argon gas in neon is a happy gas, and it makes people feel good. That's why it's in casinos, brothels and bars, because it's a hedonistic, feelgood thing. Now it's all being replaced by electronic lighting which is completely different, and people who don't know the difference, they see it as a light, but if you know the difference... In Miami for example there's some neons there that are fifty years old; they're all historically protected. And then places like Margate, they've just all been stripped away.

Can you tell me about writing your thoughts and phrases in neon?

First thing, I've got unusual handwriting. Other people could do it and it would just look wrong. Also, my neons are really special. they are hand-blown and hand-bent, and are taken directly from my drawings. They're not done on a computer, they're not done by machine, they're done by a human being. It's like working with a really good foundry or something, you know? It's all through me. There's a lot of artists that use machine neon, which is completely different. I also know how my handwriting works, and I know that some letters just don't work in neon. For example, if you write 'sleep', you have to really open up the *e*'s, because otherwise if I do a big *s*, a big long *l*, and then *e* and *e* and then *p*, the *e*, *e* and *p* get smaller and smaller; then the hole in the *p* would be too small, and the second *e* would be too small. So you have to understand about that. When you do the drawing you have to understand about opening the letters up, but you have to do it in such a way that it doesn't actually destroy what you've done. Also, the glass has to bend backwards behind itself. You look at a lot of people's neons and they just have the glass bending in a diagonal behind, and it looks really horrible.

Are there any thoughts you've had that you couldn't write in a neon?

There's actually some things that I've always said are difficult. How do you write a note saying to someone that you're leaving them? No matter how you write it, it's never going to be a good thing. And there's some things that should never be written in neon because they should just never be written anyway. The things that work best are all the romantic things. Also I've never been influenced by other artists' neon works, because someone like Bruce Nauman's art is just so radically different. I've never looked at Bruce Nauman and thought, 'I'm going to make a neon'. I looked at Margate and thought, 'I really love neon'.

How did your first neon come about?

How I got to make my first neon was... do you remember I used to be with Col [Mat Collishaw]? I had to have a sign for the *Tracey Emin Museum*, and I was just going to get it done in lettering, you know, painted or whatever, and Col just said, 'Don't be stupid, do it in your handwriting'. And I went, 'Oh yeah, that's a good idea', because I've got nice handwriting, and then he said, 'And do it in neon, you love neon'. I said, 'How do I do it in neon?' He said, 'Let's go and find out'. And so we went to a neon signmaker's. And that was over twenty years ago.

Are you lured by the sea? You do spend a lot of time on the coast now.

I love being by the sea. I really, really, really love it. I don't think I would ever want to live in the country. Even in my place in France I can see the sea fifteen miles away. I couldn't be landlocked. When I lived in Waterloo, twenty years ago, I used to cycle everywhere, but I used to love it because I cycled over Waterloo Bridge – I was always cycling over the river, backwards and forwards, I always felt connected with the water. In Margate we regularly have waves up to thirty feet, and we have the spring tides which can be really colossal, you know, really massive waves.

When did you first swim in the sea? Was it when you were a child?

The first sea I swam in was the Mediterranean. I didn't learn to swim until I was nine. But I'd go in the water, I'd go in the sea all the time. Just, like, wade around and everything, keep going around by the waves. And then I learned to swim. We did a week of learning, then I swam 25 metres, then the next week 50 metres, the next 100 metres or whatever.

You were a natural.

I'm not a fast swimmer but I can swim a really long way. Maybe now a mile or whatever. When I was younger, in Turkey, I used to swim from one bay to another bay, maybe swimming a mile and a half from one place to another. I can't do that now. And then in Australia I swam in giant waves. I've swum in loads of different seas, but I've never swum in the Dead Sea which I'd like to do. You can just float on it really easily. I've swum in lots of different lakes. Yeah, I love it, you're right. And I love going in different water. I understand the difference of the water, I like the feeling of it and understanding it. I grew up by the sea, so, you know, some people grow up in the country climbing trees, I grew up throwing myself in the water, so it's a different kind of relationship. It's a *familiar* thing.

You've talked a lot about swimming in different seas, and I've seen you go plunging into the water in Miami. What is it about swimming for you?

Well, it could be because you're weightless, number one. You're in another element, a completely different element from what you're usually in. There's two things about the water: one, it's engulfing you and surrounding you, which is quite a fearful thing, but another thing is it's quite comforting – it's holding you, so it's kind of womb-like, isn't it?

The colour of your neon She Lay down Deep Beneath The Sea *really captures the colour of swimming up into the light.*

Yeah, I'm aware of that, but that isn't why I chose the colour. It was two things: one, I wanted a sea colour, and a colour that I've never used before – I don't know why, I just hadn't used this particular turquoise; two, I've got a fantastic Polaroid photograph of my dad in the sea from about thirty years ago, and in the Polaroid the water is exactly that colour, that neon, almost like the same kind of shimmer on it as well.

Isn't that incredible? So actually that very particular Mediterranean colour?

Yes. I don't think you could get more Mediterranean if you tried, really.

What's so inclusive about neon is that anybody walking in from the street, anybody who doesn't know anything about contemporary art, can understand your neon. Yet it's from a deeply personal place.

Yes, it totally came from something really personal. Around the time when my dad was dying, I went to my house in France and the gardener had slaughtered all of the olive trees. I'd wanted them pruned, but they were cut right back. What they should have done was cut every other branch out, but they didn't, and I went outside and I just knelt on the ground and started crying because of what they'd done to the trees. My dad knows everything about olive trees and at that time my dad was really ill. I knew he was dying. I thought, 'If my dad could have come here, he would have done it all for me and made sure it was all alright'. I was crying because my dad was dying, but I was also crying for the olive trees. And then the weirdest thing was that it was Palm Sunday, and that is the day when everyone whips each other with olive branches, so the whole thing was just really kind of bizarre. So when I did the drawing of the woman crying in the olive grove, *She Lay Down* (2011), the trees went and everything... and the figure just looked like she was lying not on the ground, but on the seabed. And then I thought about the immensity of the weight of water, and how there's nothing that you could do about it, you just have to surrender. It's like lying on the bed of the ocean with the whole weight of the sea on top of you, but you just lie there motionless, and it doesn't hurt.

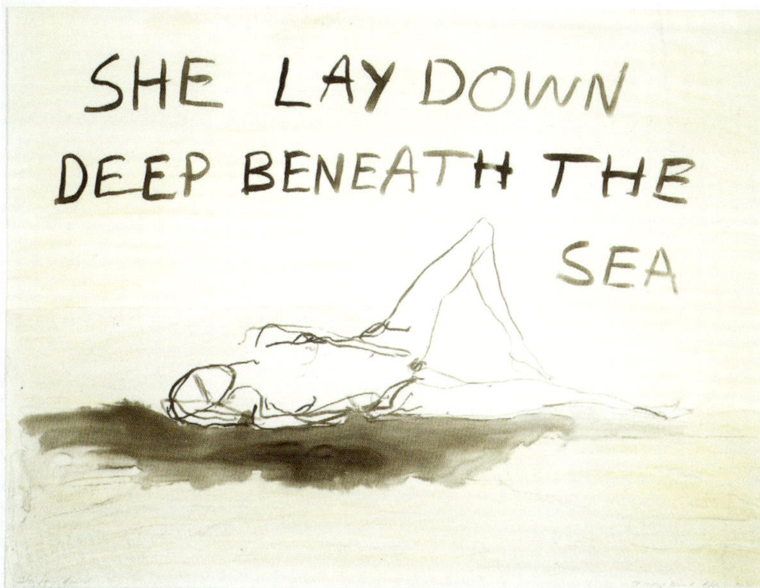

Tracey Emin, *She Lay Down*, 2011. 56 × 73 cm (22.05 × 28.74 in)
© Tracey Emin. Courtesy Counter Editions, London, photo: Andy Keate

I remember that you've talked to me about drowning in the past.

I did drown. I drowned in the Mediterranean and I was dragged out of the water, unconscious. I remember it. It was fantastic – it was like all your most beautiful feelings in the world. So I came up with the title *She Lay down Deep Beneath The Sea* after my dad died. When he died, I had to surrender to that idea. Some people are so overwhelmed by grief, they never recover, do they? They have a mental breakdown; their life is never the same again. Well of course it's the same, but they can't recover from it. When your parents die, you've no choice but to accept the situation. You know, it's part of the status quo of our existence. You just have to accept it.

Yes you do.

See you by the sea sometime.

I hope so.

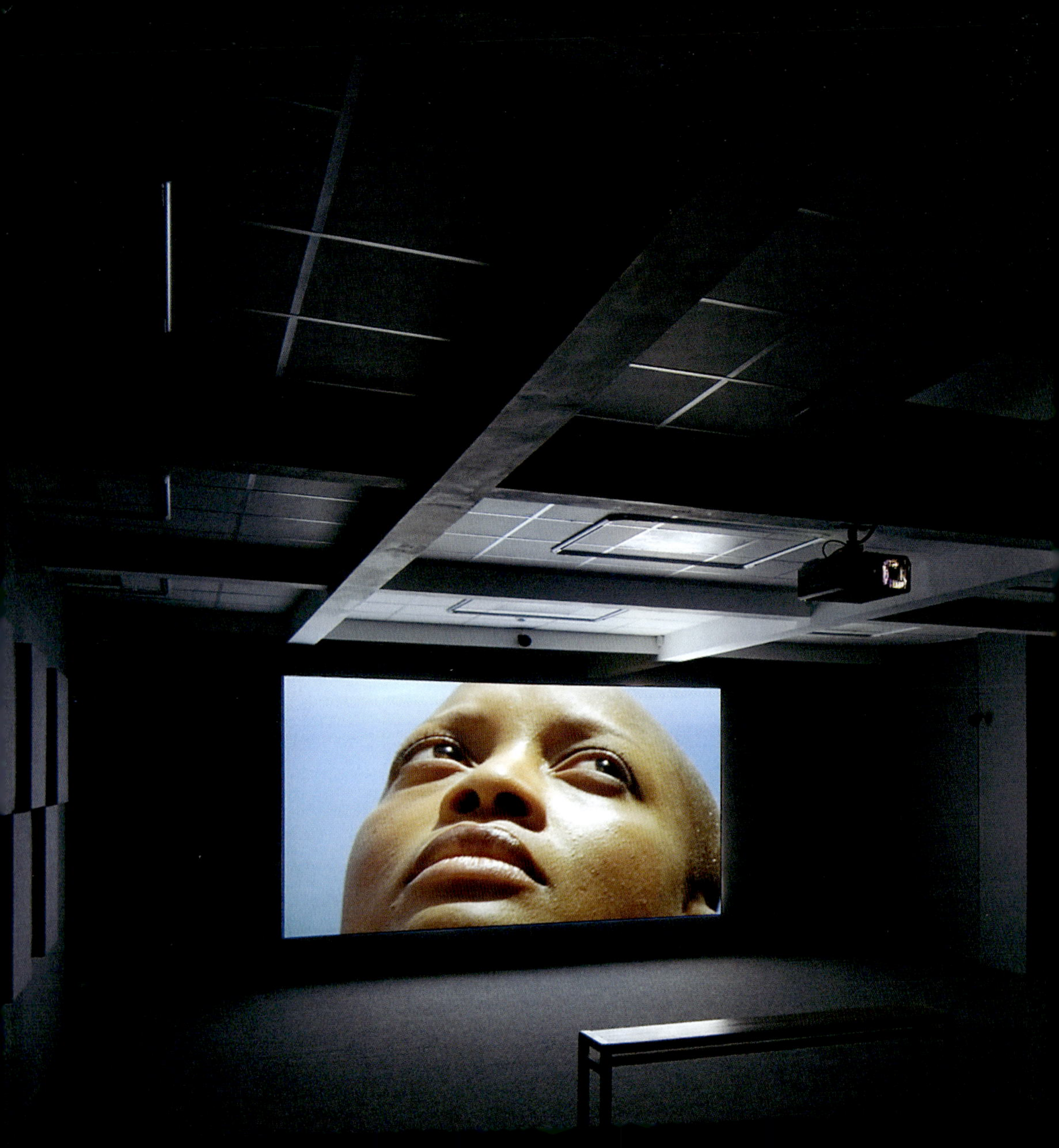

ISAAC JULIEN

THE LEOPARD (WESTERN UNION: SMALL BOATS), 2007

In The Leopard (Western Union: small boats) *you explore – as you have done previously in your films* True North *(2004) and* Fantôme Afrique *(2005) – the idea of the sublime, and of diaspora. Your mother travelled by ship from the Caribbean to Southampton in the Fifties, to come and live in England. What has she told you about that journey?*

My mother always talks about how, when she arrived in Southampton from Saint Lucia, she thought it was London. Then she realised she had to get on a train to finish her journey. That's something which interests me: people coming to a new city or different place, their sense of geography. My mother, for instance, was always getting lost. She also talks about the voyage, about being seasick, nervous and scared. But at the same time, it seems to me like she had fun, and I think she enjoyed that seven-week journey. She was twenty years old, just a young woman, and she was heading towards a really strange place.

Was she on her own?

She was on her own, although she knew she was going to be met. But I think she was someone who immediately wanted to go back. It came as a shock, the cold weather, all the acclimatising.

OPPOSITE: Isaac Julien, *The Leopard (Western Union: small boats)*, 2007 (installation view, *Ship to Shore: Art and the Lure of the Sea*, John Hansard Gallery, 2014) Single screen installation, 16mm colour film transferred to High Definition, 5.1 surround sound (19 mins 51 secs). Courtesy the artist and Victoria Miro Gallery, London. Photo: Steve Shrimpton

In your early films, such as Paradise Omeros *(2002), you show that transition, the differences in colours and culture.*

You know, my mother arrived knowing the names of all the English flowers. She could sing in Latin, but she never understood what she was singing, so her relationship to Catholicism remains ambivalent. There were other familiarities, such as with the Queen of England. That Queen is *her* queen, and it's something which embodies both a deep respect and a strong identification. Things are never simple, like 'people are oppressed because of colonialism'. There are always too many kinds of identification that can cut across nationalistic boundaries. That's even more the case now because we have greater globalisation, worldwide advertising and a revolution in telecommunications. But concepts around *créolité* – borrowing, let's say, with all its transformations, tragedies and enrichments – those are concepts which have informed a lot of my work. It's not just the Caribbean and the ways in which it's been seen. For me, it's been more about all the oscillations, all the comings-to and partings-from that happen around a region.

I've always been interested in how this is expressed physically, psychologically and, of course, aesthetically. When I've continued to explore the creolization process, it's often been in the context of migrations. When people set off to seek something, what do they 'know' about it? How do they envision their hopes, and what has informed their expectations? These kinds of questions are both ancient and modern. The idea that people can feel a strong identification, whether or not it's valid, underpins the old cliché of mythical 'streets paved with gold'. There are always all those aspects, and then there's the reality.

You've described in your book Riot *(2014)*[1] *how your mother loved the area of Italy around Lampedusa because it reminded her of home. And your film is suffused with colours. There's the Palazzo Valguarnera-Gangi with its gold and sea greens and its staircase bannister, like a glorious wave.*

For my mother, Sicily and all of southern Italy replicate many aspects of the Caribbean. It's not just the climate. I think it's also the architecture, particularly in Palermo. For instance, at the Gangi Palace, one staircase has this baroque wave formation impregnated in its design. Sicilian culture has all these aspects which are very Mediterranean yet also almost tropical.

The palace where some of the scenes are set is a key location in Luchino Visconti's film The Leopard *(1963)*[2] *and, at times, the way you shoot the scene with the particular light in the palace rooms transforms them into a mythical Atlantis in our imagination. You were speaking about 'streets paved with gold'. Those rooms have that mythological atmosphere, the sense of that imaginary place that you've never been to.*

In a way, the Palazzo epitomises the sort of ideal people are searching for. It's a literal representation of 'the better life', although, of course, it's faded and it's no longer available. That non-availability, in a sense that's what people are dying for – dying to have this better life in heaven. But Visconti's *The Leopard* is one of Italian cinema's great masterpieces. He himself was actually Luchino Visconti di Modrone, the Count of Lonate Pozzola, i.e. a descendant of that same feudal past. He had access to all this hidden aristocratic detail and history, and the screen is filled with it. The ballroom sequence takes an hour and it's really entrancing. What I wanted to create was a corollary of that, with a different kind of choreography inhabiting the same space. The structures of that palace are so rich, so baroque and rococo, that one feels it embodies the whole world of Western art. It suggests the ongoing seduction of Western ideas, the whole way they get seen as a kind of Utopia. Honestly, it's like looking at *gold*. Mine is a very porous reading, however, because these meanings are not at all new. Visconti's film has feudal Sicilians worried about losing their good life to the middle-classes. Now there's another group being viewed as the same kind of menace. But that's part of my point; this is a fear that's being merchandised over and over.

It's very poignant because your film talks of journeys by sea: the actual reality of migrants going in a boat and perhaps not being able to swim, the desperation of the overcrowding, the horrific dying – because when the migrants are pitched into the sea they drown. Your scenes of drowning have a balletic, ambiguous and terrible beauty.

I myself can't swim. I have a sort of phobia of the sea. But I also believe that, whilst they might not admit it, water is very often a traumatic sign for black subjects. I think my visceral reaction to the sea is connected to the whole question of slavery, to everything the sea represents in terms of voyaging. The sea, water, boats and vessels – they have a

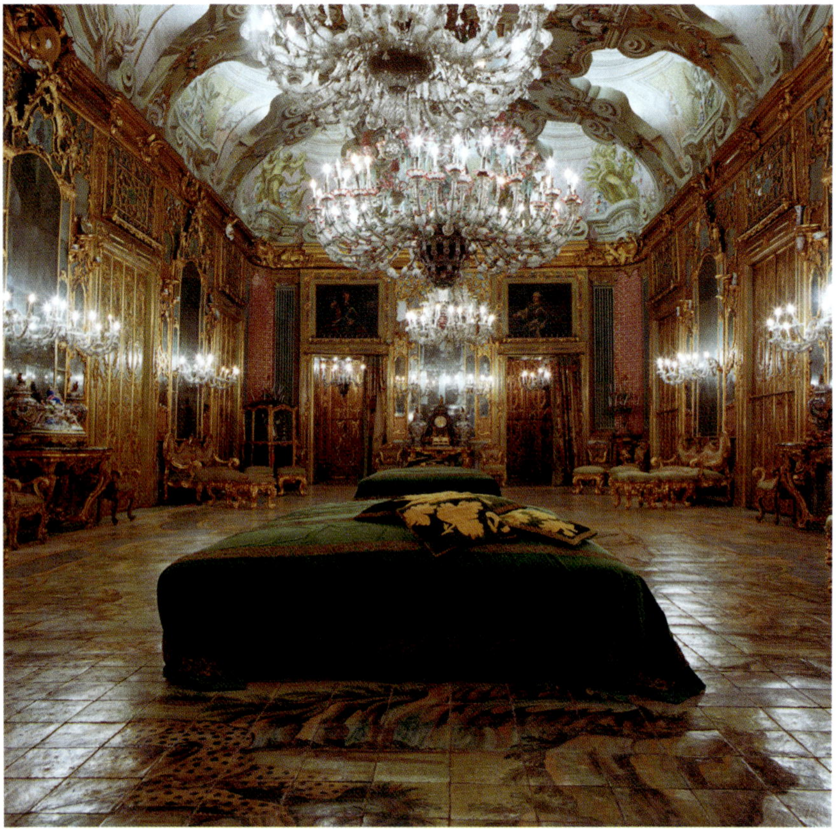

Isaac Julien, *The Leopard (Western Union: small boats)*, 2007
Single screen installation, 16mm colour film transferred to High Definition, 5.1 surround sound (19 mins 51 secs). Courtesy the artist and Victoria Miro Gallery, London.

deep ambivalence for black Atlantic cultures, because of the way the formation of those cultures was connected to the Atlantic. Essentially those are spaces which represent a certain experience of slavery and modernity, one that's really quite difficult. I think there is an unacknowledged relationship to aspects of submersion and sublimation, terror and horror.

Also we have the contrast of drowning and the seemingly idyllic holiday location – families splashing around in the water – as a kind of traumatic juxtaposition. It is a brilliant piece of filmic narrative, embracing the

I also wanted to talk about the sound in Western Union, *as it's powerfully evocative.*

The film uses some BBC news recordings, but while we were there we also recorded nautical radio from the various boats. So there's a lot of synch sound from the actual locations, feeding into our reconstructions and used as abstract sound. Research for the sound often begins before I shoot any imagery. Basically, the image usually follows the sound – certainly in terms of editing and making montage decisions. The whole idea is to create different collisions with the images.

Then there is the haunting singing.

That's Oumou Sangaré, a famous African singer. We got permission to use the refrain from a pop song she had made about never knowing when our lives are going to end. It's like a poetic treatment of the theme.

Can we also talk about the choreography?

The choreographer, Russell Maliphant, is fascinated by film, and he wanted to explore its relation to choreography. Also, back in 2006, Sadler's Wells embarked on an intriguing experimental programme. This had people like Russell, with Robert Lepage and Sylvie Guillem, making work about a transvestite spy who lived during the 18th century. With regard to dance, it was the moment a crucial conversation began. So there were several reasons for my choosing to work with it.

One of the central challenges, though, was thinking about the different stories that had been told to us by migrants, about how we could best express and juxtapose those narratives using dance. In terms of viewing expectation, we wanted to create a rupture and to come up with a more empathetic connection. In this, we were helped by using the actor Vanessa Myrie: Vanessa plays Adriana, a mythical character whose name is derived from "Adria" – the city after which the Adriatic Sea is named. She plays a witness character and you're never sure about her. Is she someone who's made the journey? Is she looking at the journey from North Africa, or is she contemplating making that journey herself? Also, she's a stand-in for one specific survivor. Thus, all in all, she operates as a kind of phantom. The work juxtaposes the documentary elements and the reconstructed elements in a border space between life, the port, and the sea. There's a mixing of all these incredibly beautiful landscapes – I liked being able to juxtapose the way those function with the way other histories lie beneath them. I also liked creating the idea of a tension between something which looks so sublime and the more deadly realities hidden within it. I call this a "contaminated sublime" and, in my work, it's been a frequent strategy. I like that viewers are both attracted to and repelled by such images. What I'm talking about is something which has been discussed by Paul Gilroy as "the slave sublime", in his book *The Black Atlantic* (1993).[3] It's one way to look at a certain type of modernity – for instance, the one achieved by the song *Strange Fruit*,[4] which was written as a protest against American racism and the lynching of African Americans. That song is very beautiful and it can sound enchanting, but, undeniably, it's also truly terrifying.

NOTES

1. Bruno, Giuliana, Paul Gilroy, Stuart Hall, bell hooks, Kobena Mercer, Laura Mulvey, Mark Nash, and Isaac Julien. *Riot.* Museum of Modern Art, 2014.
2. *Il Gattopardo* (The Leopard). Dir. Luchino Visconti. Titanus, 1963. Film.
3. Gilroy, Paul. *The Bla*ck Atlantic: Modernity and Double Consciousness. Verso, 1993.
4. Holiday, Billie. Strange Fruit. Commodore, 1939.

OPPOSITE: Isaac Julien, *The Leopard (Western Union: small boats)*, 2007 (installation view, *Ship to Shore: Art and the Lure of the Sea*, John Hansard Gallery, 2014) Single screen installation, 16mm colour film transferred to High Definition, 5.1 surround sound (19 mins 51 sec). Courtesy the artist and Victoria Miro Gallery, London. Photo: Steve Shrimpton

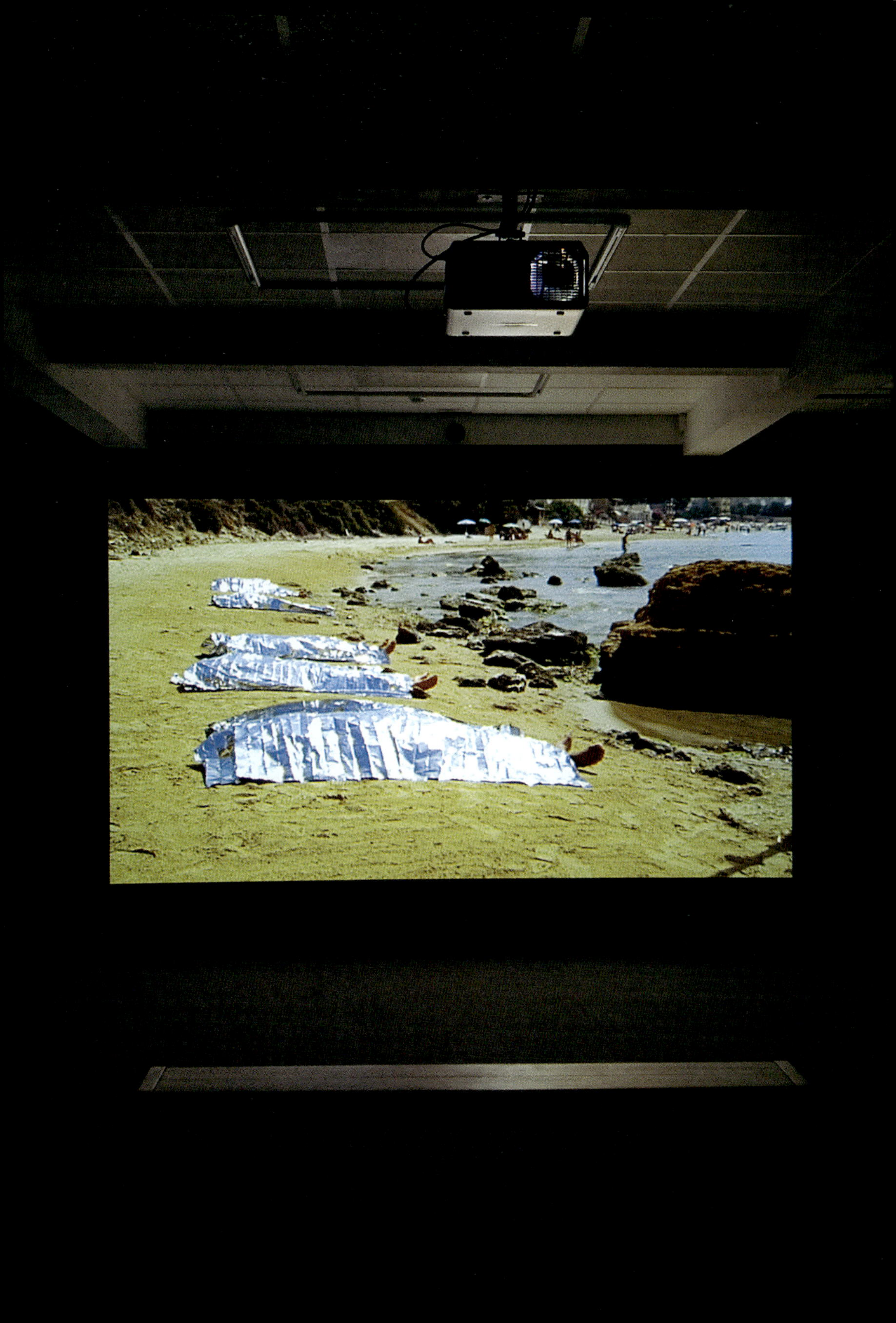

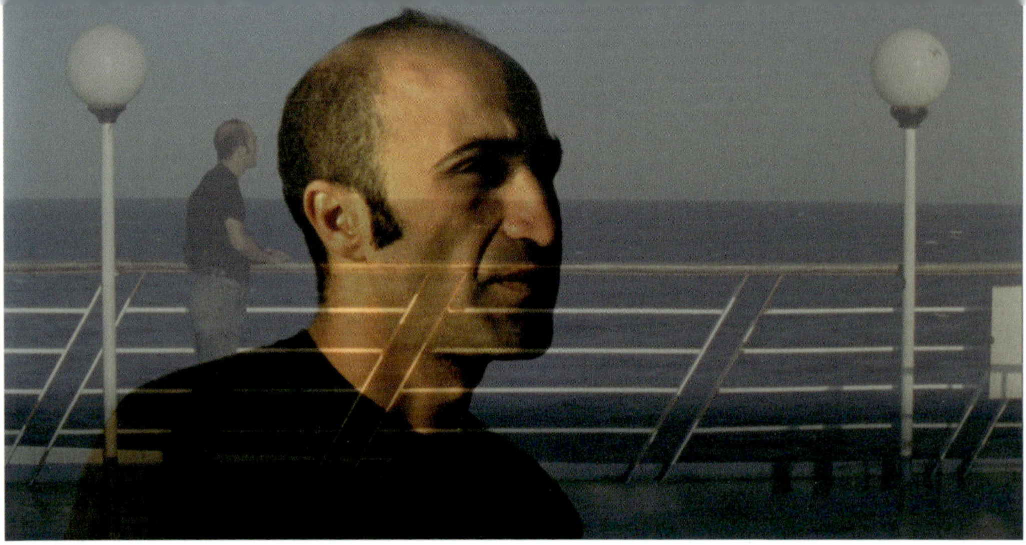
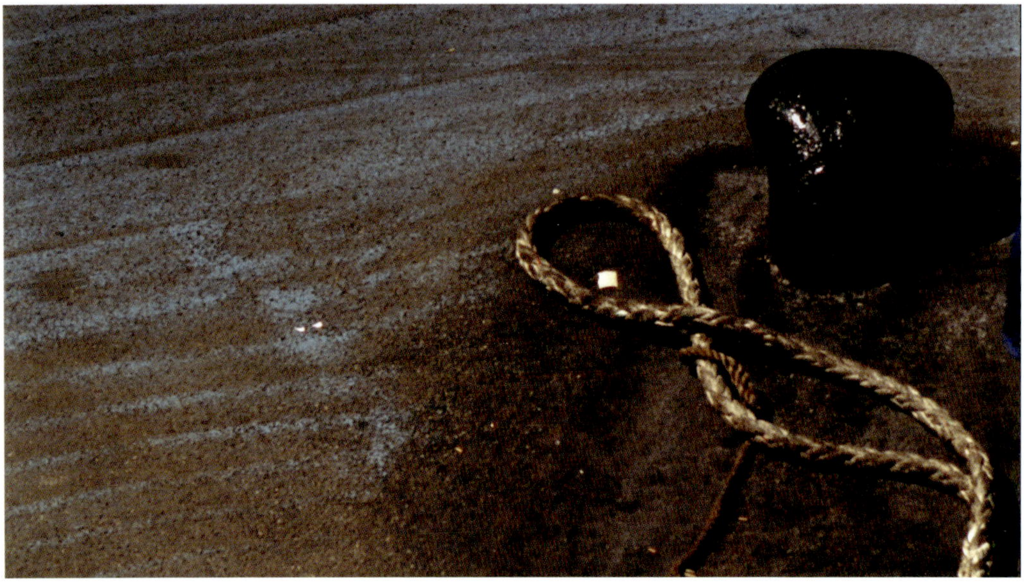
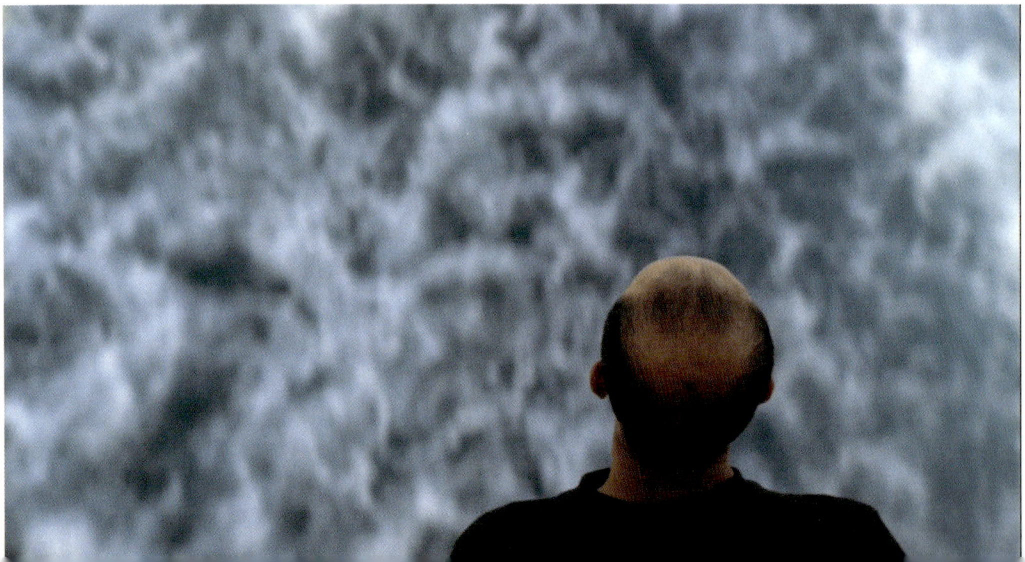

ZINEB SEDIRA

MIDDLESEA, 2008

MiddleSea *is a beautiful, complex work and an enormous projection. Why did you want the projection to be so large?*

It was conceived in 2008 for a particular space called The Wapping Project in London, where it was placed in the middle of the space. Because I shot in film – Super 16 mm – I knew the quality would actually hold at that scale.

What inspired you to make this film?

MiddleSea came out of another project called *Saphir* which I showed in The Photographers' Gallery in 2006. *Saphir* was set in and around the port of Algiers, and in the Hotel Safir, a French colonial building in the capital. *Saphir* was all about the passage between France and Algeria, and the strong ties between the two countries that still exist, despite Algeria being decolonised over 50 years ago. After filming *Saphir* I started thinking about the significance of the space between the two countries. All the boats that come through the port are from France, particularly Marseille, and I thought it would be nice to make the story of the stretch of sea between Algiers and Marseille the Mediterranean. So it made sense for me to carry on, to make a second part of *Saphir*, if you like, using the same actor, Samir El Hakim. But this time I wanted to do it on a single screen, shot on film, unlike *Saphir* which was a two-screen piece, shot on HD.

OPPOSITE AND FOLLOWING PAGES: Zineb Sedira, *MiddleSea*, 2008.
Single screen projection shot on Super 16mm film (16:9 format) (16 min)
Video still. Courtesy the artist and Galerie Kamel Mennour, Paris

For me that stretch of sea is an open space, the space of freedom, but it's also the space of enclosure, a barrier between one land and the other. So you see the actor walking in the space – you don't know where he's going, whether he's going back to France from Algeria or whether he's an immigrant living in France who is going back to Algiers for a holiday.

Why film, why did you decide to swop media?

Well *Saphir* was set in the city, and was mainly cityscape-based, though we did have some seascapes. I knew that *MiddleSea* would be a seascape, that there would be some amazing shots of the sea and of the boat – and because we were filming in the Mediterranean Sea, in the summer, I knew that film would be much more appropriate for the imagery that I was going to capture. Also, I had an appropriate budget to do it. So we decided to take a film crew on the boat – the *Tariq Ibn Ziyad* ferry – that goes from Marseille to Algiers and vice versa. So it's a return journey. Within the film you don't really know where you are, whether you are in France or in Algeria. You do see the architecture of Algeria at one point, but because it's French architecture you don't actually know. People don't seem to realise that it might be Algeria, they automatically think it's France, and that confuses them. So there is a lot of ambiguity in terms of where you are.

How did you find working with film?

I loved it. I love the quality of the image, it's really very beautiful. You get much more detail, and you get a lot of grain. I like that. I find it more three-dimensional, less flat than HD somehow. But then film's much more complicated – it's much more costly, there's more equipment and it's much larger. And you really need someone who knows about it to do it, so you need a Director of Photography, or cameraman or woman. So it's organised totally differently from when you have HD.

And although you shot on film, you decided not to project it on film?

I love film, but not that much, no. Projection? Nightmare, difficult. It's very expensive – you need a lot of copies; the film always breaks at some point, so you need a technician there to mend it – you know, all the problems with projected films. So I decided to put it back on HD, and that worked. I make a point of never showing it on DVD, because that would be too much of a compromise for me, so it needs to be played through a full screen mini Mac or media player, because then you keep the quality. With a DVD you lose some of the quality, especially on that scale.

The Tariq Ibn Ziyad *has a large capacity, but you filmed it empty of people?*

It wasn't planned. It just happened that we did the shooting during the month of Ramadan, and during Ramadan people don't travel because it's too exhausting, people in Algeria anyway.

There's a rhythm to the film and it's very enigmatically shot, with the casting off and tying-up sequences, and the sea and the spray. Did you storyboard it, or was it instinctive?

I'm a very messy filmmaker, so I never storyboard. I always shoot whatever situation happens – I never try to change it. So I can't really plan it in advance. I had done that journey a few times as a child with my parents, going back to Algeria from France. So I had an idea of it, and did one recce with the Director of Photography (DoP), when we decided what type of camera and lenses to use and so on. But you know, at sea – or with any filming of landscape or seascape – you are very dependent on the weather. We were just lucky to have the type of weather that we did. It could have been a windy day and then the sea might have been much more dramatic, which would have been fun.

Obviously the boat was rocking. How did you Steadicam it?

Well we used a lot of sandbags, and lots of tricks created by the DoP. We only had a small film crew – the DoP, Assistant DoP, Focus Puller and Sound Recordist – but between us we managed to create the illusion that the sea was pretty flat, though it wasn't and at times we were sick. It's a 15-hour trip, and you spend the night on there, but it never arrives on time. In fact it usually takes more like 20 hours, which was quite nice because it allowed us to have a lot of different imagery, like sunset, sunrise and so on.

By using that scale I wanted whoever watched the video to feel that they were actually on the boat, that they were on the journey with us. As far as I could, I tried to convey this idea of grandeur and the real size of it all, to see the sea as you would actually see it. There are one or two shots where if you look at it you feel a bit sick. I think that sometimes it works and sometimes it doesn't, because you always have to compromise, it can never be perfect.

Can we talk about the sound, because it's very particular and you used a well-known sound artist – Mikhail Karikis – to make it. Why did you decide to work with him?

It was the first piece Mikhail worked on with me. He's a friend of a friend. I really liked the work he was doing, and we decided to work together on this piece. I did some local sound recording with the sound recordist on the film crew (not Mikhail), and we then asked him to sketch a soundtrack with it, adding in his own sound. At first he worked with a rough copy of the film, then later with the final video as a QuickTime movie. I went and sat with him twice as he was editing, and we kind of re-juggled bits that didn't sound quite right. On the last day we edited the film in the space and he came and sat with us and adjusted the sound according to the new edits.

He's added some very particular sounds, like the radio tuning in…

Yes. There's also a bit of music at one point – that's him. He also enhanced some of the audio when things like the sound of the wind weren't strong enough. Sound recordists are like magicians, they've got so many tricks up their sleeves, and he obviously knows what he's doing. He's made an amazing sound piece, which is why the sound, and the levels of the sound, are so important. It was designed specifically for The Wapping Project. For example, there's a kind of balcony when you come in and the speakers were set underneath that. The whole balcony vibrated with sound of the bass, which affected you physically and made you feel as if you were actually on the boat. For *Ship to Shore* I had to try and re-create that experience. It was obviously not identical because no two spaces are the same, so the installation had a different impact.

How much footage did you actually shoot?

Six hours. In film time that's quite a lot.

So you edited it quite radically, down to 16 minutes. How did you manage that?

It was painful, because all the imagery was really beautiful, stunning. So you want to include everything. Obviously there is repetition which you can remove, but the concept also has to be there – it's not just beautiful images, I also wanted the tension. So we slowly cut it down, and as long as I couldn't remember what we'd taken out that was fine, but sometimes if I re-visit all the hours of footage that we didn't use, I feel like I want to go back.

How did you decide on the length of the film?

Well I tend to work with a video length of between 10 and perhaps 25 minutes. I do believe that above that it's a bit too long. I've done some slightly longer videos, but they were interview-based. Usually I tend to make them as short as possible, because I understand that the audience won't stay for too long, although saying that *MiddleSea* seems to be quite an immersive piece – people do sit and watch it.

Yes, people do sit, and they become immersed in the journey. When people are on a sea voyage, time slows as they gaze at the wake of the ship, or the waves around the hull. The swell, the spray… The film seems to act on time in the same way.

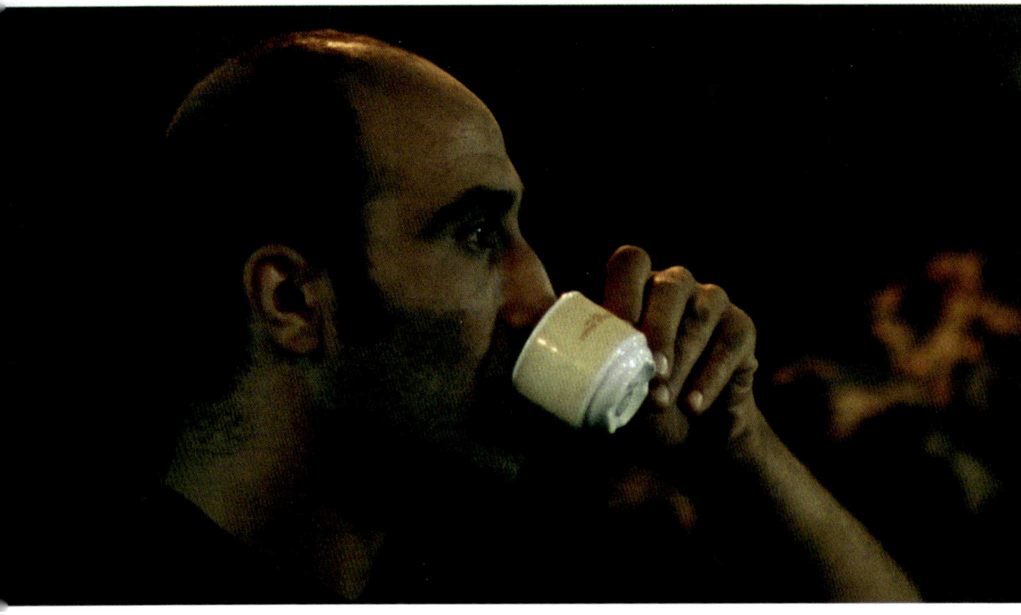

Yes. It was important to me to convey the feeling of waiting, because we're always in transit really, always waiting to arrive or depart from somewhere. But the slow pace of the film is also due to the fact that I'm a photographer, so I wanted to give it a photographic element, a photographic style. So that's why the camera sometimes focuses for a long time on things that seem really trivial, but which for me are very important, and that's what gives the video this kind of hypnotic, immersive side.

You've mentioned colonialism, migration, travel, the different, very loaded histories. How much did you want to convey about those?

Well I wanted *MiddleSea* to be a bit broader, a bit more universal perhaps than *Saphir*, which is why you don't know if you're in Marseille or Algiers (actually unless you read the text you could be at sea anywhere). Obviously physically Samir looks very much like a North African, so I knew that automatically there would be the suggestion that he's an immigrant. I mean, if you want to play around with clichés he could be an Iranian or Romanian immigrant, or whatever. So I knew that he would bring that element to the piece, but at the same time he could also

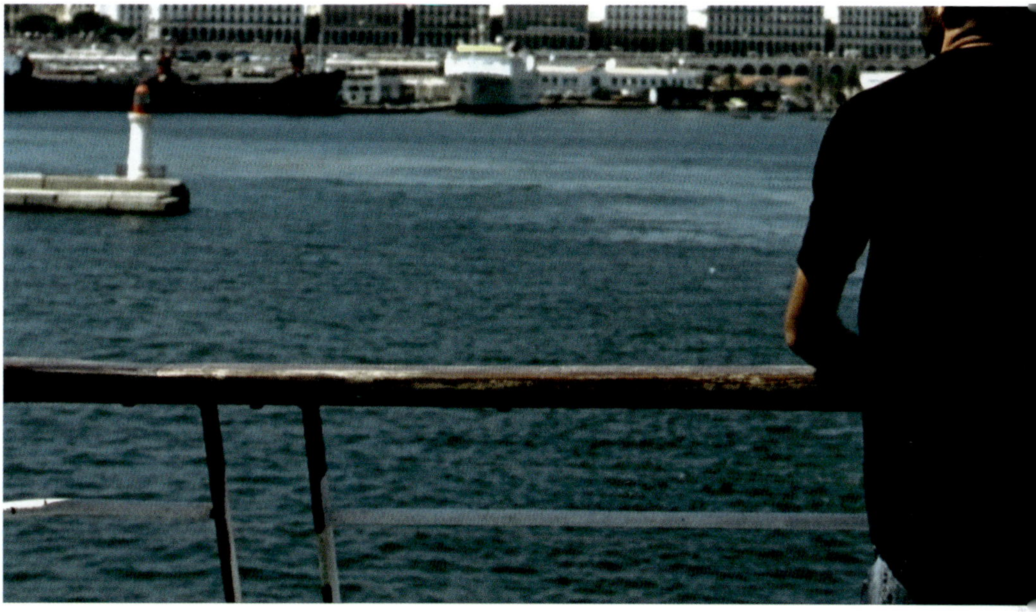

be French, because many Algerians were born in France – there were a lot of mixed marriages. So, you know, I think it's quite ambiguous.

Is that why you chose him then?

I chose him because he was in *Saphir*, so it made sense to me; but also because of his own experience of being an immigrant. Samir's done that trip many times. He's a professional actor, living in Algiers, but he went to France for a few years to see if life was better there. But he didn't like it and returned to Algeria. So he's done this trip both as a migrant and returning home. You don't know that in the film though. As far as I was concerned, he was free to act or just be himself, but being himself would almost be like acting that he was an immigrant returning home. That's why it was interesting. It would have been less interesting to me if it had been a Frenchman going to Algiers on holiday. You know, being really excited about every corner of the boat.

There are a couple of shots where he's just looking, and the way he looks is great. He's clearly contemplating – you can feel *that.*

It's quite sombre, isn't it? There's almost a kind of anxiety. You don't know whether he's coming back to Algeria, and wondering how it's going to be with the family, or his wife or his girlfriend; or whether he's going to France, and thinking, 'I'm going to leave them forever now. Oh, how I'm going to miss them.' Because you don't know. You don't know what's in his head because you don't know where he's leaving from and where he's going to. And in fact there is no arrival or departure in the film. You just don't know. Is he lost? Because immigration is also about that, having so many identities, and no longer knowing where you belong. So for me his tension was important, in the same way that the tension in the sound, and sometimes the footage, was.

The emptiness in the film lends it a tension too. It feels almost menacing. You pack so many layers into the work. Do you have a desire for your work to be political?

No, I don't have that desire, but I believe that all art is political anyway. Because of my background and what I'm known for doing – which is perhaps my work around post-colonial Algeria – my work is automatically seen and written about in a political way, and that's fine. It might not be political with a capital P, like the work of an activist, someone like Alfredo Jaar, but it is political in that sense. It's also autobiographical, because it's about my first trip to Algeria, which was by boat, and my parents' journey migrating to France, also by boat. That was when France was still just in power in Algeria – 1961 – so it wasn't the exact same boat as in the film but it *was* the *Tariq Ibn Ziyad* ferry. And I remember going on the actual boat in the film when I was ten. I've been on it a few times since.

Can we talk a little bit more about why you were drawn to the subject matter, which you've been using for some time now?

Well, my earliest video pieces were more autobiographical. I used myself, my mum, my daughter, my father. They were based very much around immigration, or diaspora, whether it was through the language, the dress or whatever. There was always this idea of journeying, of movement.

Why?

Because of my parents' migration to France, then my move from Paris to London in 1986 – funnily enough by boat in both cases. When I moved to England there was no Eurostar, so the only way you could come was on the ferry. So I got more and more interested in the ferrying, and now I've kind of left behind the autobiographical and the family. Also, in 2003 I started going back to Algeria after a good twelve years when I didn't go because of the civil war. I could have gone but it was dangerous. But my parents were living there again – they had left France and gone back in '88, just before the revolution started.

Why did they decide to go back?

Because they were unhappy. Then they got caught in the civil war. Having said that, because they had lived in France they were able to leave the country and return whenever they wanted, so they used to come and meet us in Paris. I had a younger brother and sisters living in Algiers so they couldn't stay too long, but at least I could see them. Then in 2002 the civil war stopped and I could go back, and funnily all the work I was doing around the family stopped, most probably because I now had direct access to Algeria – before, I was accessing Algeria *through* my parents in France. So I started working with the landscape and the seascape of Algeria, and in some ways Algeria became a metaphor for the family. After all, it was the land of my parents. They were born there. So when people say, 'You don't use your mother and father in your work any more', I always say, 'They're still there, but now they're in the landscape.' And in French the word for sea, *la mer*, sounds the same as that for mother, *la mère*, so I played on that, and for me the sea became a kind of metaphor for my mother.

Finally the title, MiddleSea. *How did you come about that, because titling a work's always difficult isn't it?*

That took me a long time because I really wanted it to express that space between the two countries, but I didn't want to call it 'Space In-Between'. So then I thought of 'Middle Sea', and then I decided to make it one word, without a gap: *MiddleSea*. I was happy with that.

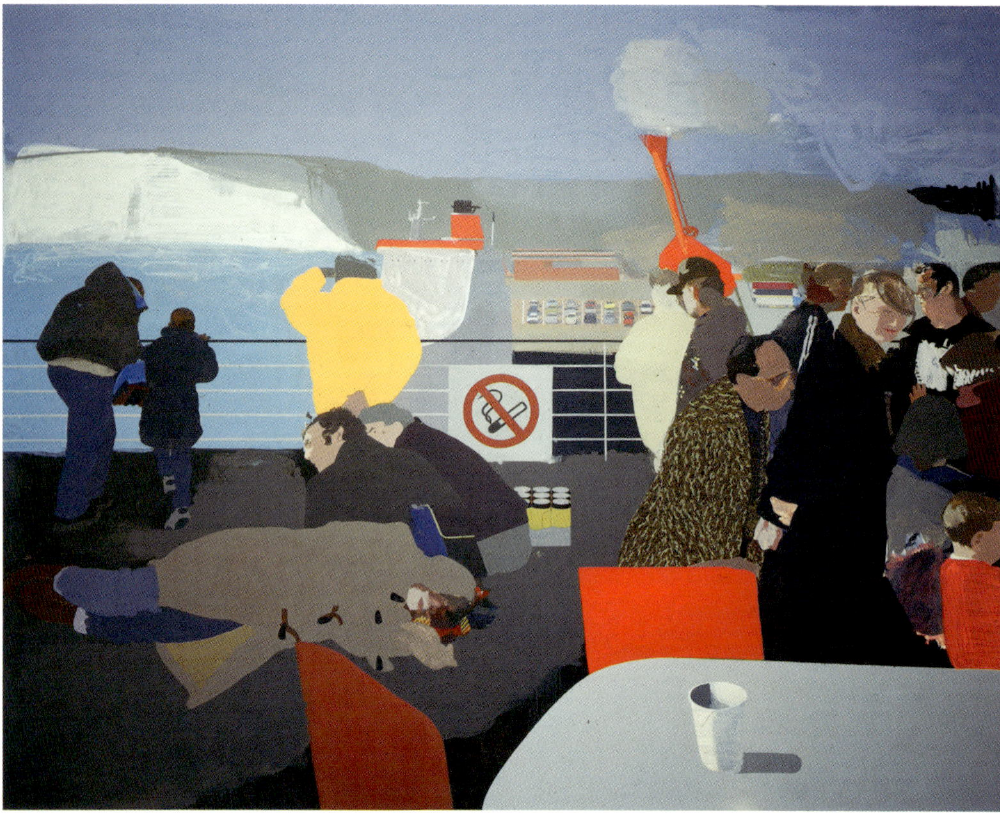

Humphrey Ocean, *The First of England*, 1998 (also pp 120–1)
Oil and acrylic on canvas. Courtesy and copyright the artist and
National Maritime Museum, Greenwich, London

HUMPHREY OCEAN

THE FIRST OF ENGLAND, 1998

Can I begin by asking what inspired you to paint The First of England?

To track back a little, in 1979 I was commissioned by the Artistic Records Committee of the Imperial War Museum to make a painting of the Navy at work. I had an interesting time at sea for a week, sailing from Portsmouth to Plymouth aboard HMS *Broadsword*, a naval frigate. Although it looked like a normal grey warship, *Broadsword* was the first computerised ship, so instead of 500 men on board it only needed 250. The men complained because what one does most on a ship is keep it clean and 'ship shape', so it just meant they had half the number of people for those duties. The painting which resulted, *Recovering the Dan Buoy, HMS 'Broadsword'* (1979–1980) was noticed by Roger Quarm at the National Maritime Museum, and twenty years later they approached me and about six other artists to make something about modern maritime Britain and the sea for the opening of the new Neptune Court.

Why did you choose the port of Dover and a cross channel ferry as your subject?

Because that's how I get over to France. I thought, 'Britain is no longer a maritime nation, in the naval sense', and although there are large amounts of containers and shipping coming into British ports, I had no direct experience of that either. I either swim in the sea or go on it by ferry and my most frequent departure point is Dover. I had been reading Alistair Horne's *The Price of Glory: Verdun 1916*,[1] about that extraordinary, pointless, ten-month battle, and it set me to thinking about the First World War and our relationship with France and Germany. I thought also of Philip Larkin's poem MCMXIV (1964),[2] with the poignant lines, 'The crowns of hats, the sun/ On moustached

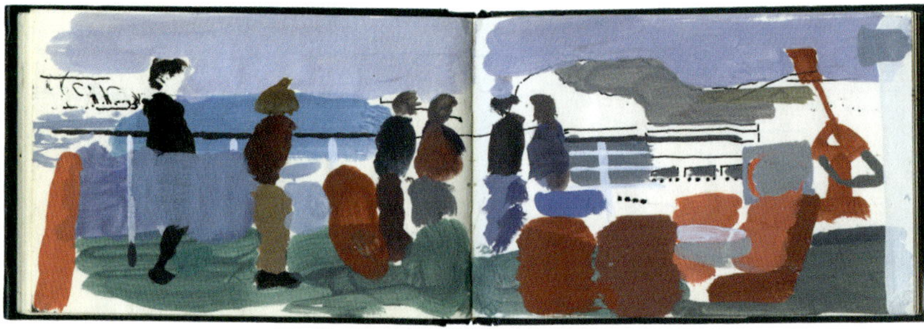

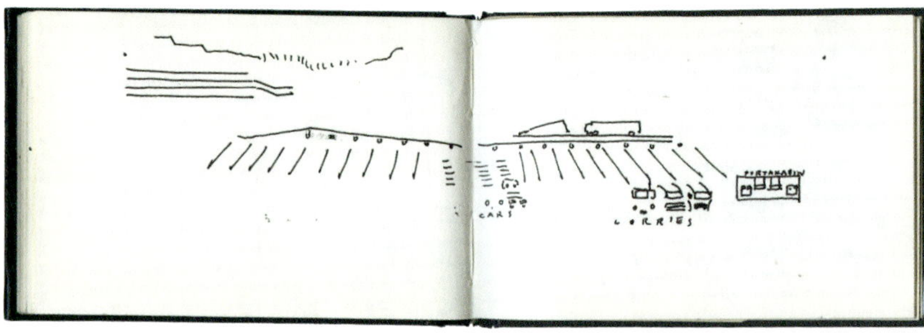

ABOVE AND OPPOSITE:: Humphrey Ocean, *The First of England*, development sketches, 1998
Courtesy and copyright the artist

archaic faces/ Grinning as if it were all/ An August Bank Holiday lark', which of course refers to the photographs we know – a black-and-white, grainy world beginning also to be documented on film, of men at the start of the First World War excited to be going to France, 'Leaving the gardens tidy', thinking they'll be home by Christmas. Tragic, really. And Larkin concludes, '...never such innocence again'. Now, cut to 1998 when I am preparing sketches for *The First of England* and everyone is making the same journey taking the ferry to Calais, only this time they are paying fifty pence each way and stocking up on whisky and cigarettes. Many of the passengers don't even disembark, preferring to stay on board what is effectively a floating shopping mall. After lunch on board and a breezy stroll on deck the ship returns and you're back in England that afternoon.

What is your painting's relationship to The Last of England *(1855), Ford Madox Brown's pre-Raphaelite work?*

The title *The First of England* came after I had done the painting.

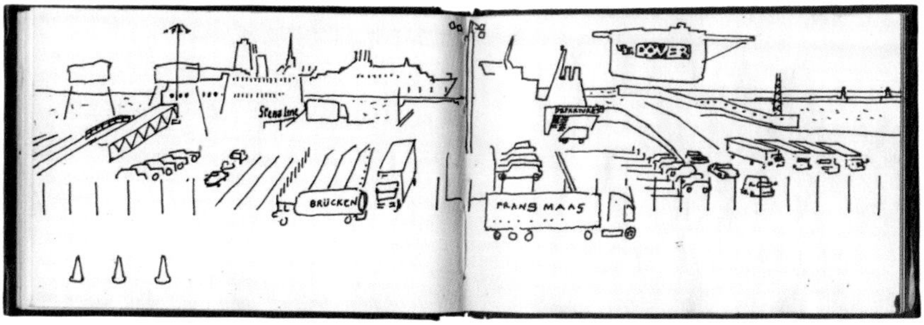

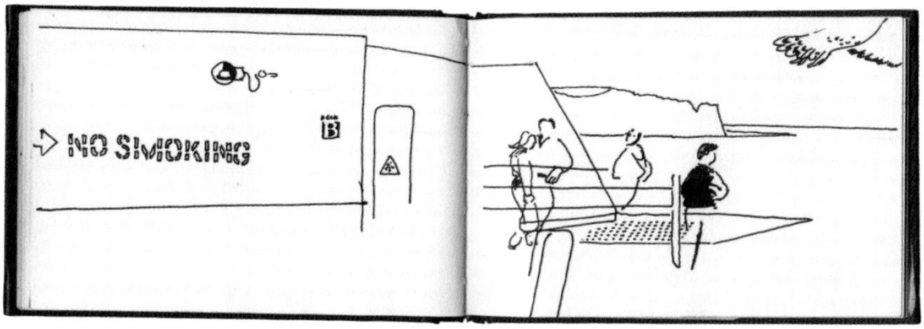

In *The Last of England* Brown is concerned with a different departure: his passengers are emigrating, seeking or driven to a new life. At that time a tearful farewell meant knowing you would not be seeing your family again for years, if at all. In my painting, most of the trippers are returning home the same day, arriving at the white cliffs with a boxful of Boddingtons beer.

What does the lure of the sea mean to you?

My father went into the Navy when he was thirteen and stayed thirty-seven years. During the war, as Mountbatten's navigator on HMS *Kelly*, he was one of the few to survive when the ship was sunk off Crete in 1941. He wanted me to be in the Navy, but I left school early, went to art school, and pretended I wanted to do interior design at first and then graphic design because I thought it would suit him to think I was capable of making a living. I was painting all the time, always had done, and remember an almost sexual frisson as I ticked the fine art painting box when applying for a degree course. I went home and owned up, 'I'm going to do painting'. My father said, 'No'. In a kind of inspired moment I said, 'It's my Navy', and he went, 'Ah, right'. I later learned something about my father and the Navy when I was on *HMS Broadsword*. Being cooped up on a ship with your fellow man requires a measure of tolerance and understanding which probably helps in moments like this.

Many of your paintings are very large. Was there a reason that The First of England *was the size it was?*

I wanted it to be almost as if you were part of it, or as if you could step into it. There's a great photograph of Barnett Newman and an unidentified woman taken in 1958 in his studio, standing about two feet away from his painting *Cathedral* (1951). As well as looking, they are experiencing something. When I went to Canterbury Art School in 1970, the accent in the teaching there was for some reason on colour field painting – Pollock and Rothko, seasoned with Frank Stella and Kenneth Noland to make it a little more contemporary – which, looking back, was strange considering that by that time things had really moved through Warhol to Smithson and Carl Andre. Although I was resolutely not making abstract paintings it must have gone in somewhere, because that thinking is still in my bloodstream. So the scale of *The First of England* is intended as intimate. I still do many of my paintings on the floor, keeping the wet paint even. And even though I respond to people, places and things that are in front of me, I cannot help being conscious of what Frank Stella called the 'paint in the tin', undisturbed.

Can we talk about the colour in your work, specifically the red?

Red is such an interesting colour, and tone has a lot to do with it. If you have pure cadmium red straight out of the tube, it can sometimes be too red, and in fact it starts to appear darker in the eye if you stare at it too long – same principle as when black dots dance in front of your eyes after exposure to very bright light. So you have to be bit careful. In *The First of England* I am just starting out, rather late, to try and deal with reds, and though not much further on now, I am still intrigued. One of the things I love on board any kind of ship is the lean and practical design. A capstan, for instance, is very close to sculpture. And then colour – think of black-and-white dazzle camouflage in WWI, or the grey of a warship. The green and white and red of this ferry slicing through the Channel makes quite a sight.

There is something quite particular about a ferry coming into dock.

Yes, compared to other forms of commercial transport it's slow and deliberate, and the lapping water brings its own sound and smell. Since the Victorians invented the railway station our points of arrival or departure are expected to look honestly industrial, and it would be an unusual day not to find scratchcards and sellophane blowing around the car park, the detritus of the departure point.

You really captured your characters and the feeling of being on a ferry: the person in your painting who really feels they're at sea, all kitted out in their yellow oilskin; the people leaning over the rail, watching the arrival; the man sleeping on the deck; and the ubiquitous polystyrene cup and No Smoking sign. How much time did you spend making sketches?

I had a rough idea in my mind. I took a ferry trip, and it seemed to me fairly obvious that really what the painting was about was a group of people. Generally I paint what's nearest to me, which mostly *is* people; and then there is the next thing, in this case the ferry. I ended up making about five or six day trips. I'd see something and think, 'Yes, I want that', or, 'Yes, I want them', pretty much like a film director might think, 'Oh, I want that person'. The person lying down in middle of the painting is Jock Scot, and standing in profile on the right is Slim Pain, both old friends who were in a previous painting of mine, *Lord Volvo and his Estate (1982)*. I wanted them to make another appearance, so I rang them up and said, 'How do you fancy a day going over to Calais?' Jock had not been to bed for three days and every flat surface he saw he was down on it pronto, horizontal.

Everything seems to balance everything else in the painting.

Yes. Painting is like bouncing a ball on a racquet – you have to dart this way and that to keep it in the air.

NOTES

1. Horne, Alistair. *The Price of Glory: Verdun 1916*. Macmillan, 1962.
2. Larkin, Philip. 'MCMXIV'. *The Whitsun Weddings*. 1964. Faber & Faber, 2001, pp. 25–26.

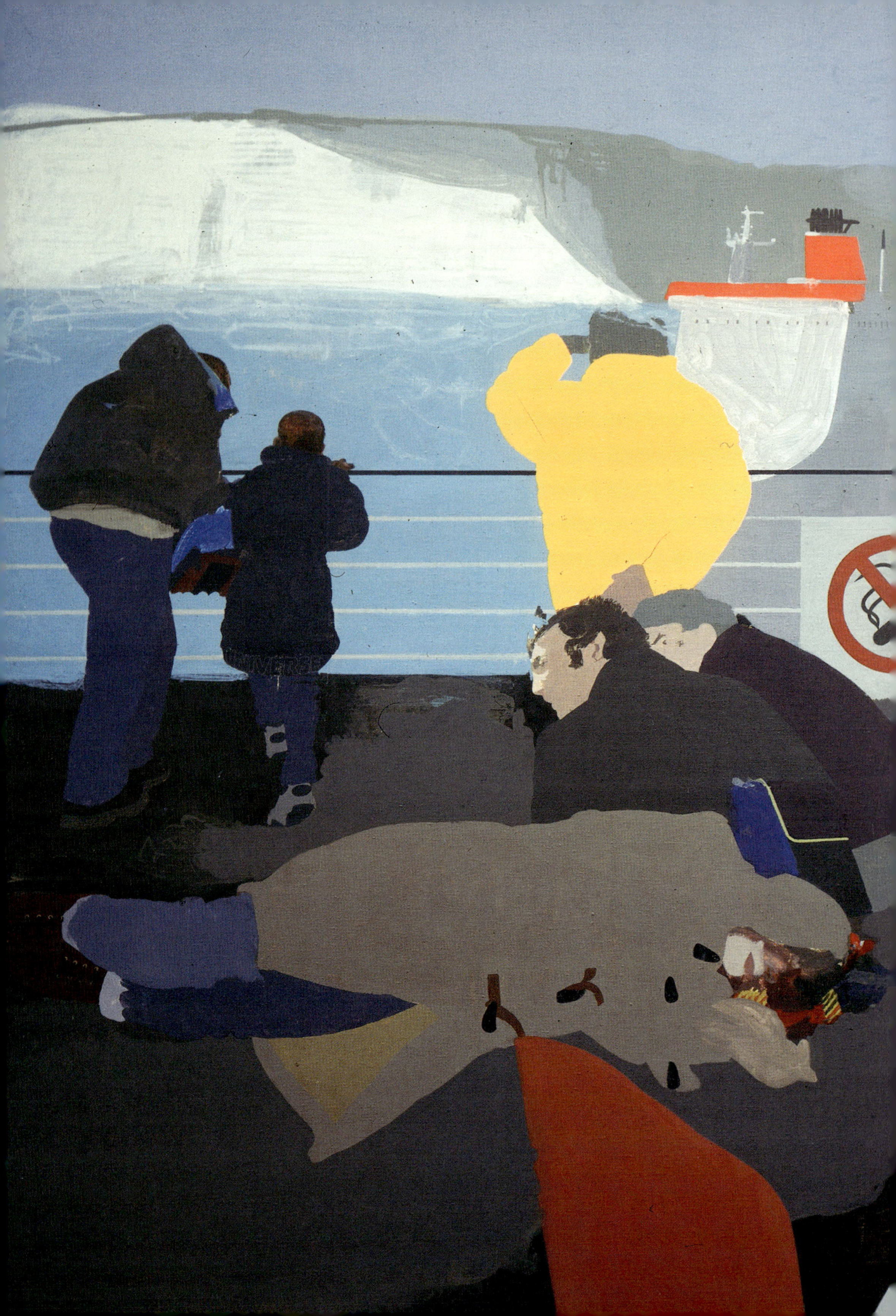

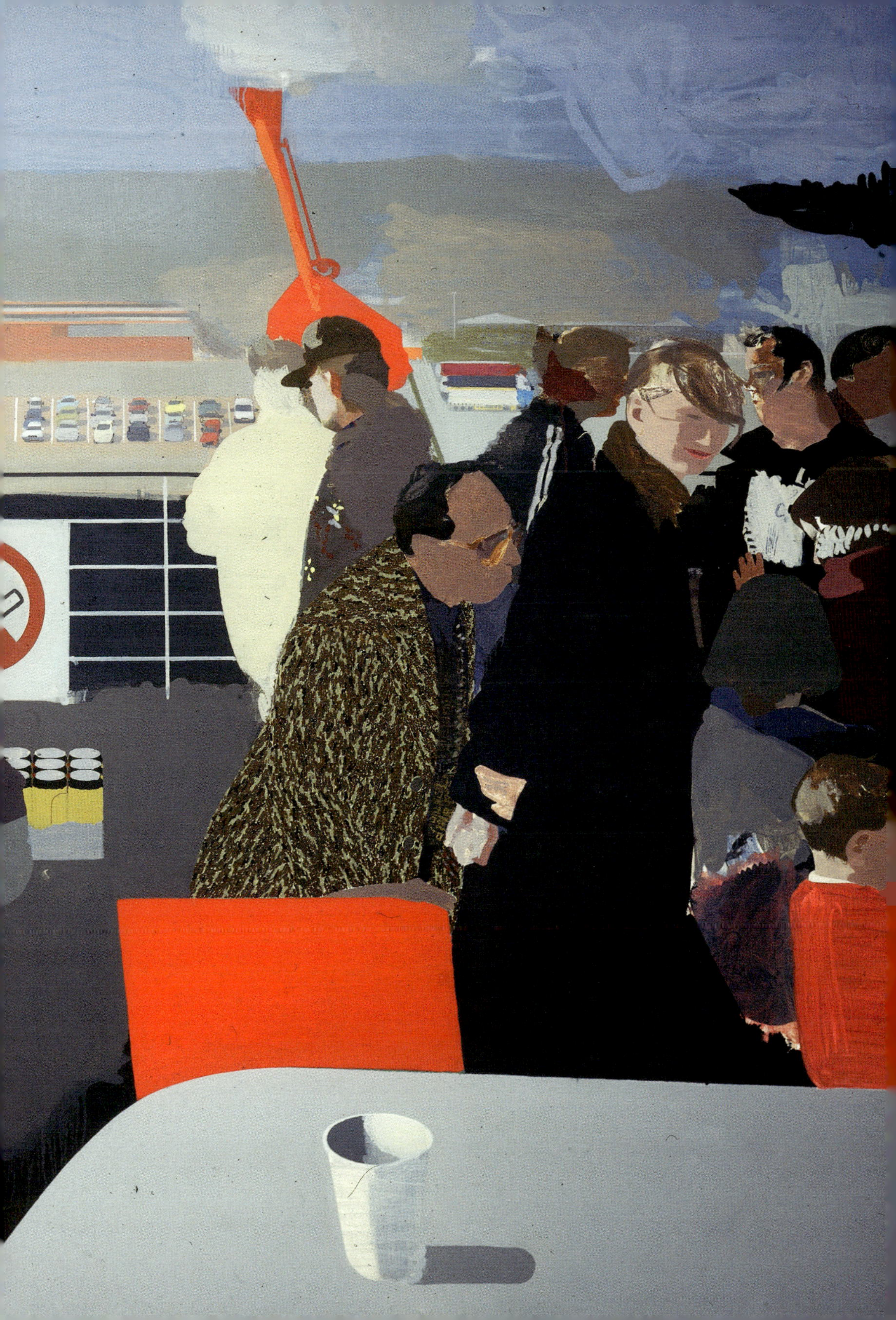

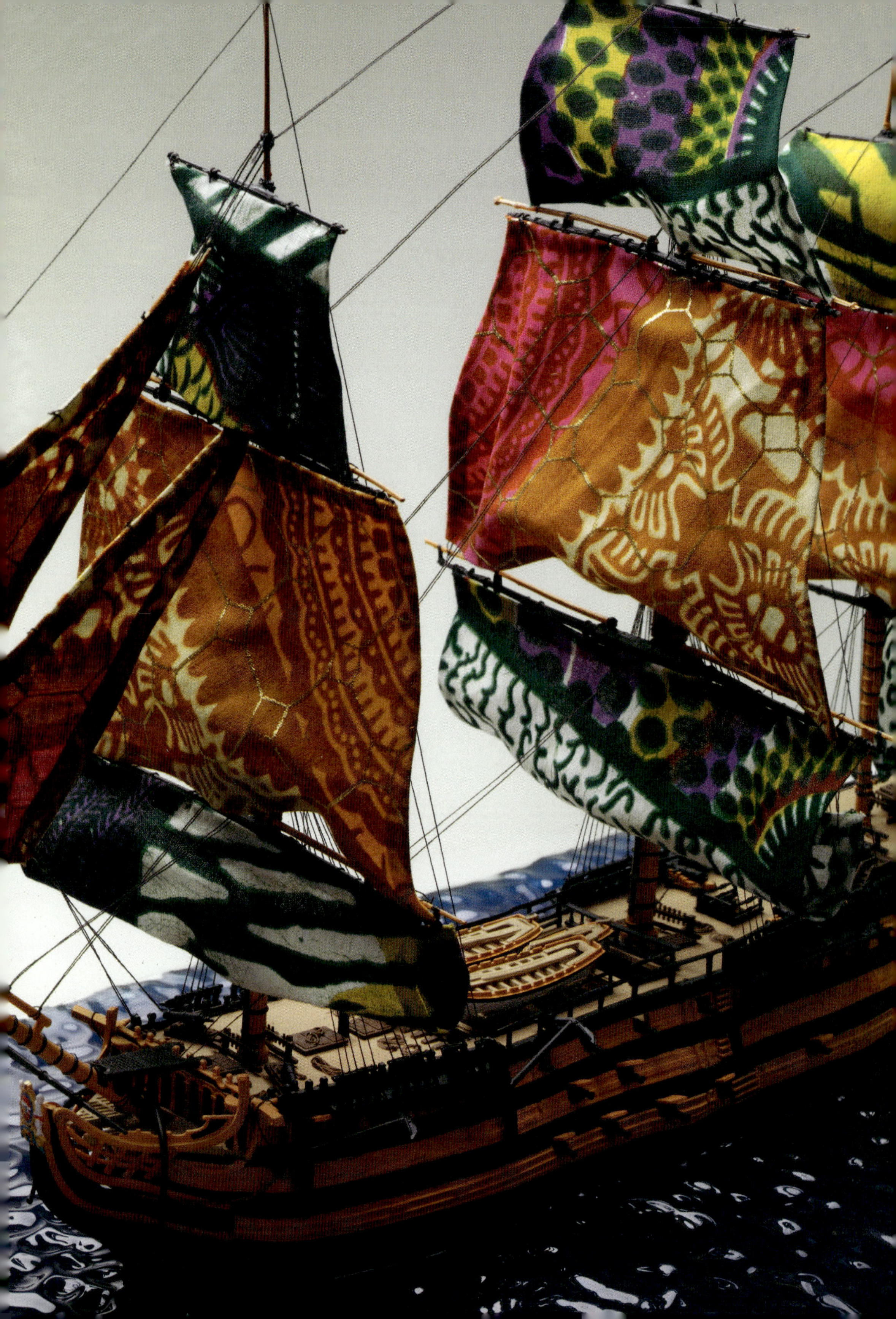

YINKA SHONIBARE MBE

NELSON'S SHIP IN A BOTTLE, 2010

Your Nelson's Ship in a Bottle *sculpture is so multi-layered, but so fitting for the space – you made it for the Trafalgar Square plinth in London of course. How did this complex idea come about?*

It just seemed sort of logical really, to contextualise the piece, to make it say something about the location.

And the idea about being in a bottle, the containment. Were you interested in ships in bottles?

Well, I remembered them from my childhood – it's obviously something that's there in the culture – but it's also sort of forgotten, you know, this old-fashioned "craft thing". I mean, in our digital world it's probably not something that children will revisit now. It's sort of out-dated really.

So did you do a lot of research into different ships in bottles? How did the idea develop?

Well this is not the first ship in a bottle I've done. I did the first one in Stockholm, and that was based on a coincidence, because I was doing this project with the Moderna Museet, and they are behind a museum for a ship called the *Vasa*. The *Vasa* was a warship going back to the 17th century that sank on its maiden voyage, so there's a kind of celebration of this failed ship, if you like, this failed voyage. That made me think

OPPOSITE (DETAIL) AND OVERLEAF: Yinka Shonibare, *Nelson's Ship in a Bottle*, 2010
Plastic, Dutch wax-printed cotton textile, cork, acrylic and glass bottle
Courtesy the artist and Stephen Friedman Gallery, London

about colonial ambitions and the use of those ships in such ambitions. And then with the plinth, Trafalgar Square, is of course where Nelson's Column is, and I was thinking about the fact that *HMS Victory* actually played a strong role in the defeat of France, the defeat of Napoleon, and that in a sense the British Empire was able to prosper because of that defeat, because otherwise France would actually have had more control of the water.

Can we talk about the sails? In, the smaller version of Nelson's Ship in a Bottle, *the sails are beautiful in the way that they catch the light and the water. I was wondering about their link to colonial history, and all the colonial references to the Dutch traders.*

Well, London today is a very multicultural city, so I think that there should be some reflection on how that actually came about, all the history. And of course a lot of it is connected to global trade, and the fabrics are very much part of those trade routes.

Yes, and of course you've used fabric in many of your works. You've also used the idea of travel, the idea of people moving from one place to another; also how cloth gets to a market, cloth that's come from somewhere else and has perhaps lost some of its references on the way. The sails of the ship are so rich in that history.

Yes, those fabrics – Indonesian-influenced fabrics produced by the Dutch – were industrially-produced versions to sell back to Indonesia. And, you know, they didn't really want them, they wanted their own domestic batik. The Dutch then tried the West African market, and the fabrics are now considered African, but they do have this history about them, which I find very interesting – that something that's meant to represent the authenticity of Africa turns out to be something which is hybrid in itself.

So were there certain fabrics, certain patterns or colours, that you felt you just had to use for the sails of the ship because of their history? What was the importance for you of the different types of patterns in the sails?

Well, for the actual *Ship in a Bottle*, the large version, I didn't use ready-made fabrics, I actually designed them myself – in the style of

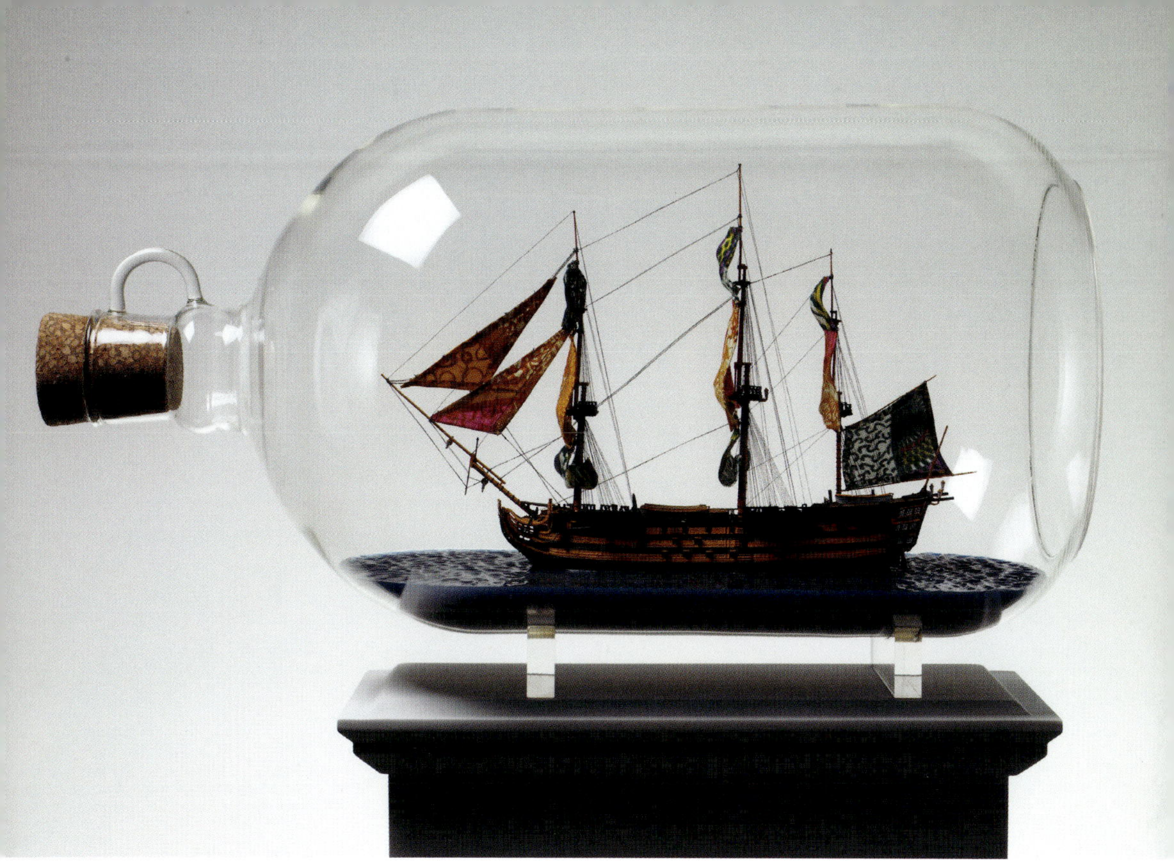

ready-mades, but designed – because they had to be UV-protected and very special fabric. So I used African designs, and kind of modified some of the typical designs of other batik fabrics. In the smaller versions of the *Ship in a Bottle,* I used ready-mades. But I'm very interested in colour and pattern anyway, so I tend to juxtapose patterns, and sometimes – because I was trained as a painter so I'm actually very visual – I deliberately break the rules of colour: I use complementary colours, or colours that somehow should not go together but then they do. So there's a lot of visual dialogue.

The whole idea of the Dutch Wax fabric on those sails, and the colours, is really important. I know you love these fabrics: you collect them and use them and, as you say, you make your own as well. Have you always been interested in the tradition in the fabric?

This is kind of part of the story behind my work. I was actually almost forced to start looking at the notion of authenticity, and what it actually means, by a conversation I had with one of my tutors when I was at college. I was making work, political work, you know, about *perestroika* in Russia and things like that, and my tutor said, 'You're of African origin aren't you? Why aren't you producing authentic African art?' And that was where the question of authenticity started for me. You know, if you're English, do you have to make work about Morris Dancing? That's where the question sort of began for me really, that the fabrics are almost a kind of metaphor for origins and the construction of identity. For example, the kilt, I gather, was actually a sort of English construction for the Scots. I'm fascinated by those kinds of cultural constructions. And so the way that I look at fabrics, I think it's more a sort of cultural study really, almost anthropological, in that I'm trying to actually understand human culture and material culture and the relation of that to history.

Can we talk now about the passion you have for the history of your pieces, because a lot of your work's really so much about that? Things like emigration, colonialism, industrialisation…

Well, I think that most people like records of history. I mean the mere fact of me having this conversation with you in English and not in Yoruba – Yoruba is my first language – has a strong historical reason behind it. So in a sense I guess in my work I'm taking that contemporary identity and trying to understand our history and where we've actually come from – that from the clothes we wear, the fabrics that we adorn ourselves with, to the words that we utter, you can actually read our history. I'm very interested in the historical background to the kind of contemporary manifestations of things.

And of course ships by their very nature not only carried cargo from one place to another, but also humans, and all those people had their own cultures and languages. And I think that's part of Nelson's Ship in a Bottle. *Traditionally ships had a mix of different backgrounds among the people who sailed them. I love the way that that goes into the sails of this piece.*

Yes, I mean on HMS *Victory* itself – because I visited it in Portsmouth – they did say that the sailors were from all different backgrounds: it wasn't just Caucasian, it was very mixed; the crew was multicultural.

Did you want Nelson's Ship in a Bottle *to be a political piece as well?*

Well, I think essentially a lot of my work is about paradox. So actually on the one hand some people saw the piece on the plinth as me celebrating England, celebrating Nelson, almost a nationalistic piece, a celebration of Nelson's achievements. Then there were other people who saw it as me actually subverting the power of the empire through this symbol of empire. But then I don't really say anything about it: I leave people to draw their own conclusions about what it is. I think that's the beauty of art, in the sense that it's open-ended, and it's up to the audience to draw what they want to draw from a work of art, depending on their own prejudices and experiences.

Could you comment on the different scales of the piece? Obviously with the larger version for the plinth in Trafalgar Square you were looking up at the ship, but of course in the smaller gallery work what you have is a completely different perspective – you're not looking up *at it.*

Well obviously a gallery work is not necessarily the same as public art. You know, it's a question of context, really. I think it's just space-appropriate to have it as a smaller piece for an exhibition, and then to have the larger public artwork. You know that the Maritime Museum now has the larger version? They have the largest collection of Nelson memorabilia there.

I know you've always been interested in history because you've made many works about that, but does the sea itself inspire you?

Well, I've always been aware of it, because I grew up in Lagos, which is by the Atlantic Ocean, and I did go to the seaside a lot when I was young. I don't think I'm a natural sailor though, so I'm not drawn to it. I mean on the edges it's fine, but when you go out quite far, that's when I get seasick. The last time I was at sea, I think I was whale watching and I was as sick as hell because it was quite rough. So I wouldn't say I have a conscious interest in the sea, no.

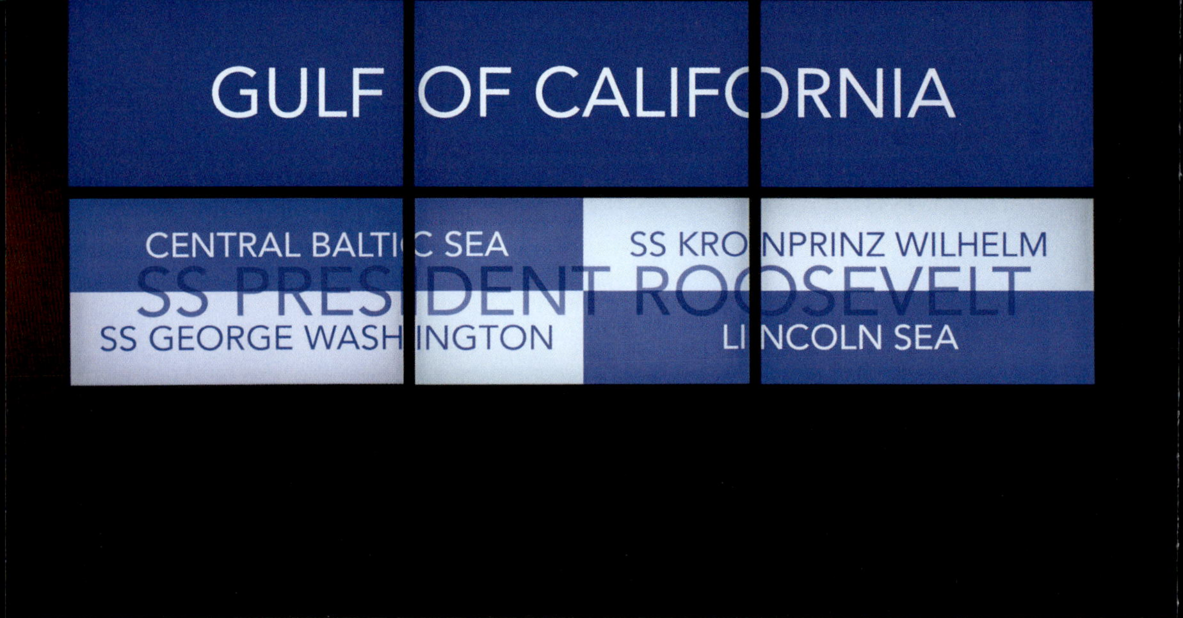
GULF OF CALIFORNIA
CENTRAL BALTIC SEA
SS KRONPRINZ WILHELM
SS PRESIDENT ROOSEVELT
SS GEORGE WASHINGTON
LINCOLN SEA

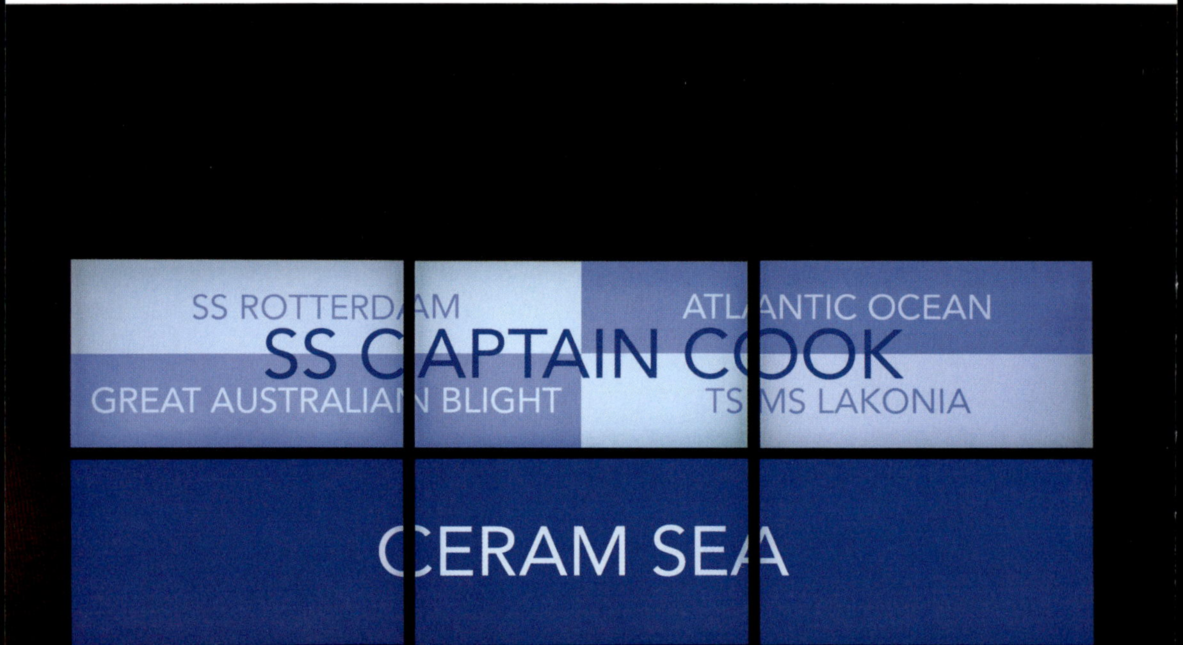
SS ROTTERDAM
ATLANTIC OCEAN
SS CAPTAIN COOK
GREAT AUSTRALIAN BLIGHT
TSMS LAKONIA
CERAM SEA

LANGLANDS & BELL

INTO THE BLUE, 2014

Into the Blue *is a multi-layered artwork where you have deployed your characteristic aesthetic of exploring various complex systems linked to the sea, so can we begin by talking about its inception?*

Nikki Bell [NB]: *Into the Blue* is really about the language of the sea, and the relationships between people, places and global histories. Historically, the seas have been zones of access and communication, and in a sense the blue and the white composition resembles a flag – and flags are one of the most enduring mediums of communication. Also blue is the colour of the sea, the sky, perhaps infinity and the horizon.

With Into the Blue *you began with lists, so can I ask about the rationale behind the names of the cruise ships, the seas, and the oceans included in the work, and the criteria for selection?*

NB: Well, we wanted to look at all the seas of the world, and combine them with the names of randomly chosen ocean liners, so that was the inception of our idea. So we researched an extraordinary list with wonderfully evocative, poetic names.

Ben Langlands [BL]: We also noticed that many of the ocean liners' names are seas as well, which we thought was interesting, and would enable us to start playing off different names against each other.

Thinking about your previous work, such as Who's Afraid of Red Black and Blue? *(2005) or* Moving World (Night and Day) *(2008), and all the tracking that you've done – literally chasing names or words – did you find a rhythm emerging in this work, a poetic rhythm?*

OPPOSITE AND OVERLEAF: Langlands & Bell, *Into the Blue*, 2014
Multi-channel digital animation archived as video, displayed on 6 screens
(14 min, 44 sec looping, silent). (Installation view, *Ship to Shore: Art and the Lure of the Sea*, SeaCity Museum, Southampton, 2014) Courtesy the artists.

NB: There is a poetic rhythm. Also, it triggers a multiplicity of different associations that we have all grown up with. They have to do with personal histories, cultural histories, the connections between places and peoples, and perceptions of distance, time and space. All of these things are inter-connected.

BL: There are strange coincidences in the names. For example, there is one quite obscure name, an ocean liner called *SS Rio Atrato*. The Rio Atrato is a river in the Chocó region of Colombia. I happen to know, because I travelled up it by boat in the early 1970s, to a place called Riosucio, meaning 'dirty river'. It's a tiny little village only accessible by boat, deep in the jungle. After that point, there are only indigenous inhabitants. So these names that suddenly appear in the work can be anywhere, and mean different things for different people. For example, the inland sea in Japan, or the islands of Japan, or the Arctic, or the Antarctic – distant and far-flung places, and names we remember from childhood, which we first learned in geography or history. And they're very evocative – like the *Windrush* or the *Titanic*. They can also be associated with more recent events, like the sinking of the *Costa Concordia*: These names and these vessels have massive associations for us.

NB: Yes, ocean liners carry our hopes and expectations, and are linked to our home or place of origin. *Into the Blue* reflects these associations. It also portrays movement. It's like waves: networks linking the liners and the seas rise and fall on the screen, so places appear and disappear, and as their identities surge, exchange and dissolve into each other, they're making a restless search across the world – from ship to shore!

BL: The structure we were working with was very logical: 128 seas of the world, repeated and combined with 256 boats, randomly chosen. That gave us 256 modules, and then we divided them up into groups of 32, which is the largest number of the smallest modules that you can fit on the screen at one time and still be able to read the text. Then we gradually stepped up the module size, thereby also reducing the number of modules on the screen from 32 to 16 to 8 to 4 to 2 to 1. It's a mathematical system in terms of the way the animation is structured, but the names of the boats are intuitively chosen and randomly paired with the seas and oceans. And then we decided to enlarge some over others for personal, aesthetic or associative reasons. So it's a real mixture of quite a strict system, combined with personal, intuitive preferences. I suppose it has this in common with life in general – the discovering of a kind of order, but all orders are disrupted by reality, no orders survive contact with everyday events. And so the order of shipping and the global order of geography is disrupted by political histories, economic histories and personal associations. In a way, that's common to all our work, in that we are often seeking out, discovering, interested in, the order inherent in architecture, in buildings or cities, or different types of language, or communication systems – and then exploring them and unravelling them, disconnecting them, and reconnecting them in different ways, because they tell us about the relationships that we have with each other, with places and different entities, whether they're political, economic or geographical.

NB: Water occupies two thirds of the world. Southampton has double tides with more rising water 17 hours a day, allowing access to the ports by the largest container and cruise ships in the world. Our piece is dual-structured – there's a doubling, and there's two of us. In fact what's interesting is that some names of the ships we chose are repeated

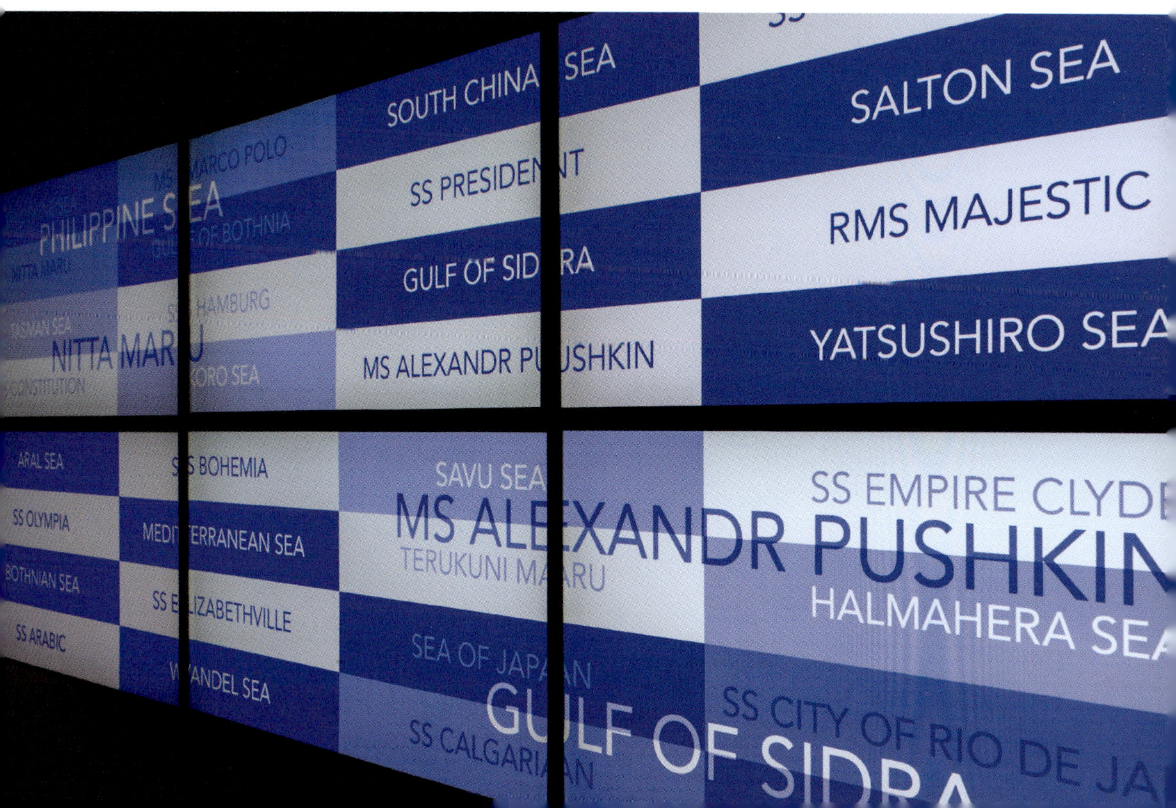

over time and history. They also reflect what could be described as the heyday of ocean liners, because now more people travel by aeroplane. I think we're in a new age now, and a new age of travel, and I think that cruise liners coming into Southampton, because it's such an accessible port, has been sustained in an incredible way.

Were you aware at the beginning how many seas and oceans there were, including the inland seas?

NB: I think we were quite surprised.

BL: There are different interpretations of what a sea is, and it's not actually completely accepted exactly how many there are.

Is this the first work you've made specifically on a maritime theme?

NB: Well, we made a piece called *The Language of Places* (1999). This was a digital animation as well, but then also extended to a wall painting.

BL: Yes, but that was based on global communication and access via international airports and air travel. It uses the three letter codes that identify destinations around the world, like JFK or LHR, LAX.

You also made a work that used NGO *codes.*

NB: One of the works we made when we went to Afghanistan, yes.

These are interesting because they contain a code that is loaded with historical or political meaning, in the same way that the Sea of Galilee is absolutely loaded with history, but has never been abbreviated or shortened and yet is a code for a whole history.

BL: Yes, so the names in *Into the Blue* still function much like codes.

Like the East Siberian Sea, the Indian Ocean and some of the other names, which are really loaded metaphorically with colonialism or war.

NB: Yes, which is why in a way we also hoped that these pieces would be accessible to people from all over the world, because they could identify with different aspects of them in their own way.

Also some of the ships are named after landlocked countries, such as the SS Uganda.

BL: Yes, and some of the *seas* are landlocked, like the Great Salt Lake. And then you have seas like the Aral Sea that have virtually disappeared, largely through global change, environmental destruction or damming for irrigation projects.

I love the ebb and flow of the installation, and everything that is encapsulated in the names. One thing I started thinking about was the ships' registrations, because they would be registered in different countries and continents, flying under different flags.

NB: Well, the blue and white were important as the colours of flags. We went to see the *Turner and the Sea* exhibition at the National Maritime Museum (2013–14), and there were wonderful paintings of battles where you could see all the flags so vividly. So in a sense we're alluding to this tradition of the flag, saying, 'This is who we are', and, 'We're here!' They're referring to the fact that in battles, flags announced the invading armies. National flags were often provocatively waved or hoisted.

Finally, how different did you find working with the digital screens, because you haven't made a work in this way before?

NB: We like to use the technology of our moment, to make new works in a way that's relevant to the time in which we're making them. So it felt really right to work in this new medium for the first time.

BL: The work came together once we'd decided on using the screens. We devised the animation to work with them. They suited the longer word lengths because they're very horizontal, so we were fortunate in that respect. The development of the work, technically, conceptually and aesthetically, emerged together as a whole in the Sea City Museum in 2014, and, as you've observed, encapsulates the lists we compose and the working aesthetic evident in our other artworks.

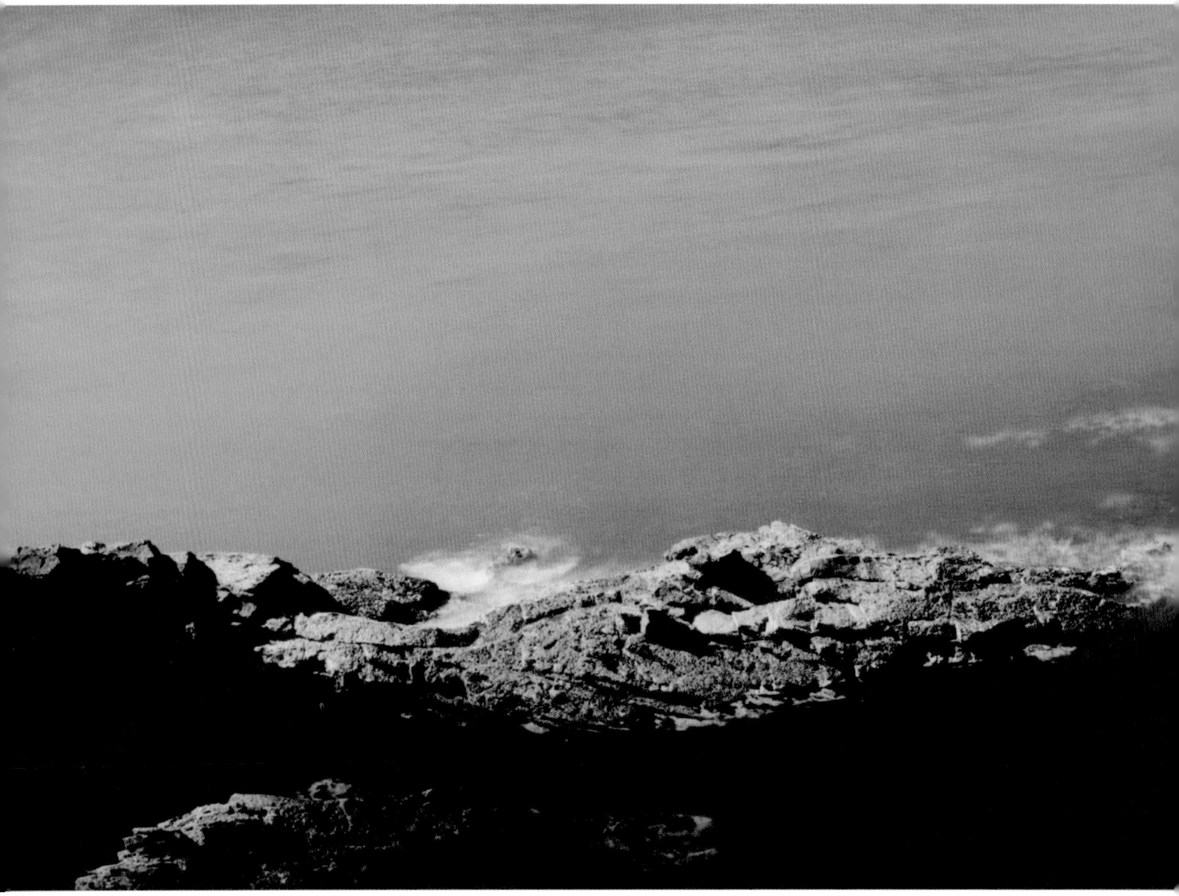

Thomas Joshua Cooper

Near North-most – The North Atlantic Ocean and The Pentland Firth Strathy Point, near Dunnet Head Sutherland, Scotland, 3/3, 1991–2001

102 x 137 cm. Selenium and gold chloride toned silver gelatin print. Courtesy the artist

THOMAS JOSHUA COOPER

THE WORLD'S EDGE
– THE ATLANTIC BASIN PROJECT –
AN ATLAS OF EMPTINESS AND EXTREMITY
1989 – ONGOING

What does the lure of the sea mean to you, and how has it informed your work?

There is something compulsive in the lure of the sea, this strange liquid environment that creates sound, moves back and forth and envelops. The sea has an apparent unlimited immensity, and I think we find ourselves compelled towards these points where the edge of the land meets the beginning of the sea. I'm an American, who has been transplanted from the New World to the Old World. I've lived in Britain for over half my life. I started to think about that in relation to William Manchester's book *A World Lit Only by Fire*.[1] The last chapter was devoted to the Portuguese sailor Ferdinand Magellan. The world changed unequivocally when Magellan and his crew finally managed to circumnavigate the world. I started to think, 'Is it possible for me to stand on the physical edges of all of the continents surrounding the Atlantic basin, with my back always to the land, and try to imagine the difficulties, excitements, opportunities, dangers, dilemmas, horrors and sometimes the delights of bringing something that was not necessarily wanted, but that, because of the force of politics or just human desire, was brought from one place to another'. I thought that if I could do that, then maybe I could also speak in some kind of a voice that would touch others about longing: longing to understand where we belong, how we become what we are, and who finally we might be.

That was the beginning of a project that I started in 1990, with a circumnavigation of Scotland, and then a circumnavigation of Britain, moving then to the west and to the southwest of Europe, where all the explorers and discoverers left from. When Magellan left on his voyage, he undertook a twenty-four hour vigil at the Cape of St Vincent, and I re-enacted it, making a picture every six or eight hours, and thereby began a journey that has taken me from Africa to the northernmost point of Antarctica. If I complete it, I'll be the first person in the world to have circumnavigated the Atlantic basin from all five continents and both poles by land. But going back to the lure of the sea, in a way I think the circulatory system of the blood moving through the body is very much tidal, perhaps an equivalent to the movement of the sea. There's something remarkably human about the need to be near this kind of liquid environment, and I'm compelled towards it, unto the end of time. One thing I've learned from wave particle physicists is that every wave in the sea is actually unique. It's like a fingerprint.

Have you encountered any difficulties when making your images?

The thing is that it's often really difficult to get to these sites. My photograph *"Force Majeure", The South Atlantic Ocean…* (2006–2008) was made when I was coming back from the northernmost point of Antarctica. I travelled by a very small boat – there were just four of us. I was out for nearly three months. Horrible, not fun. We ran out of water, food and fuel. We'd just crossed The Drake Passage, the most difficult sea passage I know of in the world, and we got to where there was a small inlet with a lighthouse 'at the end of the world' and knew we were in dangerous waters. Then the boat broke. The Argentine army would not allow us to land anywhere to mend it, so we had to declare *force majeure*. While the captain spent four days fixing the boat, I went around and made one final picture from the land.

We see the different materiality of water in your photograph South – The Mid Atlantic Ocean Cape Manuel, Dakar… *(2004). We are looking down at crashing waves with beautiful flecks of light and motion on the water.*

Cape Manuel is closest to the capital city of Dakar, but it is surrounded by the army base that commands and protects that part of Senegal. Civilians just don't get in. My guide, a wonderful Senegalese man, said that he knew a place where the fort wall had a break, so we snuck in at night, onto a cliff. We saw a spectacular finger of land extending into the sea and lit by moonlight. I used a long exposure in order to photograph this compelling formation. This spar of land is a notorious people-trafficking point, from both the local islands and the Cape Verde Islands themselves. Regularly the poor souls who try and get from the

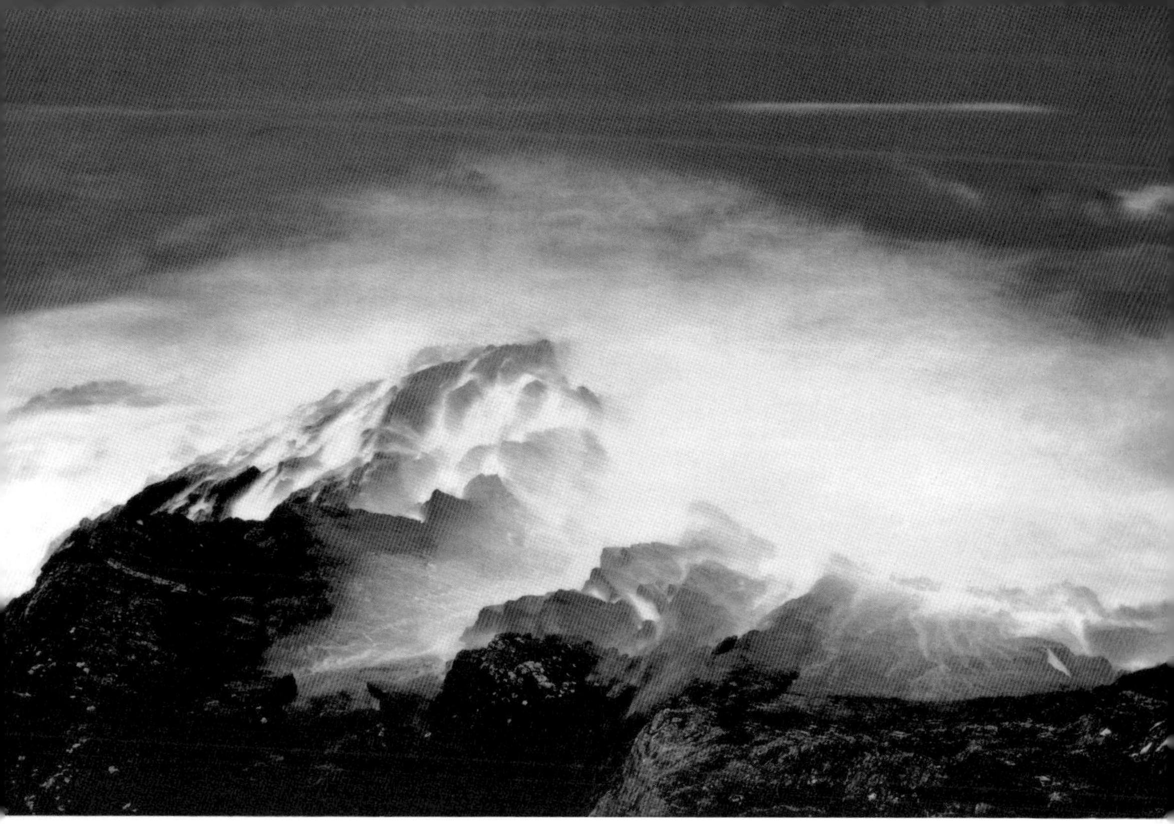

Thomas Joshua Cooper
"Force Majeure", The South Atlantic Ocean, Looking Towards Cabo San Juan from "The Lighthouse at the End of the World", Cabo Lasserre, Isla de Los Estados/Staten Island, Tierra del Fuego, Argentina, 2008. The Southeast-most point of all South America. 54°, 2006–2008
102 x 137 cm. Selenium and gold chloride toned silver gelatin print. Courtesy the artist

Cape Verde islands onto the African continent to head north often drown. They're viciously dangerous waters, and shark-infested. There is this compulsion towards the sea. It attracts because it appears to be so generous, but it's also just brutally neutral.

The Mid North Atlantic Ocean, Ponta das Gaivotas, The Isle of Madeira… *(2002–2003) is a very different seascape.*

On that particular site I did my inevitable circumnavigation, looking at where Columbus would have sailed from. He went from a little island below Madeira, then on to the Canaries and finally to the New World. This ended up being the last picture I made while I was on Madeira. I am looking down from an elevated view: I try to remove horizons, removing the figure-ground capacity to move through a picture. If you have a horizon or a recognisable object in any two-dimensional picture plane, the eye naturally travels to it, and you start to physically as well as mentally move out of the picture. I try to stop that movement as much as possible by eliminating horizons, unless I need to use them specifically to do something. In this instance I decided to make a 'painting' of the sea with white on black, so white caps of water on this very strange and choppy, rocky, horrible sea edge: the volcanic rocks just rip boats from that island. I made a very deep, dark surface of white flecks on black. I thought, 'I'll try to describe both the physical and emotional difficulties of being someplace both foreign and uninvited'.

Your photograph Moonrise over "The End of the World" – Furthest West – The Mid North Atlantic Ocean… *(2002) is also steeped in history.*

The Ancient Greek geographer Ptolemy, who lived in the 2nd century AD, actually helped influence most of the renaissance explorers, through his book *Geography*,[2]. Ptolemy designated a spot on the furthest south and west island of the Canaries, El Hierro – its westernmost point, Punta Orchillo – as the prime meridian (zero degrees longitude), or the end of the Ancient World. He wrote at length about it, and I thought, 'I have to get there.' So I get there and see the red cliffs over the sea, at an elevation of about 300 feet, and it's just wonderful. And I think, 'OK, I need a horizon now', so, I stood on the westernmost point of the Canaries, at the designated zero-degrees longitude of the Ancient World. I was there close to the spring equinox, and there was an early crescent moonrise, so unusually I left this sliver of moon in the top right of the picture. Ansel Adams, whom I knew and loved, made a famous photograph called *Moonrise, Hernandez, New Mexico* (1941), one of his great pictures – a very spontaneous and difficult photograph for him to make – so the title is both a smile and a nod towards his inspiration.

Can we talk about moonlight for a moment, because you are setting yourself another challenge, working in such low light.

I just love it. Whenever it's possible – when there's a full moon and I'm out in the field and can make a picture – I'll do it, no matter what. The light is so lovely, and what's great is that the exposures can range from several minutes to over two hours. Moonlight is soft silver light,

Thomas Joshua Cooper
Moonrise Over the End of the World – Furthest West – The Mid North Atlantic Ocean "The Lighthouse at The End of the World", Faro Orchillo. The Isle of El Hierro. (Near the West-most point of the entire Canarian Archipelago and the furthest extent South-West of the Old World). The Canary Islands, Spain, 2002
102 x 137 cm. Selenium and gold chloride toned silver gelatin print. Courtesy the artist

unlike sunlight, and I'm just compelled by it. Somehow physically, and therefore emotionally, I'm moonstruck. One of the things I've found is that light softens as you get closer to the northern and southern continental edges. I've had to learn to work whenever and wherever I am, because I only make one picture in each place, and if, for instance, I'm at a place in the jungle, at noon, when the light is at its brightest – as I was several times in South America – there is no choice. But what's wonderful is that whether the light is very bright or there's very little light, you just see differently. There's a very lovely, strange little book called *Wisdom Sits in Places* by Keith H Basso[3]. about place-naming among Western Apache people, where the names tell stories and convey history and sense of place. It's made me think about how the 'wisdom'

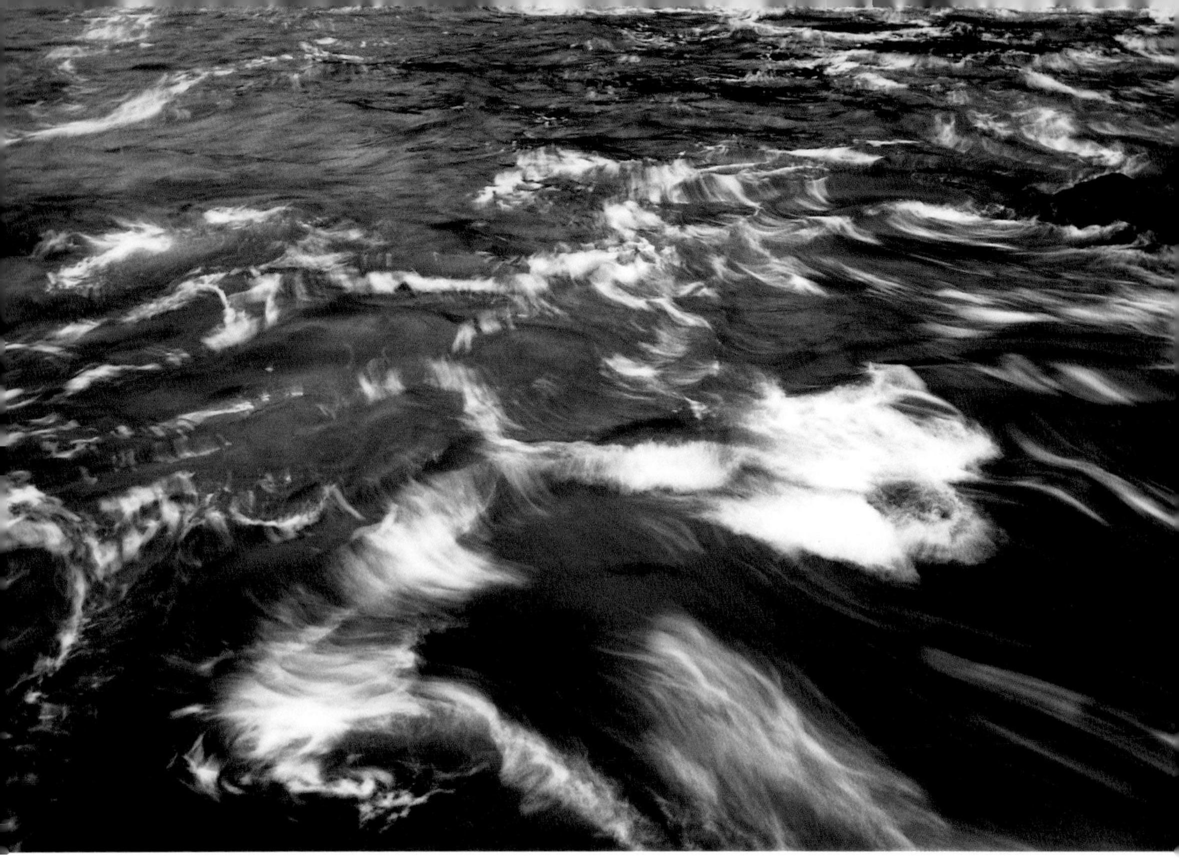

Thomas Joshua Cooper
The Three Great Rivers. Wind whipped. Looking towards Delta Amacuro – The Orinoco Delta. Golfo de Paria – The Gulf of Paria – Boca Grande and Bocas del Dragón – The Dragon's Mouths. Punta Piedra, Promontorio de Paria, Península de Paria. Sucre, Venezuela, 2005, 2005/2006.
Part 2 of a 3-part work, 2005–2006. 71 x 91 cm. Selenium and gold chloride toned silver gelatin print. Courtesy the artist

of place at different times of day can be communicated in real terms. In my work I try to make those 'conversations' with place clear and accessible.

Your titles are very poetic. For example, Wind whipped. Looking towards Delta Amacuro – The Orinoco Delta... *(2005), or* Thick early morning river mist. The confluence of the Rio de la Plata... *(2006) in your* Three Great Rivers *work.*

I use words very specifically. What I realise is that, although I've dedicated my life to the visual world, the titles do a variety of things: With *Wind whipped...* I tried to not so much tell as suggest that the physicality of the time, the place, the nature of the light – be it last light, first light, heavy rain, high mist, or wind whipped – may not necessarily be evident in the picture, but they give the local conditions of the picture, their reason for existence – the human-environment relational response. I'm also trying to make a visual atlas. The overall project is called *An Atlas of Emptiness and Extremity*, and that, of course, is meant to be physical, emotional and conditional in terms of response to the landscape and trying to live in the circumstances of emptiness and extremity. Whilst the pictures are un-peopled, the principal condition of response is the emotional connection that occurs through the experience of viewing. I hope this is translatable metaphorically, otherwise I've made some serious life mistakes. The description of the mist in the *Thick early morning river mist…* title is important because sometimes it's so palpable and deep you can touch it – you can move your arm through it, and when your arm comes back you've made a hole in the thing! Those *OrInoco Delta* and *Rio de la Plata* images are companions to a piece I made at the mouth of the Amazon on the Equator [*The Three Great Rivers: Sunrise on the Equator-zero degrees latitude- "The River Sea" at the mouths of El Rio Amazanas – The Amazon River, the mouth of an unnamed stream and the South Atlantic Ocean. Uulture Beach, Ilha Mexicana, Para, Brazil, 2006*], all three in different kinds of physical conditions. I'm trying to suggest the continental waters; that the main rivers of the continent fill into the vessel of the ocean, bringing a circular sense of refreshment that the circulation system in the body does as well.

Can we talk about your camera now? You use an antique camera and specially-made photographic plates?

Yes. I bought my 1898 Agfa field camera and enlarger in 1965, for £300. When I bought it, I was working with a traditional 35 mm. camera and I thought, 'What have I done? What am I going to do with this?' Essentially, from 1967 till 1969 I spent occasional moments trying to learn how to use the camera, and by 1969 I realised I loved it. What I'd figured out by then was that I was interested in slowness. The early pioneers of photography really had to look hard at what they were working with, and that charmed me. I thought, 'OK, the longer it takes for me to look, the more likely it is I might see something.' So in 1969, at See Canyon in California, I did an 8 mile walk with my heavy

Agfa camera thinking, 'I'll make something'. I walked and walked. It was a beautiful place, but I couldn't see anything that made any sense to me. I got to the top of the rim of the canyon, I turned round, and all of a sudden I saw the picture that I'd hoped for, because I had a different point of view. It was April Fools' Day, and I made the first of three vows in my life: that I would use this camera; I would make pictures outdoors for the rest of my life; and I would only ever make one picture in any given place. When I've figured out what to look at, I usually turn my back to it – it's a ritualised thing. And if I make a mistake, that's it. I never go back. I'm interested in creating some kind of a conditional relationship with things that are generally not seen, to be able to represent responses.

You work exclusively in black and white, but you say you miss colour?

I've been making black-and-white pictures for over 50 years, but yes, I miss colour. I love colour. I do add colour to the prints after the actual printing process, for the emotional possibilities, with a series of chemicals that create slight colour washes over the top of them. They're imperceptible for the most part. Depending on what I'm doing, I add a layer of red-to-burgundy, using a chemical called selenium, then sometimes I add a layer of very light deep blue, using gold chloride – liquid gold – over the selenium. This creates a permanent archival surface on the print. I'm one of the last of the dinosaurs, using a process that actually no longer exists in contemporary photography. The paper I use was made by a German company that went bankrupt in 2006. I have the last remaining stock of this paper in the world and I'm working down the pile. When it's done, I'm done. The same with the film: nobody makes film any longer, and I often hand-make the chemistry. One of the things that I'm interested in is 'deep printing'. What can a piece of paper that's flat do, or yield, that allows the believable illusion of three dimensionalities? Tactility is also essential to everything that I do. The sense of touch is entirely superficial for most digital print surfaces, and that is a severe loss to me. So in my pictures I emphasise through tone what I think is the deep emotionality of the infinitely grey space between black and white, and the possibility for a resonant sort of physical illusion as well as emotional nuance. My thought processes are sometimes very laborious and sometimes very spontaneous, but the pictures are the result of a history of consideration.

Because I make everything in the field, I don't develop the negatives till I get back to the darkroom, and failures can occur. In South America, because I had to go through so many very crude x-ray machines from country to country and border to border, 100% of the film was spoiled, so I had to print through that basic destruction of the quality of the negative to make a print. In Antarctica because of the extreme cold, there was a lot of physical damage to the negatives.

There is something rather marvellous about the physical imprint on the print itself.

Absolutely. When I was in Tierra del Fuego, at a point called Sancti Spiritus on the Argentine-Chilean border, there was a huge snowstorm. The snowflakes were the size of 50p pieces, and I was just sodden on this cliff edge, with border guards on both sides. I'm making my one picture, and they're out with their guns and thinking, 'What the hell is this guy doing here? Nobody ever comes to visit.' I get back and realise that so much snow has fallen that it's faulted part of the negative and made a big black glob on part of the image, but the glob was so perfect that it made the picture. There's no possibility of a mistake-free zone because the working conditions are so extreme. If I got overwhelmed by it I'd have to quit, because it's impossible. I now try to make sure that people see the marks on certain types of pictures, that they understand it's field stress, and that's the way it is. These are handmade prints, made in extreme circumstances.

Finally, can I ask you about The South Atlantic Ocean. Ponta Copacabana. Copacabana Beach… *(2006). That photograph is so different from the stereotype.*

I had to go there, to Rio, in part because I wanted to see what the city was like. The night before I made both pictures in the *South Atlantic Ocean* work, I was walking on Copacabana beach. Walking on the top level of the beach is safe at night, but if, as I stupidly did, you go down to walk along the water's edge – within 300 metres of all the Rio nightlife – you find feral gangs who live along the water's edge. I was attacked from both sides by young kids with knives and had to run for it, because if they could, these kids were going to take whatever I had, my life included. It was like something out of a zombie movie, and it

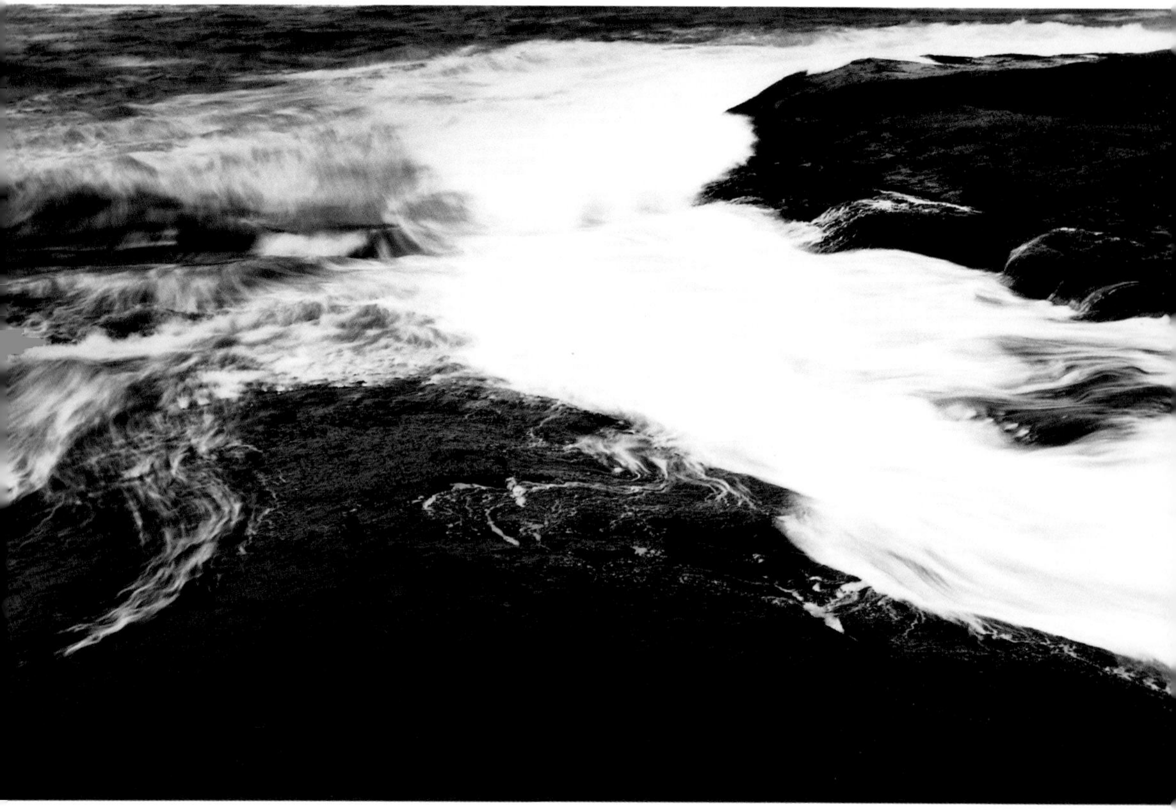

Thomas Joshua Cooper
The South Atlantic Ocean. Ponta Copacabana. Copacabana Beach. Rio de Janeiro, Brazil.
Part 2 of a 2-part work, 2006.
71 x 91 cm. Selenium and gold chloride toned silver gelatin print. Courtesy the artist

scared the living Jesus out of me. So the next day I went back. I love Brazilian music, and went to the bar where Tom Jobim wrote *The Girl from Ipanema*[4] to have a Caipirinha, my favourite drink of all time. And I thought, 'OK, talk about the harshness, here, on the beaches. Let's indicate something different than the kind of playboy image of sun and surf that is actually also part of this social condition here". So I made the harshest pictures I could. They're both really early morning pictures because I didn't want anybody around, and I needed access to some sites that were very popular for sunbathing, a circumstance which I do find very foreign I have to admit, because I sunburn easily. But the pictures were just about that unexpected sense of terror, being chased silently, no noise. I thought, 'OK', as I always do, 'Face, if you can, the things that frighten you, and make pictures about them.'

And you have done that.

Yes, I have, but also, thinking about the different seas in my work, there is the fact that something so obviously, immediately clear and understandable as water, seemed to me to require the courtesy of a time, of understanding. I've become alert, simply through the study of time in relation to the ocean's edges, and this has taken me by surprise. I've never been bored by the sea or being near it, the sea is so huge. And my response to a strangely difficult and not necessarily immediately understandable material substance like the water's edge has become remarkably allowing of accident and discovery. It leads to understanding. The fingerprints of the ocean are everywhere, and they're unique in every instance. I just can't wait to introduce myself to as many of them as possible.

NOTES

1. Manchester, William. *A World Lit Only by Fire: The Medieval Mind and the Renaissance – Portrait of an Age.* Little, Brown, 1992.
2. Ptolemy, Claudius. *Geography. c.* AD 150. Translated by Edward Luther Stevenson. Cosimo, 2011.
3. Basso, Keith H. *Wisdom Sits in Places: Landscape and Language among the Western Apache.* University of New Mexico Press, 1996.
4. Jobim, Antônio Carlos Brasileiro de Almeida (Tom). *The Girl from Ipanema.* Verve Records, 1964.

Mark Power, *Wight*
Saturday 18 February 1995
Northwesterly backing southwesterly 6 or 7, increasing gale 8 for a time. Showers then rain. Good becoming moderate or poor.
Silver gelatin print, sandblasted text on glass. Courtesy the artist

MARK POWER

THE SHIPPING FORECAST, 1993–1996

As a child you discovered your father's home-made photographic enlarger in the attic. Can you tell me about finding it? Did that mark the start of your interest in photography?

I had no idea what it was. We brought it downstairs, and then I remember going out with his old Voigtländer camera and some black-and-white film. I took some (probably very bad) pictures of trees. He then helped me process the film and make some prints, although looking back I'm not sure he really knew what he was doing.

When he was in the Merchant Navy my father had taken on the unofficial role of 'Ship's Photographer', which largely consisted of him taking photographs of oil tankers on the very distant horizon, always immaculately straight, predicting his future career as an engineer. It was the first example I'd ever seen of a typology, since all the ships were the same size and in the same position, albeit tiny and very far away. Sadly I lent them to a sculptor friend to use during his degree show and we never got them back. I'd love to make a little book of them now. I do remember being very excited by the alchemy of it all, but that's nothing unusual. It never crossed my mind that photography could be a career. I don't believe I saw a photography exhibition until I was about 20, a show by Don McCullin. That was what really sowed the seed for me.

You went to Brighton to do your Fine Art degree. Did you do any seascapes or coastal-related works when you were there?

Most of my time was spent in the life-room drawing from the figure, but in my final year I did gravitate to the beach. I painted and drew a number of seascapes in stormy weather. I was very influenced by people like Frank Auerbach and David Bomberg – you could say my pictures were very 'painterly'. Unfortunately (though it didn't seem so at the time) they were all sold at my degree show. I've no idea where they are now, but in any case I soon became more interested in photography, which overtook any interest I had in pursuing a career as a painter.

What does the lure of the sea mean for you?

Well, sailing dinghies were very much a part of my childhood. As I said, my father was in the Merchant Navy and has always loved the sea. When I was seven he built me my first dinghy, an Optimist, just 7ft 6in long with one sail, in the garden. My interest in sailing dinghies, or rather racing them, grew throughout my childhood and blossomed in my teens until, in my early 20s, I was sailing very competitively in a Laser, a single-handed dinghy with an enormous following. As well as sailing at club level three times a week, I also competed in the National Championships every year. I used to do reasonably well, although I was never competitive enough to get to the very top. I hung up my wetsuit when our daughter was born, just before my 40th birthday.

Did you listen to The Shipping Forecast *as a child and why does it hold such an attraction for you?*

I wouldn't say I actually *listened* to *The Shipping Forecast* as a child, but it was always there as a sort of wallpaper backdrop. When I began working on the project it became obvious to me that I wasn't alone; there was a whole generation, or generations, for whom *The Forecast* meant something similar. It evokes a warm and cosy feeling, bringing back the happiest childhood memories. So in 1990, when I discovered a tea towel in the RNLI shop in Great Yarmouth showing a map of those elusive sea areas, I was instantly fascinated. Suddenly it dawned on me that these were *real* geographical locations. As I read through the names on the map all sorts of images flew into my head, and I guess the

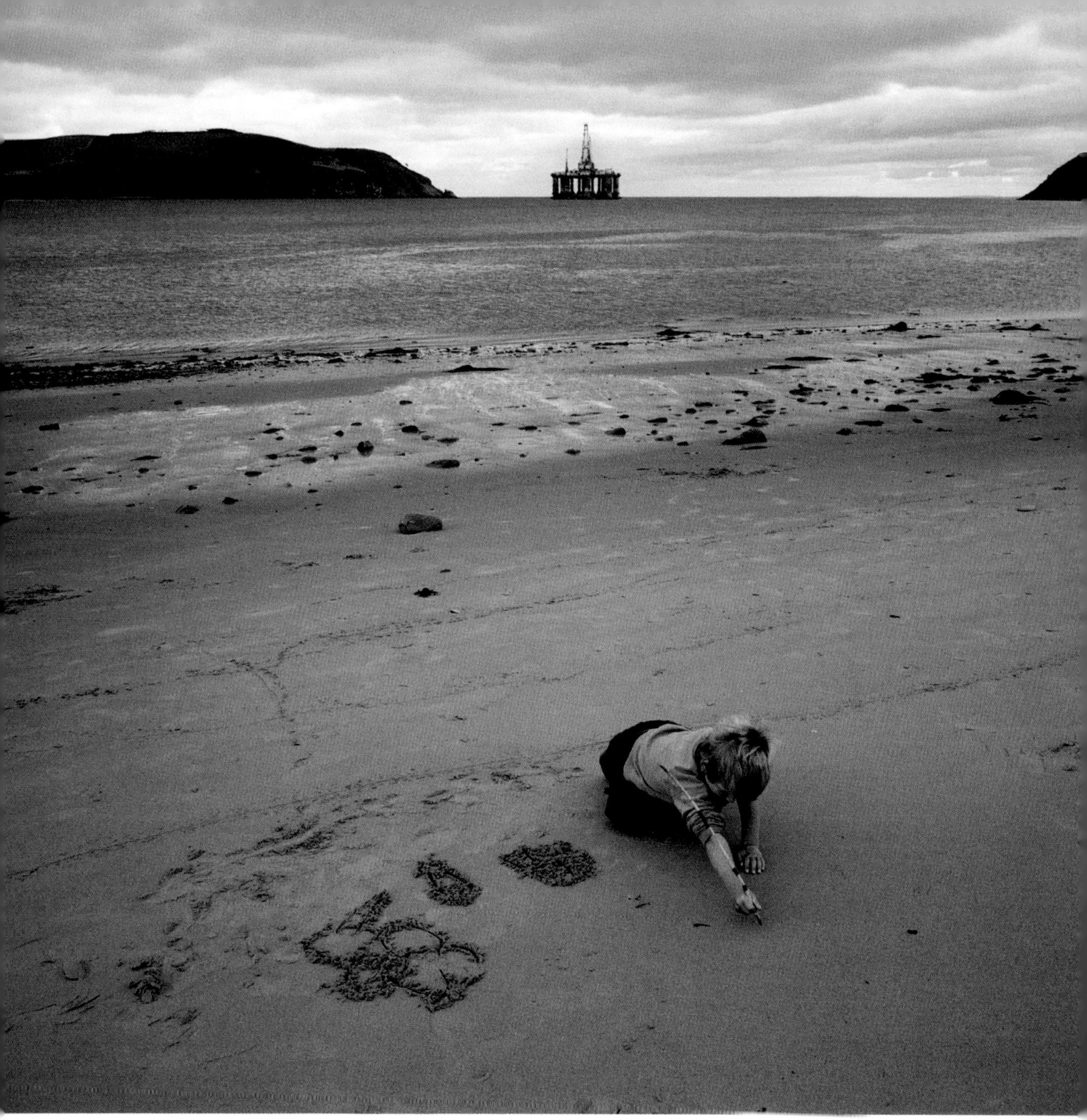

Mark Power, *Cromarty*
Saturday 21st August 1993
Westerly veering northwesterly, 4 or 5, occasionally 6. Showers. Good.
Silver gelatin print, sandblasted text on glass. Courtesy the artist

idea for *The Shipping Forecast* project was born at that very moment, even though I didn't begin for another two years. I thought it would be an interesting idea to visit all 31 sea areas and see if the reality of what I found bore any relation to the imaginary landscapes that had developed in my head over all those years. Somewhat typically, I didn't really think about the logistics of actually doing it, which is why it took four years to complete. It really was a massive undertaking, but when I began I gave no thought to either the time or the money I'd need to finish it. I'm afraid I learned no lessons from the experience.

You decided to title your works according to the 0600 shipping forecast on the day the images were taken. Can you expand on why you made that decision?

The 0600 forecast is the first broadcast on the BBC during the day, therefore it seemed sensible to continue that strand throughout. There were enough other elements in the work that were chopping and changing, so I wanted the use of the forecasts to be consistent at least. I developed a relationship with a fellow at the Meteorological Department in Reading who was interested in the project, and he would send me a copy of the same forecast the radio presenter would read from. I'd make a reasonably tight edit of recent work, send him the dates I needed, and he would send me the relevant information back, by post. I had to pay £1 photocopy fee for each one.

Can you talk about how you went about taking the images for The Shipping Forecast, *and the challenges that you faced?*

When starting a new project, particularly one that you think is going to take some time to complete, there are certain decisions to be made. What format am I going to use? Is it going to be in colour or black-and-white? Stylistically (for want of a better word) what are the pictures going to *look like*? At the time I was very interested in Tony Ray-Jones, Chris Killip, Raymond Moore and others of that ilk – all were influential.

How did you plan the visits to all 31 sites?

I began very locally, in sea area Wight, which is where Brighton (where I live) is. It was there that I worked out the sort of photographic 'language' I wanted to use. As the project progressed and the years passed by, I realised that I'd left all the more inaccessible areas until the end. There were certain places in the middle of the Atlantic that were tricky to get to, and countries like Norway and Iceland were just downright expensive. I applied to the Arts Council for funding, and failed, but then out of the blue I was awarded a £25,000 grant by the Mosaic Foundation in Luxembourg. It doesn't take much knowledge of geography to know that Luxembourg doesn't have a coastline, so conceptually the work would've meant very little to them. However, they must have seen some merit in it and that money enabled me to complete the work, put money into the book, and make the exhibition as I'd wanted it.

Why did you decide to take all the images in black-and-white?

Of course, black-and-white photography and nostalgia go hand-in-hand. The *Forecast* had already been around for some 70 years, and it had played a part in so many lives, so it seemed sensible to use it. Also, black-and-white pictures are a further abstraction of the world, since obviously we don't see like that. It was never my intention to produce definitive images of what sea areas Dogger, Fair Isle, Cromarty – or any of the others – actually *looked like*. They are just fleeting impressions, very much led by a reaction to the disappointment I felt when discovering that the reality of the situation bore very little reference to my imagination. There is also another reason. It's much easier to sequence pictures in black-and-white than in colour. You don't need to be concerned with weather conditions since everything is homogenised into tones of grey. You can sequence according to subject and form, and you don't need to worry about one picture having a blue sky and the next a white one. It meant I could go out and work in any weather.

You were working with quite a cumbersome analogue camera. What were the advantages or disadvantages of working in this way?

Actually the camera wasn't very cumbersome. I used a Mamiya 6, rather like an overgrown plastic Leica, and with a very good lens. Each roll of film gave me just 12 pictures, so there was a cost involved, which tended to focus my mind. I was careful with the number of exposures I made: in any given situation I would limit myself to perhaps three or four pictures. I processed the films myself in my darkroom, made

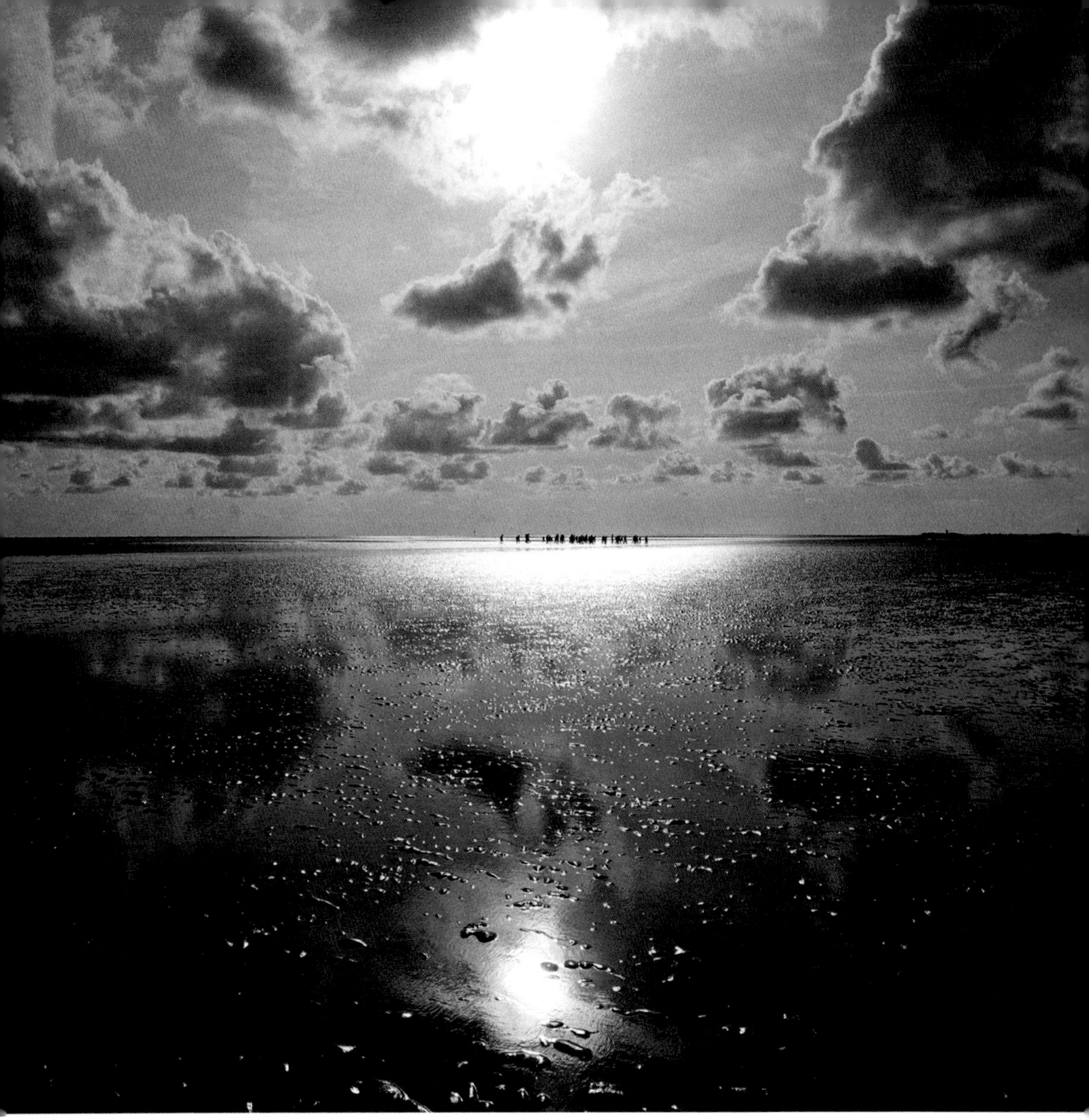

Mark Power, *German Bight*
Thursday 24 August 1995
Northwesterly 4, backing southwesterly 5 or 6. Rain later. Good becoming moderate.
Silver gelatin prints, sandblasted text on glass. Courtesy the artist

contact sheets, and then hundreds of little prints. I immersed myself in the work, living and breathing it every day.

Can you talk about how you set about taking each image and how long it typically took to get 'the one'?

This is an interesting question, because I was able to spend a lot of time in some areas (most notably Wight, where I live), while for others I was only there for a matter of minutes. I reached sea area Sole by a Met Office research flight, skimming along at just 50 feet above the waves. I took just three pictures of the sea, pretty much all the same, and a couple more of the pilots using the extraordinary banks of instruments, and that was it. Because of the difficulty in getting there I was content with the picture I eventually used… it seemed adequate. On the other hand, no matter how much time I spent in sea area Wight I couldn't make a picture I was happy with: my expectations were that much higher.

You have talked previously about the real and imagined space of The Shipping Forecast. *Can you explain what you were embedding into your images in terms of truth and fiction?*

The pictures do seem to float somewhere between reality and imagination. An important aspect of what I was trying to do was to make pictures that were quite mysterious and difficult to 'understand'. It's important to know that for two or three years prior to starting the project I'd been working as a magazine/newspaper photographer. In those days (and it may still be the case today) a media photographer's role was to try to prove that what the writer was writing about was factually 'correct'. In other words, your pictures had to contain as much information, and be as easily digestible, as possible. Naturally, when I started *The Shipping Forecast*, which I was making purely for myself, I rebelled and started to enjoy producing pictures which didn't explain themselves at all. I was looking for a kind of visual metaphor for the complexity of the language used in *The Forecast*, which we understand (to some extent) because it's in English and we recognize the words. But the meaning of the sentences is difficult to fathom. I knew that if I could produce pictures which looked like *The Forecast* sounded (if that makes sense) then I was on to something…

How does the series relate to your work as a documentary photographer and as an artist?

At the end of *The Shipping Forecast* I felt I'd exhausted all the ways I could think of of using the camera, and I was in danger of repeating myself. I gravitated immediately afterwards to a large format 5in x 4in camera, used with the tripod, and my work became more contemplative as a result. But, technical things aside, it gave me a confidence in my ideas which I've carried with me ever since. It taught me to know that if I see things through, and have patience, something decent will always emerge. It taught me not to go home if things aren't going well. And that making good work usually – but not always – takes considerable time and effort, and doesn't happen just by sitting at home thinking about it.

When you display your prints you etch the record of The Shipping Forecast *on the day you took the images onto the frame, so that the shadow of the writing appears on the white mount of the image. Why did you decide to do that?*

The etching of the forecast onto the glass, and the shadows created when lit, emphasise the ephemeral nature of the weather. It's never permanent: the text only appears as a shadow which disappears as soon as the light is removed. It's a simple idea, but effective.

Built into the images themselves is the passage of time. Looking at these images now, which include both the images with people and those solely of the sea, do you view them differently to when you made them?

As I get older I'm increasingly looking back at work I made in the past. Of course you have to be careful that nostalgia for the past doesn't dominate the pictures, but there is no doubt that the extra layer of time passing adds something.

The first edition of *The Shipping Forecast* sold out in three weeks and it was subsequently reprinted twice. In all, 10,000 copies were sold, which means that it must have emerged from the photographic ghetto

– it wasn't only bought by other photographers. I'm very proud of the fact that the work reached a wider audience without being, dare I say, 'dumbed down'. It's a serious piece of work and the book is something I still stand by. Having said that, it's been unavailable for some years now, so I'm vaguely thinking about doing a sort of *Shipping Forecast redux*, since I'd probably make a very different edit today.

Do you still listen to The Shipping Forecast?

Yes I do, but I don't turn the radio on specifically to listen to it. If it's on it floats around as a backdrop, much as it ever did. Subconsciously, since I've now been to all of these sea areas, images pop into my head that are different from those I had before I began the project. This, to me, encapsulates the wonder and beautiful extravagance of being a photographer. It forces you out into the world to make discoveries you never thought possible.

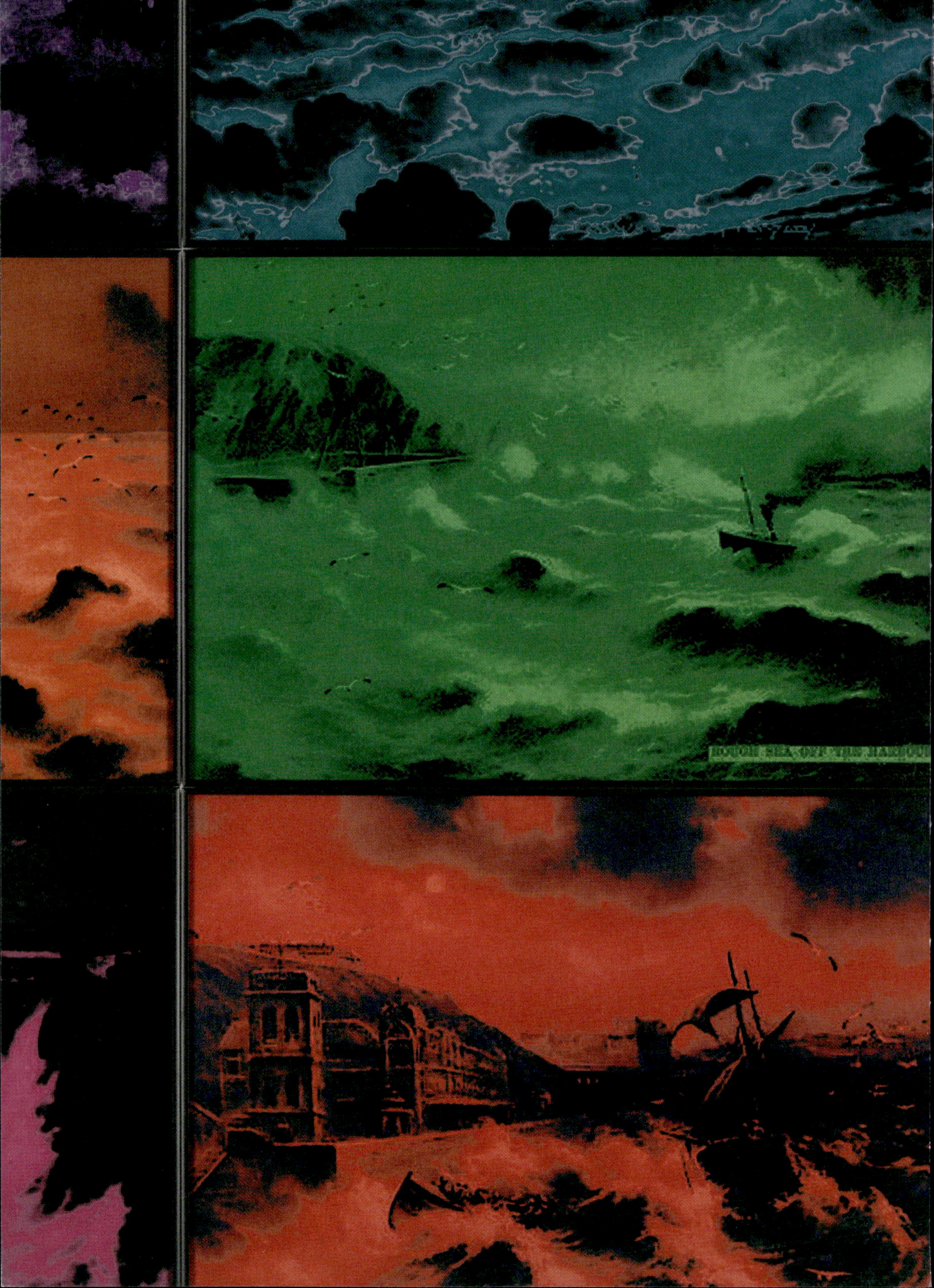

SUSAN HILLER

NIGHTWATCH, 2009

The idea of crashing waves is both a romantic and threatening image. What is it about rough seas that you find so compelling?

I've always been fascinated by the wildness of the sea. I saw so many kitsch seascapes growing up in Florida that I don't think they could have had a positive influence on my work, but on the other hand, I've always found Turner's works *Rough Sea* (*c.* 1840–45) and *Rough Sea with Wreckage* (*c.* 1840–45) wonderfully palliative. When I discovered a series of British postcards labelled 'Rough Sea' – even when sometimes the sea doesn't look particularly rough in the card's image – I was captivated.

Do you have a first, or abiding, memory of the physicality of the sea?

Well, one of my earliest memories is of being roughly tumbled about in the surf at the edge of the beach where I had been paddling. I think I was about two years old. My father came to my rescue and pulled me out of the water, but I can still remember how terrified I felt. Luckily the incident wasn't traumatic enough to destroy my enjoyment of things like swimming and boating.

OPPOSITE: Susan Hillier, *Nightwatch*, 2009 (detail)
Dry transfer archival archival prints (set of 9)
Courtesy the artist and Timothy Taylor Gallery, London

The sea enthralls us, it holds secrets and is the site of myths. What does the sea mean to you as an artist?

Oceans are unpredictable, mysterious, and – like deserts – are vast, shape-shifting, sublime. These postcards I've worked with, are a sort of miniature domestication of the sublime.

Nightwatch *is closely linked to your seminal work* Dedicated to the Unknown Artists *(1972–76), which features over 300 of the 'Rough Sea' postcards. Can you say more about what the postcards mean to you and how they inform your work? For example, in* Nightwatch *you made a very specific selection from your huge archive. What criteria did you use for the selection of the images that you've used in your work?*

They engaged me. I liked them enough to work with them and on them. What the 'Rough Sea' postcard images are saying is paradoxical and contradictory, as I believe our notions are. In most cases the images show a turbulent sea, often encroaching on or threatening human structures, and we get the impression of the sea as threatening, wild and terribly thrilling. Some of the postcards show people standing watching the sea like voyeurs watching a sexual act. These images are miniature evocations, or reminders, of the sublime elements in a seaside holiday.

I know you're interested in capturing what lies behind the artefacts in your artworks, what is not overtly present in an image, but influences in an unconscious way. What initiated your interest in the forgotten artists who photographed and hand-tinted the original images in the postcards?

Yes, in some of the postcards where the original image is photographic, hand tinting has been added. We tend to think of this process as an automatic mechanical process, but by comparing several examples based on one initial image, it's easy to see that each tinter interpreted the image completely differently. Aspects of imagination, fantasy, or whatever, inevitably enters the process. Human beings are not machines; they express their creativity in their ordinary, mundane working gestures. So in my enlarged re-imaginings of the postcards I'm following in this unacknowledged creative tradition.

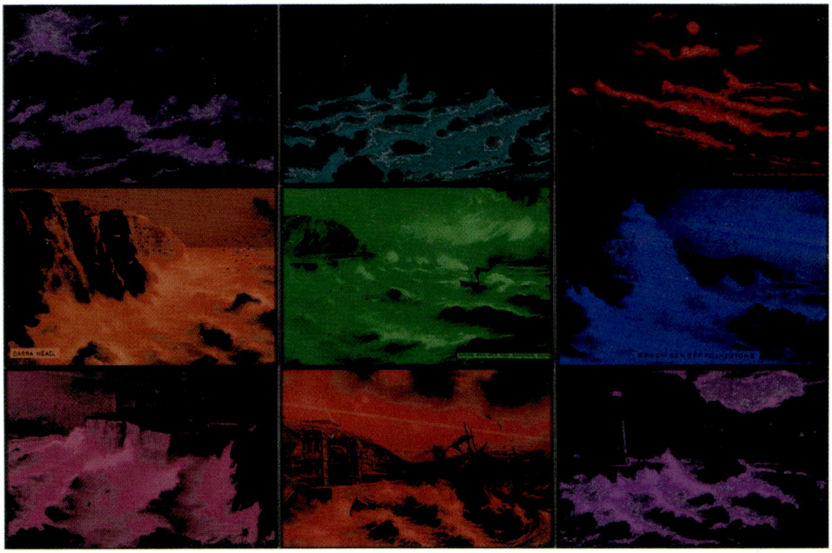

Susan Hillier, *Nightwatch*, 2009
Dry transfer archival archival prints (set of 9)
Courtesy the artist and Timothy Taylor Gallery, London

So the tinted colours hold a lot of meaning. Traditionally hand-tinting was used in an attempt to heighten the realism of black-and-white photographs, but in Nightwatch *you have chosen to enhance the postcards' tinted images further, using acid colours in compelling, toxic hues, which in a sense is doing the opposite.*

Exactly. I used them because they seemed to be, as you say, compelling, unnaturalizing nature.

In Nightwatch you have enlarged the images onto dry prints. Why have you chosen that particular medium?

'Dry print', in this context, is another way of saying 'Giclée print'. What I used to do by hand, working directly on the images, has evolved to enjoying the possibilities of digitization, but rather than being a shortcut, this approach has turned out to be as laborious – bad word, but you know what I mean – and as time-consuming, as any other form of painting. The print series started as a direct result of my earlier classificatory practice of working with the postcards, which themselves seamlessly incorporated the variety of ways in which their production involved both photographic and painting techniques.

Nightwatch *is an evocative title, with references to the history of art, history and politics. Is it important for you to add another layer of meaning to your work?*

I do think good art achieves the status of metaphor, and I try to keep that in mind.

When you first began using postcards in your work they were commonplace objects. How has your relationship to them changed in the age of digital communication?

They've become old-fashioned and rare, and people love them for their nostalgic value. I'm not immune to that but it's not my major interest.

You've previously suggested that your work shifts from scientific analysis to a romantic consideration of the feminine forces of the sea, which you are interested in exploring. Do you still see this as a major factor in your series?

Maybe what interests me now is something more like the ambiguous gender or the alteration of characteristics traditionally labeled feminine with characteristics traditionally labeled masculine? The shape-shifting nature of the sea? Or, a little bit deeper, the sea as a metaphor for the unconscious? Something like that. Since *Nightwatch* I've made a few other works in this series, with titles like *Dark Moonlit Nights, Roughly by Night, Roughly in Dreams* – you will understand, I think, where I am going with this. Years and years ago, one of my first works was called *Towards an Autobiography of Night* (1983), and I guess this is an abiding fascination for me.

You've spoken in the past about your fascination with how the sea 'invades' the land, the masculine and feminine aspects of that?

In my notes to the early postcard work *Dedicated to the Unknown Artists* (1972–76), now at the Tate, I quoted the Victorian romantic novelist Marie Corelli, who wrote about "Earth the Beautiful and her Lover the Sea"[1]. I myself don't tend to attribute gender to earth or sea, but I suppose in a more traditional way of thinking, the stability of earth and the wildness of the sea were thought of like this.

It's been commented that your work is about 'ghosts: the unknown, subliminal, haunting and hidden relics of our past and present lives'.[2] Is this how you view these images?

Yes. I'm interested in our collective unconscious, so work with things and ideas that are just out of sight but present enough to disturb and puzzle us. I like to work with materials that have different layers of meaning, and contain things that have been forgotten and overlooked, like these postcards, which might appear mundane on the surface, but become special as soon as you pay attention to them. There is something elusive, uncanny and fascinating beneath the surface of what seems at first easy to understand.

NOTES

1. Corelli, Marie. *The Treasure of Heaven: A Romance of Riches*. Constable, 1906, p. 180.
2. Fitzgerald, Chelsea. 'Susan Hiller @ Tate Modern'. *Whitehot Magazine*, 2011. www.whitehotmagazine.com/articles/susan-hiller-tate-britain/2234

OVERLEAF: Susan Hiller, *Rough Moonlit Nights (Cyan)*, 2015
Archival pigment print on Hannemuhle photographic paper
edition – 250 + 5 a/p
Commissioned by Camden Arts Centre for the 50th anniversary edition series

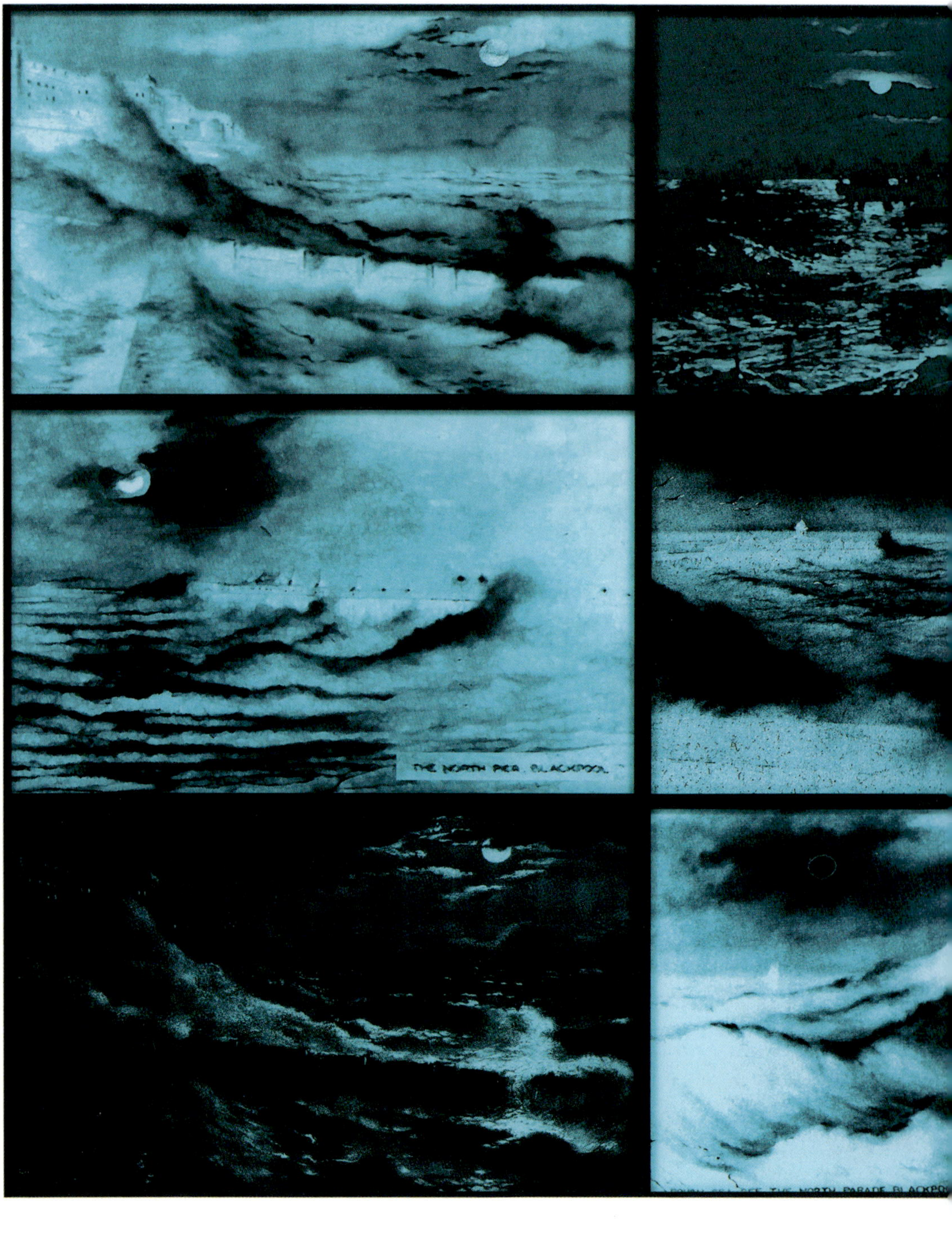
THE NORTH PIER, BLACKPOOL

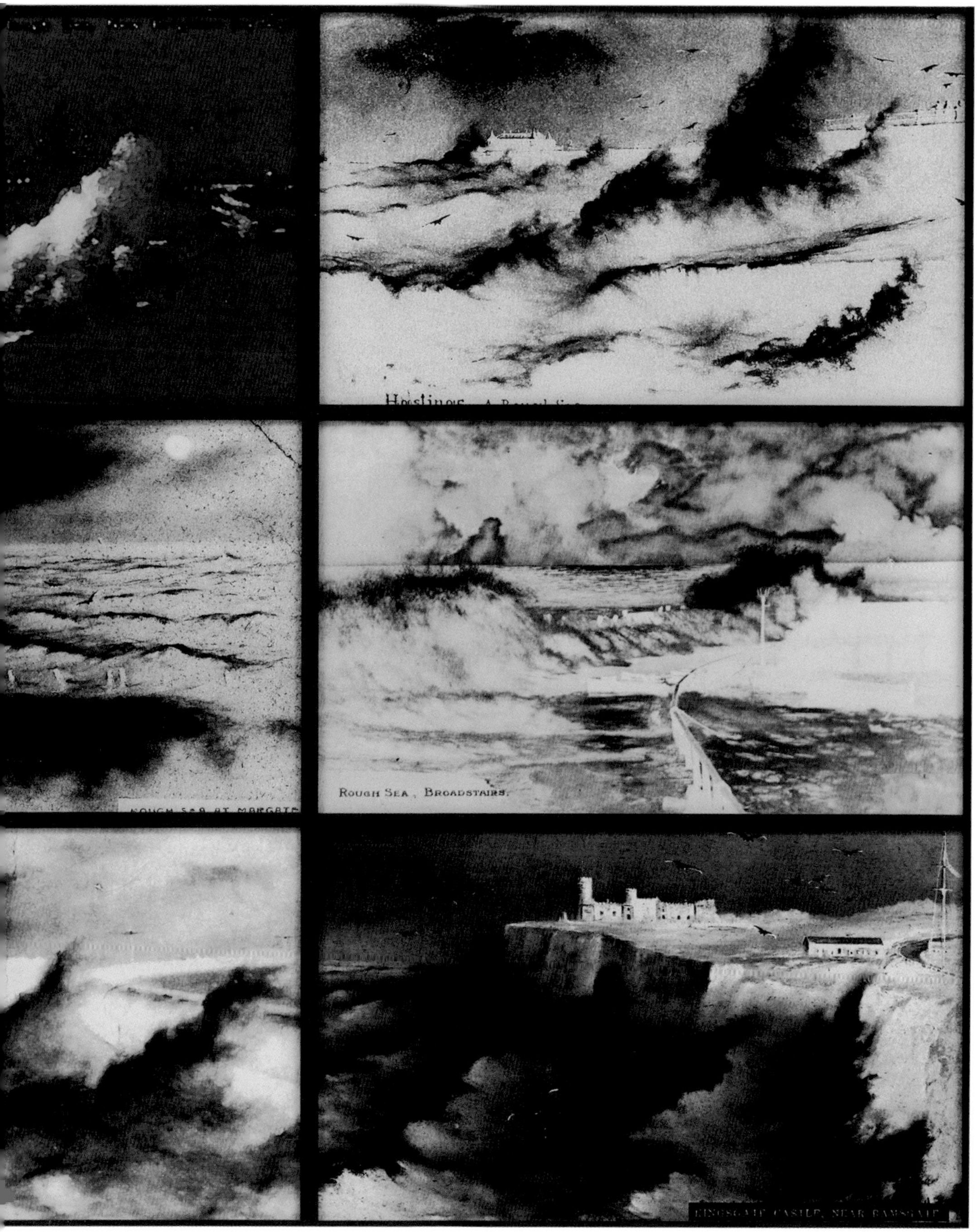
Rough Sea, Broadstairs.

ARTIST BIOGRAPHIES

CHRIS BURDEN

Chris Burden was born in Boston in 1946 and lived and worked in Los Angeles, California, where he died in 2015. In 1965, he moved to California and studied at Pomona College and the University of California. His performances redefined the possibilities of the medium; his sculptures sought to extend the limits of the physical. In 1999, Burden exhibited at the 48th Venice Biennale. In 2013, the New Museum, New York presented *Chris Burden: Extreme Measures*, that marked the first New York survey of the artist and his first major exhibition in the United States in over twenty-five years. *Ghost Ship* was a main attraction – suspended on the outside of the building – and it remains to this day a semi-permanent public sculpture.

THOMAS JOSHUA COOPER

Thomas Joshua Cooper was born in San Francisco, California in 1946 and currently lives and works in Scotland. He studied at Humboldt State University in Arcata, California and at the University of New Mexico. Cooper founded the Fine Art Photography Department at the Glasgow School of Art in 1982, where he remains a Professor. In 2009, he achieved a Guggenheim Fellowship in Photography, and in 2014 he was elected a Fellow of the Royal Society of Edinburgh. Cooper's work is held by over fifty museums and public collections including Art Institute of Chicago, Chicago; The Museum of Fine Arts, Houston; Los Angeles County Museum of Art, Los Angeles; Tate Britain and the Victoria and Albert Museum, London.

DOROTHY CROSS

Dorothy Cross was born in Cork, Ireland, in 1956 and lives and works in Dublin. She studied at Leicester Polytechnic, England, and at the San Francisco Art Institute, California. Working in sculpture, film and photography, Dorothy Cross examines the relationship between living beings and the natural world. During the 1990s, the artist produced a series of works using cow udders, which drew on the animals' rich store of symbolic associations across cultures to investigate the construction of sexuality and subjectivity. In her art she amalgamates found and constructed objects. In 1993, Cross represented Ireland at the 45th Venice Biennale. She has exhibited internationally in group and solo exhibitions including: The South African National Art Gallery, Cape Town; Beijing Art Museum of the Imperial City, Beijing, China; Tate St Ives, Cornwall; Irish Museum of Modern Art, Dublin; Camden Arts Centre, London; and the ICA London.

TACITA DEAN

Tacita Dean OBE RA was born in Canterbury, UK, in 1965, and lives and works in Berlin and Los Angeles. She studied at Falmouth University and the Slade School of Fine Art where she received her MA. Adrian Searle has written that, "Dean's work is carried by a sense of history, time and place, light quality and the essence of the film itself. The focus of her subtle but ambitious work is the truth of the moment, the film as a medium and the sensibilities of the individual". She is one of the Young British Artists (YBAs), was a nominee for the Turner Prize in 1998, and was elected to the Royal Academy of Arts in 2008. She has had numerous exhibitions worldwide. Her recent solo exhibitions in 2018 include the Royal Academy of Arts, London, The National Gallery and the National Portrait Gallery, London.

TRACEY EMIN

Tracey Emin was born in London in 1963 and studied at Maidstone College of Art and the Royal College of Art, London. She represented Great Britain at the Venice Biennale in 2007 and was elected a Royal Academician in the same year. In 2011, Emin became Professor of Drawing at The Royal Academy of Arts, London, and in 2013 she was awarded a CBE. Her solo exhibitions have been shown in Hufkens, Brussels (2017), Château La Coste, Aix-En-Provence (2017), Galleria Lorcan O'Neill, Rome (2015), White Cube, London (2014), MoCA, Miami (2013), and a major survey exhibition at the Hayward Gallery, London (2011) amongst others. She has also exhibited her work in a series of dialogues with past masters she admires, in exhibitions at Turner Contemporary (2017), Tate Liverpool (2016), Tate Britain (2015) and The Leopold Museum, Vienna (2015).

SUSAN HILLER

Susan Hiller was born in Cleveland Ohio in 1940. She has lived and worked in London since the 1970s, during which time her practice has greatly influenced new generations of artists. Inspired by art movements such as Fluxus, Minimalism and Surrealism and informed by her early study of anthropology and her commitment to feminism, Hiller's work presents a free-flowing narrative, juxtaposing and combining such formative influences into a powerfully articulate visual investigation of both the mundane and the extraordinary.

ISAAC JULIEN

Filmmaker and installation artist, Isaac Julien CBE RA, was born in London in 1960, where he currently lives and works. His multi-screen film installations and photographs incorporate different artistic disciplines to create a poetic and unique visual language. His 1989 documentary-drama *Looking for Langston* garnered a cult following. He has had solo exhibitions worldwide including the Americas, Canada, Africa, the Netherlands, Sweden, Ireland and France. Julien's work is held in collections that include: Tate, London, the Museum of Modern Art, New York; Centre Pompidou, Paris; the Solomon R. Guggenheim Museum, New York; the Hirshhorn Museum and Sculpture Garden, Washington DC; the Albright-Knox Art Gallery, Buffalo, New York; Fondation Louis Vuitton, Paris; the LUMA Foundation, Arles; the Kramlich Collection and the Zeitz Museum of Contemporary Art (Zeitz MOCAA), Cape Town.

CLAIRE KERR

Claire Kerr was born in Wallsend, UK, in 1968 and lives and works in Dublin. She studied at Magdalen College Oxford University, Wimbledon School of Art, and Dun Laoghaire Institute of Art, Design and Technology. Kerr's paintings interact with art-historical and contemporary sources, often 'performing' representation itself. Small in scale, her work combines a meticulous technique with conceptual ambiguity, inviting the viewer to 'see differently' something superficially recognisable. Kerr has exhibited widely internationally, including at the Royal Hibernian Academy, Dublin, the Museum Sinclair-Haus in Bad Homburg, and Espacio Artkunstarte, Madrid.

STEFFI KLENZ

Steffi Klenz was born in Germany in 1979 and currently lives and works in London. She trained at the Royal College of Art in London. Her photographic practice has been consistently preoccupied with the built environment, critically exploring the notion of place and spatiality. Her work unfolds in urban places and buildings, but it is not architectural photography; instead it uncovers unexpected narratives and traces of history embedded in the place. She has exhibited widely in museums and galleries in the UK, Europe and America, including, the New Art Museum, Walsall; SeaCity Museum, Southampton; Tate Liverpool, Liverpool; FotoMuseum, Antwerp; LA Centre for Digital Arts, USA; the Phoenix Art Museum, Arizona; Künstlerhaus Bethanien, Berlin; the Fine Art Museum, Luleå; Museum Künstlerkolonie, Darmstadt and the Finnish Museum of Photography, Helsinki.

LANGLANDS & BELL

Artists Ben Langlands (born in London, in 1955) and Nikki Bell (born in London, in 1959), began collaborating as Langlands & Bell after meeting at Middlesex Polytechnic in London, in 1977. They are based in London and have exhibited internationally since the early 1980s. They explore the complex web of relationships linking people and architecture and the coded systems of mass-communications and exchange we use to negotiate an increasingly fast-changing technological world. In 2002 Langlands & Bell were commissioned as "War Artists" to visit Afghanistan. In 2003 they won a BAFTA and were shortlisted for the Turner Prize for *The House of Osama bin Laden*, the trilogy of art works that resulted from their visit. In 2016 they unveiled a permanent installation *Beauty Immortality* at Piccadilly Circus Underground station, London. Major solo exhibitions include *Internet Giants: Masters of the Universe* at Ikon Gallery, Birmingham, 2018, and Sir John Soane's Museum, London, 2020.

HUMPHREY OCEAN

Humphrey Ocean was born in Sussex, UK, in 1951 and lives and works in London. He studied at Tunbridge Wells, Brighton and Canterbury Art Schools and has been a Royal Academician since 2004. Ocean is a contemporary painter with a long association with portraiture. His work is in the British Council, Wolverhampton Art Gallery, National Portrait Gallery, National Maritime Museum and Victoria and Albert Museum. He was awarded an Honorary Doctorate by the University of Kent. Ocean has exhibited widely including Tate Liverpool, The Whitworth Art Gallery, National Portrait Gallery, Dulwich Picture Gallery, Christine König Galerie, Vienna and Sims Reed Gallery, London. He is Professor of Perspective at the Royal Academy of Arts.

SIMON PATTERSON

Simon Patterson was born in England in 1967, and was one of the Young British Artists (YBAs) of the early 1990s. His work often involves the way that language and images interact. In works such as *The Great Bear* (1992) and his 2002 *Cosmic Wallpaper* at Warwick University, Patterson blends the classification and definition of world history, science, and pop culture. In *The Great Bear*, Patterson replaced names of train stops on a map of the London Underground with those of soccer stars, philosophers, scientists, and other cultural and historical luminaries. Patterson's work has been shown at a number of major institutions, including the Museum of Modern Art, the Brooklyn Museum, the Victoria and Albert Museum, and Tate London.

MARK POWER

Mark Power was born in Harpenden, UK, in 1959, and lives and works in Brighton. He studied at Brighton Polytechnic and after graduating, travelled for two years around